Telling
the
UNTOLD
STORY

Telling
the
UNTOLD
STORY

How Investigative Reporters
Are Changing the Craft of Biography

Steve Weinberg

University of Missouri Press
Columbia and London

Library of Congress Cataloging-in-Publication Data

Weinberg, Steve.
    Telling the untold story : how investigative reporters are
changing the craft of biography / Steve Weinberg.
        p.   cm.
    Includes bibliographical references and index.
    ISBN 0–8262–0873–8 (permanent paper)
    1. Biography as a literary form. 2. Investigative reporting.
3. Journalism—Authorship. I. Title.
CT21.W45   1992
808'.06692—dc20   92–17674
                                                           CIP

∞™ This paper meets the requirements of the
American National Standard for Permanence of Paper
for Printed Library Materials, Z39.48, 1984.

Designer: Rhonda Miller
Typesetter: Connell-Zeko Type & Graphics
Printer and binder: Thomson-Shore, Inc.
Typeface: Elante and Globe Gothic

CONTENTS

Telling
the
UNTOLD
STORY

INTRODUCTION

I come to this book as a practitioner of biography, and as a student of it. I write biographies, review biographies by other authors, derive knowledge and pleasure from them. Biography helps me understand the lives of others in new ways, so that I can understand my own life better. As the advertisement for the cable television program "Biography" says, "Get Involved in Someone Else's Life."

The in-depth delineation of character at the center of biography is a difficult, noble task. It is practiced full-time by a small number of authors. It is practiced consistently well by a much smaller number. This book will focus on those who practice it well. It is different from previous books about biography in many respects, emphasizing as it does how recent book-length biographies by contemporary authors with investigative journalism backgrounds—who relentlessly follow paper and people trails left by living or recently dead influential figures and who use compelling narrative techniques sometimes borrowed from fiction—are revealing character in original and important ways.

Imbedded in that capsule description is the assumption that the training of biography's practitioners influences the substance of what they write—and the training of today's best biographers is quite different from that of past generations. Generalizations are dangerous because there are always exceptions. But I will generalize anyway. Until about 1975, most biographers considered to be at the apex of the craft were academics—specialist university professors, think-tank residents, or unaffiliated scholars with advanced degrees, often doctorates. Their books tended to be nonjudgmental about the subject's intellectual, emotional, and moral character; the focus tended to be on the public lives of long-dead subjects, leaving private matters in the closet or bedroom or wherever.

1

Telling the Untold Story

Stephen Oates, among the best of the academics writing biography, has described the phenomenon: "These would-be biographers are often specialists in some field who decide to write a biography of someone who made a contribution in it. Too often, such authors are mainly interested in offering a new interpretation of their specialty—say, a new assessment of colonial class antagonisms or a new angle on the narrative poetics of Herman Melville. For these authors, biography serves chiefly as a showpiece for their own erudition."

Oates, who earned his Ph.D. in history from the University of Texas in 1969, said he had to learn how to act like an investigative journalist while researching his biography of Martin Luther King, Jr. Oates was having difficulty getting reluctant sources to talk: "The trouble was, my parents had raised me to be a gentleman. I took 'no' to mean 'no.' Now I had to impersonate an investigative reporter—I had to be aggressive, devoid of shame, and rude if necessary, and I had never to take no for an answer. Nothing in graduate school had ever prepared me for this. I was terrible at it. I hated to intrude on other people's privacy, to ask them to remember things that could be painful. Who gave me the right to do that?"[1]

Most journalism school graduates, as well as experienced journalists without university training in journalism, have no such reservations. Partly because of that, today many of the best biographers come from journalism backgrounds. Most are college-educated, but do not have doctorates. Most are generalists, not specialists. Many style themselves as investigative reporters unaccepting of the previous tradition. A 1991 cartoon by Eli Stein in the *Chronicle of Higher Education* captures the current situation. It shows a library patron approaching the stacks. One aisle is marked "Fiction." The next aisle is marked "Muckraking (formerly biography)."[2]

Comparing the Lyndon Johnson biographies by Robert Caro (a newspaper investigative reporter turned biographer) and Robert Dallek (a Ph.D. historian teaching at a university), Nicholas Lemann commented in the *New York Times Book Review* that someone with Caro's background "can now attempt a magisterial multivolume political biography of Johnson that concedes no ground to professional historians. . . . There is a substantial difference in feel between Mr. Dallek's Johnson and Mr. Caro's, but it springs from the way in which the two authors handle their material, not from a great disparity in the basic information they have at their disposal." Lemann said he was looking forward to the next Johnson volumes from both biographers, but that Caro's "will surely make" the fascinating cast "memorable in a way that is beyond Mr. Dallek's literary capabilities."[3]

Such handling of material in new ways and novelistic writing are part of the genre as practiced by many investigative journalists turned biographers. All this can go too far, of course. *Washington Post* literary columnist Jonathan Yardley noted that lately "biography has become as much a journalistic genre as a literary one; indeed, in the realm of popular culture it has become solely journalistic. Biography in this sense exists not to explain and understand but to eviscerate and exploit, and its methods have less to do with literature than with guerilla warfare. . . . What the genre now demands are a ferretlike determination to dig up facts, or factoids; a nose for the sensationally newsworthy; a talent for innuendo and selective interpretation; an insensitivity to nuance or human ambiguity; a gift for choosing subjects whose lives are bottomlessly fascinating to John Q. Boob, not to mention thee and me."[4]

Yardley's concern is, sadly, valid in some cases. In general, however, biographies by investigative journalists are responsible. The contemporary dominance of biography by journalists, although a major shift, is not completely surprising. The best journalism has long been the ultimate scholarly activity, which I define as learning everything that can be learned about an individual (or institution, or issue), then communicating that knowledge compellingly and clearly. The top journalists turned biographers bring ready-made to the craft traits that tend to come less naturally to specialized academics: they know how to obtain hard-to-find, previously private information on a variety of subjects from government agencies and private repositories; how to convince reluctant sources to talk; how to write clearly for readers of all levels rather than other holders of doctorates; how to compose at the word processor before the deadline is long past.

That said, this book is not meant to be, and will not be, a monument of praise for biographers trained as journalists; neither will it be a monument of criticism for biographers trained as university scholars.

By honing in on quality biography as practiced by investigative journalists, I hope this book will add to the knowledge about the craft. There have never been many books about the doing of biography. In the past two decades, the number has, happily, increased, but there are still gaps. This book is an attempt to plug one of the gaps—to explore how and why more and more investigative journalists are producing quality biographies of influential contemporary subjects.

What is already out there about biography falls more or less into three categories. One category is the how-to book aimed at the would-be practitioner; a representative example is *The Biographer's Craft* by Milton Lomask. (I have provided further information about all books mentioned throughout the text in the Bibliography.)

The second category is the anthology of biographers talking about their particular books. A few of the anthologies contain remarks by journalist-biographers whose subjects are contemporary figures, but the collections tend to be dominated by academics who write about literary figures and/or those long dead—altogether different enterprises from doing books on persons alive and powerful. The anthologies tend to make for easy reading, being heavily anecdotal. The selections are so idiosyncratic, however, that it is difficult to extract universal truths about the craft. A representative example is *Telling Lives: The Biographer's Art,* edited by Marc Pachter.

The third category is the academic study; these rarely include even a paragraph about contemporary biography. Such books usually have limited distribution through university presses, and thus can be difficult to find in bookstores or in public libraries. A representative example is *Ultimately Fiction: Design in Modern American Literary Biography,* by Dennis W. Petrie, published by Purdue University Press.

This book is intended to redirect the discussion. To accomplish that goal, I have written connecting pieces that explain the who, what, when, where, why, and how of modern-day, journalist-based biography. In preparing this book, I have interviewed contemporary journalist-biographers, studied their writings line by line, obtained permission to reprint their own versions of how they did what they did, and drawn on my own experiences. If this book succeeds, it will give biographers new ideas for telling lives more powerfully, give reviewers an increased understanding they can bring to writing about biographies, give publishers the motivation to commission more quality biographies of living subjects, and give readers a consumer's guide for better evaluating the lives they have chosen to examine.

The biographies I will discuss in-depth tend to be muckraking in nature, which means they contain at least occasional revelations embarrassing or damaging to the subjects. It is legitimate to ask whether the subjects deserve Judas as a biographer. But it is equally legitimate to wonder whether society is better served by having Paul as the chronicler.

The book will unfold in this way, chapter by chapter: One, an overview on the state of contemporary biography, and how we got here. Two, an examination of Robert Caro's watershed biographies of Robert Moses and Lyndon Johnson, with samples from his work as well as informed commentary and reportage by others about his work. Three, an explication of the techniques used by Donald Barlett and James Steele while writing exposés of individuals for the *Philadelphia Inquirer* and while composing their Howard Hughes and Nelson Rockefeller biographies, with samples from their writings. Four, an inside view of my techniques and experiences researching and writing an unauthorized biography of Armand Hammer. Five, an examination of shorter-form biography in newspapers and magazines. Six, ruminations on current and future perils of investigative biography.

Given all that I have promised, I should spell out what this book is not intended to be. It is not an exhaustive history of biography through the ages, a scholarly critique covering all permutations of the craft, a thorough how-to primer for would-be biographers, a textbook on investigative journalism, or an anthology of biographers discussing their work, although it contains elements of all that.

Because of my emphasis, my desire to fill a gap, this book gives short shrift to biographies of historical figures. Delineating the characters of Thomas Jefferson or Leonardo da Vinci or Queen Victoria or Andrew Carnegie is important, but a vastly different enterprise from successfully telling the life of a current politician, artist, monarch, or tycoon. This book also gives short shrift to biographies of novelists, painters, composers, and other artists. Chronicling such lives is important, of course, but the success of such a biography is grounded in a critical analysis of the art itself—again, a vastly different enterprise from what I am undertaking to explain.

In addition, I have omitted in-depth treatment of short-form biography by journalists writing in newspapers and magazines. Some of it (especially in slick, upscale monthly magazines such as *Vanity Fair* and *Esquire*) is outstanding, but it is not the same as book-length biography. Just as most novelists fail to excel as short-story writers and vice versa, so do most periodical profile writers fail to excel as biographers. I have reprinted two superb periodical profiles in Chapter Five, though, because there is much that book-length biographers can learn from them.

The delineation of character, when done well, relies on diverse talents. An accomplished contemporary biographer must be an investigative journalist, historian, psychologist, sensitive interviewer, gossipmonger, and compelling storyteller rolled into one. The best biographies capture life at a deeper, more intense level than does any other form of literature. Through biography, we learn how other individuals have handled the struggle between freedom and fate. Leaving a mark on this earth beyond one's immediate family is unusual; biographies tend to be written about people who have managed to leave such a mark. Biographers scratch beneath the subject's personal myth, looking for the slippages and the fittings.

The living of a life is more difficult than the chronicling of it, but the chronicling is certainly no simple task. That is why only a few of us write biographies, while many of us read them. Ultimately, telling somebody else's life fully, fairly, and compellingly is probably an impossible task. But it is important to keep pushing the limits of the possible; the quest matters. I hope this book will be an inspiration to writers, reviewers, publishers, and readers to collaborate on that quest.

CHAPTER ONE

From Plutarch to Pathography

When Robert Caro finished his biography of Robert Moses in 1974, he marked an end to seven years of research on the man who profoundly influenced the look and feel of twentieth-century New York City, simultaneously influencing urban planners the world over. *The Power Broker: Robert Moses and the Fall of New York* won the Pulitzer Prize for biography as well as the Francis Parkman Prize, awarded by the Society of American Historians to the book that "best represents the union of the historian and the artist." It was quite an accomplishment for a former newspaper reporter turned first-time biographer.[1]

But *The Power Broker* did more than win accolades for Caro—it also deeply influenced the modern-day craft of biography. Biographers had a new model: the nearly thirteen-hundred-page book was much longer than the average biography; artfully written, sometimes using techniques from the realm of fiction, while still adhering to the chronology of Moses's life as he lived it; daring in its analysis of Moses's motives; unusual in the depth of its portrayal of Moses's times, as well as his life; heavily dependent on previously secret documents; quintessentially muckraking; and done by an investigative journalist, not a historian or urban planning professor. Caro's success opened the gates for other journalists to write biographies of controversial, contemporary subjects.

Caro's book contrasted starkly with the other biography winning a Pulitzer in 1975: Dumas Malone, a Ph.D. historian at the University of Virginia, received the prize in the history category for his six-volume, thirty-four-hundred-page life of Thomas Jefferson. Unlike Caro's book, with its large dollops of muckraking about a still-living figure, Malone's admired its long-dead subject without reservation. Malone commented that after his thirty-eight years of researching the Jefferson

7

volumes, the former president had "withstood microscopic examination even better than I expected. This is not to claim that his judgment was always right, but no one can read his voluminous state papers without gaining increased respect for his ability." Malone was far more loath than Caro to analyze his subject's motives, noting, "I must confess that even with the benefit of hindsight, I have often found it extraordinarily difficult to arrive at a defensible judgment as to what he ought to have done."[2]

Nothing in the long but sparsely documented history of the biographical genre predicted the emergence of Caro and other investigative reporters as authors or the impact they would have. Until the mid–1700s, biography of a single life was not even generally practiced. What some scholars have called biography before 1750 consisted largely of "putting together groups of lives, the groupings being determined by social rank and function, or by profession," as Reed Whittemore described it in *Pure Lives: The Early Biographers*. He examined such scribes as Plutarch (46–120 A.D.), Aelfric (circa 1000 A.D.), and Giorgio Vasari (sixteenth century). "The ancient biographers found fewer warts, and did not go to Freud for help in finding them," Whittemore said. In his companion volume, *Whole Lives: Shapers of Modern Biography,* Whittemore said of the early practitioners that "they did not explore the home sources of Alexander the Great's greatness, but the signs in the heavens at his birth."

James Clifford found in his survey *Biography as an Art: Selected Criticism, 1560–1960* that "the earliest biographers in England had little curiosity about the nature of their art. They knew what they had to do, and did it. Their purpose was edification. Their justification was the glory of God, through the praise of His saints. Describing a truly holy person, their works would succeed or fail to the extent to which they taught Christian virtue and strengthened wavering faith. They had no conceivable desire to create rounded characters. Indeed, such an ideal would have horrified any self-respecting hagiographer. A saint or a king was obviously set apart from ordinary folk, and it was the duty and the prerogative of the writer to emphasize these differences."

James Boswell's biography of Samuel Johnson, published in England during 1791, marked a watershed in the evolution of the genre. Boswell's massive book (1,492 pages in one recent trade paperback

From Plutarch to Pathography

edition) received lots of attention upon publication and has stayed in print for two centuries. Unlike many of his predecessors, Boswell gave deep thought to how to tell a life. He concentrated very definitely on a single person, fitting in psychological speculation (pre-Freudian, of course) and exposing a few warts. I find Boswell's Johnson interesting to read, yet not particularly helpful as a model in pursuing my craft. Boswell seems too uncritical, too anxious to be seen as the willing hagiographer of a great man. Yet many biographers, especially from academia, say Boswell's work resonates in their own.

Nineteenth-century practitioners and theorists of biography worked under Boswell's influence, sometimes extending the boundaries. They began asking new questions, many of them in the realm of ethics: for instance, how much should a biographer reveal of the subject's private life—a lot, nothing, or something in between? Biography as a profession began to take hold in the United States during the 1850s, embodied by James Parton, generally considered to be the first professional full-time biographer in the United States. Parton's subjects included Horace Greeley, Aaron Burr, Andrew Jackson, Thomas Jefferson, and John Jacob Astor. Following Parton, professional biographers began to combine theory with practice, refining the mixture from book to book.

In *Whole Lives*, Whittemore summarizes the theoretical progression after Boswell, explaining how his volume begins "with Thomas Carlyle's inwardly driven (but hardly sexually driven) heroes, and move[s] from them . . . to Freud's inward selves. And with Freud and his successors I come to our world of capitalism, individualism and the subconscious, where all biographers must now be diligent students of self even if not lovers of it."

Ah, Sigmund Freud. Probably few contemporary journalists turned biographers have read Freud in depth; fewer (if any) have read Freud in the original German. Despite their relative ignorance of what Freud really believed, biographers invoke his ghost often; if they fail to do so, reviewers of biographies and scholars of the genre wonder why. When Freudian theory permeates biographies of contemporary subjects by investigative journalists it is ironic, because Freud was no friend of biographers. Peter Gay, in *Freud: A Life for Our Time*, quoted an 1885 letter in which the subject, explaining why he was destroying his correspondence, said he had "almost completed an undertaking which a number of people, still unborn but fated to misfortune, will feel severely. . . . Let the biographers labor and toil, we won't make it too easy for them." In a separate letter, Freud wrote a potential biographer that anyone practicing the craft "commits himself to lies, to concealment, to hypocrisy, to embellishments, and even to dissembling his own lack of understanding, for biographical truth is not to be had, and, even if one had it, one could not use it."

Despite the stretched-out history of the genre from Plutarch to Freud, the direct spiritual ancestors of Caro's work were Lytton Strachey's four biographical essays, published as *Eminent Victorians* in 1918. Strachey's lives of Florence Nightingale, General Charles Gordon, Cardinal Henry Manning, and Doctor Thomas Arnold were artfully presented, with an emphasis on "the inward creature." Strachey, born in England in 1880, revolutionized mainstream biography during his fifty-two-year life. Probably more than any other single work, *Eminent Victorians* moved biographers and publishers away from books that worshiped their subjects toward a more critical genre.

The preface to *Eminent Victorians,* despite its brevity, influenced writers and critics of biography who might not have bothered to read the entire book. Strachey said, "It is not by the direct method of a scrupulous narration that the explorer of the past can hope to depict [the Victorian Age]. If he is wise, he will adopt a subtler strategy. He will attack his subject in unexpected places; he will fall upon the flank, or the rear; he will shoot a sudden, revealing searchlight into obscure recesses, hitherto undevined. He will row out over that great ocean of material, and lower down into it, here and there, a little bucket, which will bring up to the light of day some characteristic specimen, from those far depths, to be examined with a careful curiosity."

When he wrote *Eminent Victorians,* Strachey was consciously trying to influence the craft. He hoped that his profiles would "prove to be of interest from the strictly biographical no less than the historical point of view. Human beings are too important to be treated as mere symptoms of the past. . . . The art of biography seems to have fallen on evil times in England . . . the most delicate and humane of all the branches of the art of writing has been relegated to the journeymen of letters; we do not reflect that it is perhaps as difficult to write a good life as to live one." In case any readers had missed his message,

From Plutarch to Pathography

Strachey said in the preface's final paragraph that it is not the biographer's business "to be complimentary; it is his business to lay bare the facts of the case, as he understands them. That is what I have aimed at in this book—to lay bare the facts of some cases, as I understand them, dispassionately, impartially, and without ulterior intentions." Strachey was saying that a biography belongs to the author, not to the subject. His approach fit well with the increased skepticism and questioning of authority after World War I.

So, Strachey determinedly shattered the conventional wisdom about his four revered subjects—showing the frequent chasm between professed belief and actual behavior—as Caro did later when writing about Robert Moses and Lyndon Johnson. In the five decades between Strachey's best work and Caro's debut, a few biographers and theorists could be said to have influenced the practice of the craft—but none in quite the combination of ways that Caro did.

Those introductory bows now taken, Caro comes onto center stage. The combination of his research skills, his way with words, his boldness in attributing motives, and his gutsiness in writing about powerful contemporary figures make his work topic A during any informed discussion of biography over the last quarter of the twentieth century.

Reviewing *The Power Broker* in the *Washington Post Book World*, normally skeptical journalist William Greider said, "When a truly exceptional achievement comes along, there are no words to praise it. Important, awesome, compelling—these no longer summon the full flourish of trumpets this book deserves. It is extraordinary on many levels and, despite its price and length, it is certain to endure." Such praise was typical.[3]

The book had its detractors, to be sure, as Strachey's book had its detractors. It was controversial not only because of its substance, but also because of its techniques, so it was bound to spark debate—as books that shake up the established order often do. (Caro's techniques and the debate over them are treated at greater length in Chapter Two, devoted entirely to his work.)

The disagreement among reviewers was part of a decades-old conversation, involving relatively few participants, that continues to this day: What makes for good biography? There has traditionally been little discussion about the principles of biography, because until recently it was not generally considered to be a separate discipline. It seemed to be a chameleon form, depending on the views of the commentator—maybe history, maybe literary criticism if the subject was a writer, or just something to read before falling asleep at night. After the gradual acceptance of biography as its own demanding art form, there seemed a great need to go further theoretically. The discussion, sparse in the academy, rarely reached the millions of readers who buy or borrow biographies. Reviewers of biographies for book pages wrote about how the subject had lived his or her life, rather than analyzing how well the biographer had practiced the craft of telling that life.

All of that began to change during the 1970s, as demonstrated by the controversy over Caro's efforts. Ever since the publication of Caro's biography of Moses, the debate about what constitutes responsible life-writing has been fueled by a publishing explosion: during the 1980s and early 1990s, American publishers have issued an average of about two thousand biographies annually. *Publishers Weekly,* the magazine of the book industry, devoted its first special issue to biography in 1988. There is a Biography Bookshop in New York City, and separate biography sections now exist in virtually every respectable bookstore and library. Biographers themselves have become celebrities.[4]

Readers flock to biographies today. "A good many more people are interested in reading about John Berryman or Robert Lowell than are ready to read their poems," literary critic George Garrett has said. In a similar vein, readers who will never be able to vote for Edward Kennedy during a Massachusetts senatorial race seek out books about him. Some commentators believe well-written biography has replaced fiction as the preferred art form. In the words of Jean Strouse, a *Newsweek* magazine editor and book critic turned biographer, novels from previous generations "provided readers with large slices of life in which questions of character, motivation, morality, social pressure and internal conflict could be explored in great depth. People read, and still read, those books for the pleasure of imagining their way into other lives, other times, other locations—and for what comes back into their own lives from those journeys. Most modern novels—all bare bones and spare parts—do not provide that kind of satisfaction. Modern biographies often do."[5]

From Plutarch to Pathography

Biographers have even become the stuff of fiction. Virginia Woolf's satire *Orlando* set the stage with its publication in 1928. Steven Millhauser brought the satire of biography to a new generation with his 1972 novel *Edwin Mullhouse: The Life and Death of an American Writer, 1943–1954*. Bernard Malamud's novel *Dubin's Lives* (1979) is one of the fullest, best-known portrayals of a biographer protagonist. Serious novelists Penelope Lively and Alison Lurie weighed in with *According to Mark* (1984) and *The Truth about Lorin Jones* (1988), respectively. Among others, mystery writer Amanda Cross published *The Players Come Again* (1990), and thriller master Tom Hyman wrote *Prussian Blue* (1991).[6]

A. S. Byatt, in her novel *Possession* (1990), captures the widespread fascination with biography in a passage referring to scholar James Blackadder, who is unearthing the life of a long-dead poet, in competition with another scholar, Mortimer Cropper. Blackadder, Byatt writes, "had persuaded the Vicar, whom he had met at an episcopal tea party, that biography was just as much a spiritual hunger of modern man as sex or political activity. Look at the sales, he had urged, look at the column space in the Sundays, people need to know how other people lived, it helps them to live, it's human. A form of religion, said the Vicar. A form of ancestor worship, said Cropper. Or more. What are the Gospels but a series of varying attempts at the art of biography?"

An avid reader of biography, I became aware of the debate about what makes for good life-telling many years ago. In the late 1970s, I wrote a book with my wife, Scherrie Goettsch, that did not start out to be a biography, but ended up with multiple chapters of biography as part of a larger story. As I wrestled with questions of privacy and taste, the debate over standards in biography became anything but academic. Later, I conducted seven years of research to tell the life of Armand Hammer. In the early going, I put my principles to paper and shared them with my editor, Jennifer Josephy of Little, Brown and Company. Telling somebody else's life is a big responsibility; I wanted myself and my editor to be ready to shoulder it.

If that sounds hopelessly old-fashioned, consider: Biographies influence how readers view human nature in general and certain individuals in particular. A biographer holds another's reputation in his or her hands. It has always been so. Margaret Oliphant, writing in 1883, said, "The position of the biographer carries with it a power which is almost unrestrained, the kind of power which it is doubly tyrannous to use like a giant. Not even the pulpit is so entirely master, for we all consider ourselves able to judge in respect to what the clergyman tells us and we have his materials in our hands by which to call him to account . . . but the biographer has a far more assured place, and if he is not restrained by the strictest limits of truth and honor, there is nothing else that can control him in heaven or earth. . . . He has it in his power to guide the final deliverance, like that judge whose summing up so often decides the final verdict."[7]

Many decades later, Dumas Malone, Jefferson's biographer, commented that a reader, "when he picks up a biography, has no ready way of knowing in advance whether it contains a conventionalized portrait, a touched-up photograph, or a caricature drawn at the caprice of the artist. After he has read it he can pass judgment on it as a story; if it deals with a recent figure he may be able to check it to some extent on the basis of his own knowledge; and if it has to do with the more distant past he can draw upon such historical information as he may happen to possess; but, to an extraordinary degree, the authenticity of the book depends upon the intellectual integrity of the writer."[8]

Most readers of *The Power Broker,* for example, had little independent knowledge of its subject; they quite likely judged Moses forever through the lens of his biographer. That can be dangerous if a hack biographer is involved. Books do not come with warning labels that they are written by incompetent authors, and are thus hazardous to mental health—as well as truth.

The Power Broker helped many journalists understand the vital and too often unreported connections between individual character and public policy. About the same time it appeared, two other books reinforced those connections. David Halberstam of the *New York Times* and Bob Woodward and Carl Bernstein of the *Washington Post* showed that daily journalists could do small-scale biography to buttress and illuminate newspapers' factual foundations. Halberstam's biographical sketches in newspapers and magazines informed his book *The Best and the Brightest* (1972), about the Establishment figures who led

America into the Vietnam War. Woodward and Bernstein in their second Watergate book, *The Final Days* (1976), used journalistically generated biographical vignettes to help readers understand the fall of Richard Nixon's presidency.

As Halberstam said in the Author's Note to *The Best and the Brightest*:

> I set out to study the men and their decisions. What was it about the men, their attitudes, the country, its institutions and above all the era which had allowed this tragedy to take place? The question which intrigued me the most was *why*, why had it happened. So it became very quickly not a book about Vietnam, but a book about America, and in particular about power and success in America, what the country was, who the leadership was, how they got ahead, what their percep-tions were about themselves, about the country and about their mission.
>
> The men intrigued me because they were fascinating; they had been heralded as the ablest men to serve this country in this century—certainly their biographies seemed to confirm that judgment—and yet very little had been written about them; the existing journalistic defi-nition of them and what they represented was strikingly similar to their own definition of themselves. So I felt that if I could learn something about them, I would learn something about the country, the era and about power in America.

The books by Halberstam, Woodward-Bernstein, and Caro trans-formed journalists' assumptions about what they needed to know to explain public policy decisionmaking. Before, character had been left to the feature writers, most of whom were easily taken in by powerful interviewees. Now, character was the province of the investigative reporters, with Caro showing the way by writing the Moses biography.

After the Moses life, Caro labored for another fifteen years on the first two volumes of a projected four-volume biography of Lyndon Johnson. The first two volumes received considerable attention and acclaim, confirming Caro as the most influential (his critics would say most controversial) biographer working during the last quarter of the twentieth century.

Possibly the most important post–Robert Moses biography in the Caro tradition was *Empire: The Life, Legend and Madness of Howard Hughes* by Donald L. Barlett and James B. Steele, published in 1979.

Empire demonstrated that Caro's work was no fluke, that other newspaper reporters could research and write massive, compelling biographies. It became a book after appearing in shorter form as an investigative series in the *Philadelphia Inquirer,* which employed Barlett and Steele. (I detail the methods of Barlett and Steele in Chapter Three, devoted entirely to them.)

With the Moses and the Hughes books as models, experienced biographers began to rethink their techniques; perhaps more significant in the long run, novices—especially those working as journalists—took heart and launched long-form biographies of their own. Caro and Barlett-Steele contributed to an atmosphere in which publishers were paying increased sums for investigative biographies of contemporary figures that would turn out to be years in the making, reliant on documentary research, bulky when printed, and candid in their assessments.

Following Caro and Barlett-Steele into biography were newspaper and magazine investigative reporters such as Kitty Kelley (writing about Frank Sinatra and Nancy Reagan, among others), Seymour Hersh (Henry Kissinger), Bob Woodward (John Belushi), Sally Bedell Smith (William Paley), Georgie Anne Geyer (Fidel Castro), Neil Sheehan (John Paul Vann), Nicholas von Hoffman (Roy Cohn), Taylor Branch (Martin Luther King, Jr.), James Neff (Jackie Presser), Charles Shepard (Jim Bakker), Robert Lenzner (J. Paul Getty), Russell Miller (Hugh Hefner and L. Ron Hubbard), Thomas Powers (Richard Helms), John Cooney (Walter Annenberg, Cardinal Spellman), Peter Maas (Edwin Wilson), Lou Cannon (Ronald Reagan), James Reston, Jr. (Jim Jones, John Connally, and Pete Rose/A. Bartlett Giamatti), Roger Morris (Henry Kissinger, Richard Nixon), plus the duo of Peter Collier and David Horowitz (the Kennedys, Rockefellers, and Fords).

Surveying the field of Caro-era biographies, I have formulated opinions about what separates the good from the not-so-good biographies. These guidelines make the most sense when applied to biographies of contemporary influential figures. Books about historic personages must, to some extent, be judged by different standards. In comparing his biographies of Abraham Lincoln and Martin Luther King, Jr., Stephen Oates commented, "Biography becomes easier, I think, when you write about longer-dead historical figures. You don't encounter problems with family, problems with lawsuits, problems with trying to get access to letters and archival materials. . . . Writing about the man 100 years dead was by far the easier of the two projects."9

Michael Scammell, the biographer of the very much alive Aleksandr Solzhenitsyn, further explained the distinction: "Writing the biography of a living man is sufficiently hazardous an undertaking as to call for some explanation. The very word 'biography' provokes expectations of candor and disclosure that are often precluded when one writes about a contemporary. . . . It is a story that is still continuing and therefore incomplete."10

Deciding to tackle the life of somebody still living ought to be done only after deep thought, says James Walter, who has written such a biography. There is a strong presumption in Western culture that decency forbids prying into the lives of those still living. Allied to that presumption is the difficulty of telling the full story until all the facts are in. "On such grounds many scholars, and some biographers, have denied the utility of contemporary biography," Walter says. "This has had the effect of leaving the field clear for journalists who have written most of the incisive books on contemporary politics." Those journalists turned biographers find many advantages in dealing with contemporary figures, including firsthand understanding of the social contexts in which their subjects operate, access to broadcasts of the subjects that might not be preserved for long (if at all), the opportunity to view their subjects live in debates or other public appearances, and the chance to interview those around their subjects, some of whom will cooperate even when the principals will not because they believe they are part of something significant, and want to tell what they have observed.11

Any life-writer wrestling with the question of whether to tackle a contemporary subject must also decide what status to seek—that of authorized, designated, or independent biographer. A small portion of the best contemporary biographies are authorized. But the access to information that comes with authorization often can sabotage good biography. Ronald Steel, the authorized biographer of the then-living Walter Lippmann, commented that even though he had Lippmann's sanction, there were difficult times: "If certain things perplexed me, why didn't I just ask him? Sometimes I did, but the answers weren't always illuminating. Though he had volunteered to cooperate fully . . . he had not anticipated that I would ask anything 'personal.' I soon learned that his definition of personal was quite broad."[12]

An authorized biography can be as close to definitive as humanly possible. Deirdre Bair, who has written biographies with cooperation of the subjects, says readers in the not-so-distant past "tended to give the authorized biography the most respect and credence simply because the biographer has had the trust of the subject or those who were closest to the subject, and also because this biographer has had the access—which can range from unrestricted to severely limited—to whatever written or oral testimony exists. In many cases, the authorized biography is indeed the most complete work, because it has been written with access to the subject's private papers, correspondence, journals, diaries, interviews with his family, friends and professional associates, and whatever else may exist."

Bair is aware that many authorized biographies do take the form of, as she put it, "Mr. Great Person, as seen by his nearest and dearest, who are all intent, if not on his aggrandizement, at least to preserve his reputation." To guard readers against swallowing such a biography whole, Bair suggests asking "whether or not the biography had to be subjected to the approval of the subject, the heirs, the literary executors, before it was published; did the biographer have limited or unlimited access to documentation and oral testimony; did the biographer have any literary, personal, theoretical or metaphorical axes to grind through the writing of this particular life."

After publication of her biography of Samuel Beckett, Bair received requests to become an authorized biographer. She was dismayed when the requesters would "make such statements as 'but of course you won't discuss' or 'you would not want to talk about' and then they would name aspects of the lives of which they did not approve but which were absolutely vital for a complete understanding of the biographical subject."

Bair has found a middle ground as a "designated biographer," a status she attained on the Beckett book and for her biography of Simone de Beauvoir. She and the subject or the subject's heirs agree that she is the appropriate person to write the life; they grant her access to materials, but retain no authority over the final manuscript.[13]

From Plutarch to Pathography

Today, there is a dearth of high-quality authorized biographies; as for designated biographies, high quality or otherwise, they tend to be rare. Many of the best biographies, and certainly many of the biggest-selling biographies, are unauthorized, that is, researched and written independently of their subject, who might or might not choose to cooperate a little bit or a lot. Most investigative journalists turned biographers would never think of doing an authorized book and would not be inclined to seek designated status.

The unauthorized biographer almost never starts with nothing, having at the very least the subject's autobiographical writings to check for anecdotes, discrepancies, significant omissions, and psychological insights. Some authors and their publishers revel in doing a biography in the face of the subject's outright hostility, as evidenced by the case of Kitty Kelley's *His Way: The Unauthorized Biography of Frank Sinatra*. Biographies that trumpet their illicitness often contain large doses of poorly documented sensationalism, but Kelley's life of Sinatra was a happy exception—unlike her unauthorized biographies of Jackie Kennedy Onassis, Elizabeth Taylor, and Nancy Reagan.

The debate about who is best suited to write a particular biography never will be resolved. Samuel Johnson said that only somebody who had eaten and drunk with a subject was fit to write that person's biography. Certainly there is no substitute for firsthand observation, but such proximity is a mixed blessing; it can produce all manner of biases. Dumas Malone has summarized the conundrum: "We could select some person who knew the subject well and run the risk of a biased interpretation; or we could select somebody who did not know him intimately, and perhaps did not know him at all, but who at least could be depended upon to view him critically. Assuming familiarity with the field in which he labored, which was the more important, personal knowledge or what we call objective judgment?"[14]

Each type of contemporary biography—authorized and unauthorized, by a friend or a total outsider—has its advantages and disadvantages; there is nothing inherently better in either kind. So, authorized or otherwise, what qualities ought to be present in a good biography? I will suggest eleven.

First, a life should be told chronologically. Biographers as different as Caro and Malone agree on this. Caro said of Johnson, and Malone said of Jefferson, that actions of the protagonists often make little sense if viewed as isolated decisions. But those same actions become clear when viewed as the outgrowth of a previous action. In other words, a biographer owes it to readers to follow a life as it was lived—chronologically.[15]

Leon Edel, a biographer of Henry James as well as a prolific writer on biographical theory, has been the leading opponent of strict chronology. Edel and his disciples say that most readers know about a subject's life before starting the book, so why sacrifice artistry to observe the convention of chronology? Given the artfulness of Caro and others in telling lives chronologically, I find Edel's case unconvincing.[16]

The most sensible place to depart from chronology, if at all, is in the opening chapter, when the biographer is trying to establish themes that will provide the reader with a framework for better understanding. The introductory chapter of my Armand Hammer biography is set in a Los Angeles courtroom during 1976, when Hammer was nearly seventy-eight years old. After that chapter, the biography is pretty much relentlessly chronological. Robert Caro's opening scene in the Moses biography is a masterpiece of such a departure.

Biographers sometimes depart from chronology when the material seems to cry out for a topical treatment. That usually cheats and confuses the reader. Stephen Ambrose, a biographer of Richard Nixon and Dwight Eisenhower, said that while working on the second volume of the Eisenhower biography, he "was sorely tempted to do the book by subjects, breaking it down into chapters on Eisenhower and McCarthy, or Eisenhower and civil rights, or Eisenhower and Vietnam, thereby relating Eisenhower's relations with McCarthy, or his approach to civil rights, or his policies in Vietnam, from beginning to end. But I eventually decided that such an organization would make the individual subjects easier to understand at the expense of understanding Eisenhower. What I wanted to convey was the magnitude and multitude of problems that come marching up to the president for solution, and the way in which each event relates to and influences others. . . . I decided that the only way to make the relationship between events and actions understandable, and the only way to get some sense of the factors Eisenhower had to take into account in making a single decision, was to tell the story chronologically. This method of organization has one invaluable advantage—chronologically is the way it happened."[17]

Second, a good biography should provide the context of the times to help explain the life. As Milton Lomask tells fledgling biographers in his how-to book, you "cannot catch your hero simply by confining your search to what he did and said and thought. You must read all around him, poke into every niche and cranny of his life and times." Likewise, William Abrahams, a biographer of George Orwell, says, "One cannot leave the world out. Orwell was a product of his time. There is a direct relationship there that cannot be overlooked. He was deeply conscious of the world in which he lived. The Spanish Civil War was the centerpiece of his life."[18]

Writing about the context of the life can be overdone. Anthony Edmonds notes that responsible biographers "walk a middle ground, placing their subjects within a historical context and emphasizing individuality. For example, it is legitimate in a George Washington biography to describe Indian tactics, but only to the extent Washington knew them and dealt with them." Biographer Elizabeth Longford says it is not so easy as it sounds to find the proper balance. She tries to keep the narrative moving while relating events of the times by avoiding argument with prior biographers and historians and by never losing sight of the protagonist for more than a page at a time.[19]

Another part of relating the context meaningfully is for the biographer to transport herself or himself, and readers, back to the appropriate decade. Adam Ulam in his biography of Joseph Stalin expresses the need to understand the protagonist in his time as seen at that time: "We are dealing with social and political developments but also with the development of one man's personality . . . much of the Russia of the 1930s and 1940s is explained by Joseph Djugashvili's personality, but not all. We may find in Stalin's personality some clues as to why he dealt with his closest friends and associates in the way he did, but not why he was served unquestioningly by men whose brothers had been tortured and executed, whose wives had been exiled, whose sons were imprisoned, all at his orders, and why none of them felt he could express his anguish by raising his hand or his voice against the dictator . . . if one studies Stalin's life dispassionately (admittedly not an easy task) one sees how it was affected not only by the natural rhythm of human existence, but by the politics of the time and the movement."[20]

Third, a biographer must refrain from using hindsight to intrude into the chronology. Paul Murray Kendall, in *The Art of Biography,* rightly says that biographers "are sometimes tempted to comment overtly on the decision itself, before it is made, after it is made, even as it is being made. They shout at Napoleon that he must not send Grouchy in pursuit of Blucher, at Hamilton that he had better steer clear of Burr, at James that it is idle for him to attempt the drama . . . and the deafened reader cannot hear what is actually going on, is jerked away from the subject by the biographer; indeed, the deafened reader is likely to conclude, perhaps unfairly, that the biographer is arrogantly pluming himself on a prescience that has no more merit than the good luck of being born considerably later than his subject. If the biographer is to create a sense of a life being lived, he cannot leap from his own time into his subject's time to nudge the poor man in the ribs or make faces at his deliberations, like Faustus playing tricks on the pope. The grand dimension of every man's life is the opacity of the future. The biographer, if he has foresight, will exercise the willing suspension of hindsight."

Ludicrousness often results when a biographer intrudes with commentary based on hindsight. As one biographer of Theodore Dreiser introduced the author's mistress (later to be wife) into the story, the passage began, "However, fate was preparing for [Dreiser] the most protracted, searing and significant romantic attachment of his life."[21]

Fourth, a biographer should have sympathy or empathy for the protagonist, or should at least recognize the consequences of antipathy. The warning of Bernard Crick is apt for biographers from the investigative journalism tradition, who are trained to dig up the dirt: "Sympathy must be present in a biographer; otherwise one would grow sour living for so long with someone one disliked."[22]

Being sympathetic is not the same as being in love. Nobody would expect biographers of Adolf Hitler or Joseph Stalin to love their subjects. William Shirer, a Hitler biographer, commented with remarkable restraint, "I detest totalitarian dictatorships in principle and came to loathe this one the more I lived through it and watched its ugly assault upon the human spirit. Nevertheless, in this book I have tried to be severely objective, letting the facts speak for themselves and noting the source for each."[23]

Robert Tucker, one Stalin biographer, found him to be "a loathsome man," with a "bottomless depth of . . . villainy." Yet it was important to explain that villainy to the world. Tucker said it was his task to penetrate Stalin's thoughts. "Now that I have been living through the 1930s with Stalin, trying to reconstruct his acts as they first took shape in his mind, I believe that I know him well enough to be able to think things out as he did and, in that sense, to be Stalin in the process of reaching key decisions and acting to implement them." Tucker said he tried to avoid attributing to Stalin "a consciousness of his own villainy. In the effort to reenact the villain's thought, [the biographer] must attempt to understand, and if possible to show, how the villain managed to reconcile his duplicities and atrocities with his inner picture of himself as a righteous man and a good and noble ruler. This takes a bit of doing, but the whole meaning and worth of the scholarly enterprise rest upon it."[24]

That many biographers send contradictory messages to readers is no surprise: The feelings of a biographer toward a subject understandably become complicated after he or she has spent every day for years researching a life. Some biographers have undergone psychoanalysis to better decipher their relationships with those they are writing about. The experiences of such biographers have been published as *Introspection in Biography: The Biographer's Quest for Self-Awareness*, edited by Samuel H. Baron and Carl Pletsch. The major questions they explore include how and why a biographer chooses a subject; how a biographer gains knowledge of the subject's inner life; how a biographer puts a personal stamp on the published portrait; and how a biographer is influenced by the protagonist after protracted involvement. The jury is out on the experiment. Mark Schwehn, a biographer of Henry Adams, said, "Though I can promise that such an experiment will yield self-knowledge, I cannot predict with any certainty that it will make a bad biographer a good one or a good biographer a better one."[25]

Many biographers who have not been part of the grand experiment nonetheless intuit the wisdom of the effort. Ronald Steel, the biographer of Walter Lippmann, has commented that it is "impossible for the biographer to avoid superimposing himself on the subject, not because of his failings as a biographer but because of his qualities as a human being. There is no way in which we can perceive another person, or even an object such as a bridge or painting, except by imposing that object on our psyche. . . . Biography is not the assembling of a jigsaw puzzle—with each piece filling one spot only and the ultimate design predetermined. Rather it is the creation (re-creation if you will) of a human character. In that act of re-creation the biographer inevitably imposes his values, the values of his culture, upon the character he is interpreting."[26]

Allan Nevins has commented, "Nearly all human acts and traits have a significance that varies with the sympathy or antipathy of the observer. Is Jones a shifty, wavering, uncertain man? Or does he simply see both sides of an issue, so that his apparent vacillations are simply proof of openmindedness and tolerance?"[27]

Fifth, psychological analysis of the subject by the biographer, while allowable, should be practiced sparingly. It is a tricky matter. Freud, analyzing former President Woodrow Wilson, commented, "So frequently does great achievement accompany psychic abnormality that one is tempted to believe that they are inseparable from each other. This assumption is, however, contradicted by the fact that in all fields of human endeavor great men are to be found who fulfill the demands of normality."[28]

Katharine Anthony's *Margaret Fuller: A Psychological Biography* (1920) was one of the first works to determinedly delve into motives, to emphasize the "why" with some success. Her contemporaries were commenting about the potential pitfalls before Freudianism became so ingrained in the culture, before investigative journalists turned biographers began delving into their subjects' minds as well as the outer evidence of their actions. Gamaliel Bradford, writing in 1917, popularized the term *psychography*, which he said had this aim: "Out of the perpetual flux of actions and circumstances that constitutes a man's whole life, it seeks to extract what is essential, what is permanent and so vitally characteristic. . . . From this vast and necessary [chronological] material of biography, psychography selects only that which is indispensable for its particular purpose."[29]

From Plutarch to Pathography

Bradford understood the dangers, and addressed them: "It must be admitted that psychography is always in danger of degenerating into gossip. The difference between the two is simply that gossip springs from the desire to saturate our own emptiness with the lives of others, from a mere idle curiosity about things and persons. . . . Gossip makes no distinction of significance between different facts. . . . Psychography picks, chooses and rejects; in a bushel of chaff finds only a grain or two of wheat, but treasures that wheat as . . . invaluable."

A biographer has an obligation to present more than the facts, to make judgments about normality or the lack of it. Readers want to know the why as well as the who, what, when, and where. But, like a novelist, a biographer should show instead of tell, letting readers arrive at their own realizations about character, about causation and motive. Academics who write biographies tend to rely more heavily on the psychobiographical approach than do journalists turned biographers, probably because academics receive more exposure to Freudianism as they pursue their doctorates.

Stephen Oates, an academic who has worked assiduously to master the art of writing accessible biography, puts the middle-ground position well: "The key to a successful biography is a consistent and convincing interpretation of character. Sorting through his piles of information, the biographer asks what was my subject like as a human being? What was his emotional, intellectual and spiritual makeup? How did it evolve? How much was he shaped by environmental influences? How did his personality affect his reactions to other people, to events, to luck and chance? How did his personality affect his career, his impact on history? The biographer's interpretation of character is the analytical premise upon which the entire biography will depend. Even if the biographer elects to tell his story strictly as narrative, it proceeds from this analytical base. . . . To understand character and personality, does a biographer need training in psychology? Some biographers have turned to psychology and psychoanalysis for help in comprehending the inner world of their subjects. That can help, but most biographers, I think, would agree that it is not imperative. What is imperative is that the biographer have insight into character. Such insight is psychological, but it doesn't have to derive from psychoanalytical training."[30]

Leon Edel, almost certainly the most widely read, prolific theorist of biography, would go further than either Oates or I would. He encourages telling lives through the lens of psychoanalysis: "The biographer needs to discover human self-deceptions, or defenses, which they usually are. Such deceptions may become a covert life-myth out of which lives—and biographies—are fashioned."[31]

It appears to me that the non-Freudians are the more convincing, as they struggle against the simplistic, uncertain explanations of behavior that too frequently take over psychoanalytic biographies. It can be argued that we fail to know the character of our own spouse or our parents, that any biographer would be hard-pressed to predict what his or her mother was thinking at a particular moment, much less what the subject of a biography was thinking.

Mark Schorer, author of a massive Sinclair Lewis biography, resisted calls to say straight out what was wrong with Lewis: "It was precisely because I was unwilling to make such a statement that I made the book so long. I wanted to give the reader all the evidence that I coherently could which would permit him to say to himself what was wrong." Psychological theories existed to explain Lewis's actions, but Schorer said, "I don't think that the jargon of psychoanalysis would have heightened either the comedy or the pathos of that life."[32]

In the introduction to his biography of George Orwell, Bernard Crick said the psychological insight present in so much contemporary biography "may be pleasant to read, but readers should realize that often they are being led by the nose, or the biographer is fooling himself by an affable pretense of being able to enter another person's mind. . . . We can only know an actual person by observing their behavior in a variety of different situations and through different perspectives."[33]

Samuel Clemens said it forcefully in his autobiographical writings a century ago: "What a wee little part of a person's life are his acts and words! His real life is led in his head, and is known to none but himself. All day long, and every day, the mill of his brain is grinding, and his thoughts, not those other things, are his history. His acts and words are merely the visible, thin crust of his world, with its scattered snow summits and its vacant wastes of water—and they are so trifling a part of his bulk, a mere skin enveloping it. The mass of him is hidden—it and its volcanic fires that toss and boil, and never rest, night nor day. These are his life, and they are not written, and cannot be written. Every day would make a whole book of eighty thousand words—three hundred and sixty-five books a year. Biographies are but the clothes and buttons of the man—the biography of the man himself cannot be written."[34]

Sixth, biographers must concede and then explain the complexity of the human animal when looking into the minds of protagonists. This is true whether or not the biographer subscribes to Clemens's formulation, a belief that could bring despair to the biographical enterprise if subscribed to literally.

Part of the complexity biographers must recognize is that human beings are not static. That is true for the protagonist, and also for the supporting cast. In the best biographies, the people who surround the main subject evolve as he or she evolves; they change over time, and thus affect the actions of the protagonist. A biographer must try to understand all the characters in the play, not just the one with the leading role. Complexity is the watchword; if there is such a thing as simple folk (which I doubt, having never met one), biographers and publishers rarely choose them as subjects.

If a biographer lights on a theme while attempting to make sense of a life, it must not become reductionist, must not be used to purportedly explain every thought, every action of the subject. It should be considered a cardinal sin to interpret a whole life using a single formula from Freud, or any other simple notion. Human beings simply are not simple. Joan Peyser, the biographer of Leonard Bernstein, said, "I wrote recently that I was clearly unable to decide whether Bernstein was an angel or a monster. . . . It is not a question of either one or the other. He could be both, and within minutes."[35]

The anomaly amid the recognition of complexity is that the lasting biographies do have a theme or, perhaps more aptly, a central tension. Often, that tension is no more, and no less, than the struggle between free will and predestination. The best biographies are word portraits of a protagonist in conflict with himself or herself, or with the surrounding society, or both. Joseph Wall, after researching his biography of Andrew Carnegie, wrote: "It seemed to me that the one thing above all else that gave Carnegie's life an inner tension and made him the interestingly complex and often contradictory figure he was was the continuing necessity he felt to reconcile the radical egalitarianism of his grandparents, his parents and his own childhood with his insatiable desire for material acquisition. . . . Carnegie finally found the answer that resolved these tensions in his 'gospel of wealth.'" Wall understood the perils involved: "I was . . . fully cognizant of the fact that as a biographer I had quite purposefully imposed a central theme upon Carnegie's long and variform life. . . . Although it seemed patently clear to me at the time I was writing the biography that this was indeed the basic theme of Carnegie's life, I nevertheless realized it was a theme I had selected and imposed upon Carnegie. It was one none of his other biographers had chosen."[36]

A biographer must be allowed some latitude in this regard. Biographies are, after all, not life—they are an arrangement and interpretation of a life. Without a theme imposed by a biographer, a book can become chaos, a self-contradictory narration that reflects the incoherence of life. Once a plan is chosen, the biographer should be faithful to it while also maintaining as much objectivity about the contradictory evidence as humanly possible.

The biographer must concede that some actions and words will never be understood fully, and tell readers just that. Paul Mariani, biographer of William Carlos Williams, provides a real-life illustration. Mariani had every reason to believe that Williams's wife, Floss, was totally devoted. But when she died thirteen years after her husband, she chose to be cremated rather than buried beside him. "I myself chose not to speculate on the reasons for that final decision," Mariani said, "thus reminding the reader again that, in any life, no matter how long, much must remain, finally, a mystery."[37]

Seventh, a biographer must be honest with readers about filling gaps. Every life leaves gaps in the public record, what Victoria Glendinning calls "lies and silences." Gaps can lead a biographer to overemphasize periods for which there is ample documentation and underplay important periods for which the documentation is sparse. As Bernard Crick has said, "One has only the evidence that one can find. Which papers survive and which do not is largely accidental; there is no neat proportionality between the records and periods of Orwell's life."[38]

Paul Murray Kendall has noted, "There are no rules for handling gaps. Each paper trail is unlike any other paper trail. Each biographer is unlike any other biographer. The right way to fill gaps is unknown; the wrong ways are legion. Confronting a gap, the writer can but recognize that he is domesticated in imperfection; at the same time, he must respond to King Harry's call—'Once more into the breach!'— and, summoning his talents and honesty, struggle to suggest the life of his man during the blank, without either pretending to more knowledge than he has or breaking the reader's illusion of a life unfolding."[39]

One point is clear. Too many contemporary biographers, when confronted with gaps, fill them with mean-spirited suggestions and unsupported allegations. Such practices are one reason social commentators have worried about contemporary biography turning into "pathography."

A responsible biographer who accepts that some gaps are forever also accepts that research is never complete. Antony Alpers published two biographies of writer Katherine Mansfield, the first in 1953, the second in 1980. He estimated that the second version was based on twenty times more material than the first. In 1988, Claire Tomalin published a new Mansfield biography that superseded some of Alpers's research. Stephen Oates said while comparing and contrasting a spate of biographies about Lyndon Johnson: "None of the volumes, of course, offers a definitive portrait of Johnson. There is no such thing as a definitive biography. The nature of life-writing and reminiscence, the process by which one human being resurrects another on the basis of human records, memories and dreams, precludes a fixed and final portrait of any figure."[40]

New decades bring new perspective along with new information. Sometimes, different perspectives turn up virtually simultaneously. During the 1980s and early 1990s, different biographers studied the same subject at the same time—Jessica Savitch and Manuel Noriega are two cases on point. The competing books on Savitch and Noriega showed up in stores virtually simultaneously. Each time, the books contained substantial differences.[41]

Philip Ziegler conceded this about his subject, Lord Mountbatten: "It seems to me certain that within a decade, or at most a generation, a substantial reappraisal will be necessary of at least his role in India at the time of the Suez crisis, and over the reorganization of the British defense establishment. On a personal level, more evidence will by then be available about his extramarital affairs or lack of them, and his wife's remarkable career and character will be far better documented. . . . My biography will have been overtaken." Ziegler also noted that the same facts used by earlier and later biographers "may undergo a strange sea change in the intervening years. Details that seem of transcendent importance when first bruited abroad may well appear insignificant a generation later. Mountains become molehills or molehills mountains." As an example, Ziegler cited a 1941 radio broadcast by P. G. Wodehouse, in which the Englishman failed to sound harsh enough about Hitler. If Wodehouse had died soon thereafter, and if his biographer had begun work immediately, the radio broadcast almost surely would have been a highlight of the published book. But Wodehouse lived until 1975. During those decades, he regained his stature in society, so that his biographer was able to treat the broadcast's effects as transient.[42]

Eighth, good biographers go the extra mile to check out everything, never settling for secondary data when additional effort might uncover primary data. Gaps or incomplete information can tempt biographers to rely on newspaper clippings, hearsay, and autobiographical writings without subjecting them to rigorous examination. A good biographer will tell readers that secret, specifying the possible overemphases and unreliable evidence: newspaper clippings frequently are factually incorrect; hearsay might be motivated by spite and fraught with ignorance; autobiographies are often more significant for what they omit than what they include.

The best biographers never use secondary sources until all leads for primary sources are exhausted. Granted, it can be difficult to know when enough is enough. As Ziegler has noted, a biographer can never know whether he has located everything of significance that might be out there. With luck spawned by persistence, the biographer might determine the subject has left behind papers both accessible and useful. That, however, even if true, is usually just a first step, providing a rough map for what often turns out to be a futile search for biographical riches. If Smith wrote regularly to Jones, Ziegler notes, then it stands to reason that Jones wrote to Smith. But is Smith alive?

If she is, will she grant access to Jones's letters? If Smith is dead, who might have possession of her papers, and will they be available to a biographer? If Smith is a poet and Jones a prime minister, there might be hope that the letters back and forth will have been preserved; but poets and prime ministers are not born as public figures, so the biographer must ponder the odds that seemingly unimportant yet often revealing letters from Jones's youth have survived. According to Ziegler, Mountbatten at age nineteen seemed smitten by a woman named Peyton, whom Ziegler proved unable to trace. Ziegler reasoned that Mountbatten's letters to Peyton had been destroyed, but the slim possibility that they still existed was a nagging thought that any biographer would find enticing and unsettling.[43]

Witnesses certainly have an impact on accuracy, an impact that sometimes is beyond a biographer's control. By choosing to remain silent, a witness might make it impossible to fill a gap or correct a misimpression. On the other hand, sometimes the talkative sources cause more trouble than the silent ones. Mark Schorer said, "When one is writing the life of a person only recently dead, living witnesses are, of course, an essential source of information. And one discovers all too soon the burden that such evidence entails. Sometimes I wished that I had ten years more, for in that time most of those people would have gone away and I would no longer be confused by their conflicting tales and would in fact be free to say what I wanted about them. Quite as often I despaired when, just as I was about to get to an important informant, he did suddenly go away."[44]

Ziegler related similar experiences, saying no biographer can afford to let his guard down when dealing with evidence, especially when it is in the form of verbal testimony. What a letter or diary entry seems to mean can change, to be sure, as the biographer picks up more and more information during the research process about the circumstances of composition—but at least the words themselves are immutable. Interviewees, however, frequently alter their thoughts and words. They consciously lie, or have poor memories, or repeat anecdotes they think they "know" but actually have heard secondhand, or try to please the biographer by saying what they think he or she wants to hear.[45]

One of the diciest witnesses might be the subject. Doris Kearns, a Harvard University historian and biographer, watched the production of Lyndon Johnson's memoirs close up. What she observed was "a literary assembly line. I learned how unauthentic memoirs can be unless one understands the stage of life in which they are written, why they are being written at that time, and what audience they aim to please."[46]

Footnotes, endnotes, and bibliographies help readers determine the quality of the evidence. That said, the responsible biographer does much of the interpreting for the reader, pointing out where information is Grade B or Grade M instead of Grade A. After all, a biographer, unlike a novelist, operates under oath to provide the whole truth as far as it can be determined, however much that oath prevents telling a better tale.

Ninth, biographers must make hard decisions about the appropriate length of the book. Sometimes, setting out a smorgasbord of verifiable facts, and enough reasoned (and maybe even alternative) hypotheses, can help make up for unreliable or uncooperative human sources. That raises the question of how long is too long for a biography?

The answer is elusive. Sometimes, short ones seem too long. When Peter Collier, an experienced biographer, reviewed the relatively slim (274-page) Adnan Khashoggi life by *Washington Post* investigative reporter Ronald Kessler, he commented that Kessler "seems always to be huffing and puffing to bulk out the contents of the book. Subsidiary figures who play a brief role and then disappear are always introduced by a digressive portrait that tells us far more than we need or want to know about them."[47]

Many readers want evidence, but only what the biographer considers to be relevant evidence. A biographer who dumps everything from dozens of notebooks into the profile is failing to assume the responsibility of selectivity. Choosing the telling fact or quotation while discarding hundreds of others—yet not distorting the big picture—demands skills that some biographers lack, but must try to develop.

Being selective with masses of material to keep a biography at a readable, publishable length is its own skilled form of interpretation. The task is harder than ever in an age of presidential libraries with millions of documents, videotapes, and audiotapes, commercial computer databases that allow a biographer to search thousands of publications in a matter of seconds, and other resources that can lead to information overload. Most readers have no desire to buy an exhaustive biography; exhaustive too often also means exhausting. Readers pay an author (by buying the book) to help interpret a life.

Tenth, a biographer must avoid traps of illogic. David Hackett Fischer says sometimes trying to answer too many questions, trying to interpret too much, ensnares biographers. In his *Historians' Fallacies: Toward a Logic of Historical Thought,* Fischer suggests that trying to answer the question "why?" is dangerous, given the obstacles. "A 'why' question tends to become a metaphysical question . . . it dissipates a historian's energies and interests. 'Why did the Civil War happen?' 'Why was Lincoln shot?' A working historian receives no clear signals from these woolly interrogatories as to which way to proceed. . . . He can never hope to find the inner secret, maybe because it does not exist." Fischer identifies eleven categories of logical fallacy, those of question framing, factual verification, factual significance, generalization, narration, causation, motivation, composition, false analogy, semantical distortion, and substantive distraction. Fischer's warnings, while valuable, can be frustrating. Biographers indeed fall into traps of logic from time to time, but they must look for answers—including the "why"—if the enterprise is to continue.

Eleventh, good biographers must take style as seriously as substance. Many investigative biographers writing on contemporary subjects discover fascinating new material, if only by serendipity based on sheer time spent. But precious few of those biographers have the talent to tell the tale compellingly. Interesting lives can too easily be rendered pedestrian by pedestrian prose. The best biographers not only arrange the facts logically, but also provide readers with the feel of the facts.

Some of the writing techniques they use to create the feel are borrowed from fiction. Biographies and novels are concerned with birth, death, love, hate, and moral dilemmas galore. The techniques used in each genre might include scene-by-scene construction based on immersion in a geographic setting, physical descriptions of the key individuals, dialogue, imagery, symbolism, irony, contrast, and shifting points of view among various characters. Some novelists today write biographies; some biographers double as novelists.

Biographer Paul Murray Kendall figured this out decades ago, noting, "The obvious difference between biography and poetry-novel-drama is, if enormous, not quite so enormous as it appears. It will not do simply to say that biography is made out of fact (whatever that is) and fiction is made out of fancy (whatever that is). The writer of fiction, out of the mating of his own experience and his imagination, creates a world, to which he attempts to give the illusion of reality. The biographer, out of the mating of extrinsic experience, imperfectly recorded, and his imagination, recreates a world, to which he attempts to give something of the reality of illusion. We demand that a novel . . . be in some way true to life; we demand of biography that it be true to a life. There is a difference in meaning between the phrases; they join, however, in signifying not 'factual' but 'authentic'—and authenticity lies not only in what we are given but in what we are persuaded to accept."[48]

The dark side of the biography boom inspired by Robert Caro has been the large number of second-rate biographies—by journalists and academics—who lack pride or skill or native talent, or all three. There have been, unhappily, a great many of them. Some are passably researched (just barely passably), but poorly written. Some are passably written, but poorly researched. Some might actually be works of art, but their omission of endnotes makes them difficult to take seriously. Some biographies in the Caro mold would have turned out fine except for external obstacles, usually legal in nature, that the biographer and publisher were unable to overcome. (The last chapter of this book discusses in detail the troubled present and future of biography grounded in the techniques of investigative journalism.)

Nothing should be allowed to take the place of verifiable—and verified—information. Too many biographers today dig the dirt, then forget to look for the diamonds that might also be in the pile. They fall into a trap described by Jacques Barzun as forgetting to observe the maxim "by their fruits shall ye know them." Barzun explained, "It is the principle Lincoln used to confound Grant's enemies—if drinking whisky wins victories, let all the generals be given a pint of Scotch. But Grant was not a drunkard who happened to win battles. He was a military genius who happened to drink. Similarly, all our victims of biography are not idlers and profligates who were great artists on the side. They were artists whose characters were marred by adventitious elements precisely like certain other people that we all know."[49]

Poorly done investigative biographies almost always fail to show whether the transgressions exposed invalidate the subject's accomplishments. Sure, Frank Sinatra as portrayed by Kitty Kelley is a sleaze, but does that mean we should stop valuing his music? How do we explain the greatness of that music? From what traits did it spring? The very worst of the genre (Kelley's Sinatra biography is not among them; Kelley's Onassis, Taylor, and Nancy Reagan biographies are) tend to expose transgressions for exposure's sake, failing to account for the successes amid the sinning.[50]

Unfortunately, the authors of unrelieved pathographies—and hagiographies—can call themselves "biographers" along with the best practitioners of the craft. We can only hope biographer Park Honan is correct when he observes in his *Authors' Lives: On Literary Biography and the Arts of Language*, "It may cynically be said that quickly written, fluent and superficial studies win literary prizes, and that the public does not know a good biography from a dreadful piece of claptrap; but even as that is said the public's winnowing out is taking place, and I know of no abominable biography that has been cited with praise long after it was first printed. Bad biographies abound, but we do not hear of them a few months after they glitter."

CHAPTER TWO
Up from the Newsroom

Introduction

Robert Caro, an investigative reporter at Long Island's daily *Newsday* during the first half of the 1960s, left the newsroom to write books because he disliked the deadline-induced incompleteness of mainstream journalism. Little did he, or anybody else, know then how that little-noticed decision would affect the world of biography.

"I really wanted to take time to find out what happened, and time equals truth," Caro said two decades later. "What I mean is, there's never one truth about anything, but there are lots of objective facts. The more facts you can get, then when you sit down to interpret them, the closer you come to the truth. On newspapers, I never had enough time to find enough facts. I swore when I started doing books that I wouldn't write until I had explored all the avenues."[1]

Caro has researched, written, and published three massive books so far. The first, a 1,280-page biography of Robert Moses, won the Pulitzer Prize in 1975. The second and third, using 1,312 pages to chronicle Lyndon Johnson's life through his election to the U.S. Senate in 1948 (there are two additional volumes planned), were bestsellers. The first LBJ volume won an award from the National Book Critics Circle against stiff competition, as did the second LBJ volume.

Today, Caro is often called the super-reporter of our age. Virtually every commentator agrees that his research is awesome, even the historians who sniff that Caro lacks their training, seeming to suggest that he and other journalists ought to leave serious biography to the academy. But there is loud and legitimate controversy over whether his awesome research has indeed yielded the ultimate truth about his subjects. National magazines have devoted cover articles to that question; newspapers have devoted full-page features to it. Perhaps never before has an author's quest for truth been the subject of such widespread debate in the media. Caro's Johnson biography quickly became the version against which all others are measured. When historian Robert Dallek published the first volume of his Johnson life in 1991, the reviews and the reportage speculated whether Dallek's largely humane portrait had been presented as an antidote to Caro's meaner model.[2]

Unfortunately, the quality of the debate has failed to match the decibel level; the average reader knows only that either Caro has written the great biography of the twentieth century, or he has tried hard to do so but overreached and ultimately failed. In fact, Caro's work gives rise to an overriding question: can a gifted journalist with years of time and some money find truth better than daily reporters or academic researchers? If the answer is no, does that mean truth is impossible to attain? If the answer is yes, can Caro's techniques be adapted as guideposts for print and broadcast journalists, as well as other biographers, as they seek to better inform their audiences?

This chapter will examine Caro's findings concerning Lyndon Johnson, based on a dissection of the two volumes. Such painstaking examination is the only way to advance the debate about whether Caro achieved truth where others had failed, and, if he did, exactly how he did it.

The Path to Reportorial Power

Caro, born in 1936, grew up in New York City, the eldest of two boys. His mother died when he was eleven; his father, who sold real estate, carried on. Caro graduated from Princeton University with a degree in English literature and found a job reporting for the *New Brunswick (N.J.) Home News.* He began working at Long Island's *Newsday* a year later, green and Ivy League in a newsroom that did not take well to either.[3]

According to Robert Keeler's authorized history *Newsday: The Candid History of the Respectable Tabloid,*

During Caro's first few days at *Newsday*, someone assigned him to go to a Long Island Rail Road crossing, just east of the office, to get the details on a near-accident. He was so raw that he drove to the west instead, and didn't realize it until he reached Queens. When he finally got to the scene, he found a deaf man with a troubled marriage who had tried to kill himself by parking his pickup truck on the LIRR tracks. "I remember I felt like crying," Caro said. "I mean, this was the first time I had ever been at a human tragedy. I came back and I wrote this story, and I didn't even know how to write [a newspaper article]."

Once Caro had written it, Dick Aurelio, the news editor, walked over to him. He said something like, "This is a terrific piece of writing, but you don't have a lead on it," Caro said. "I, of course, knew in theory what a lead was, but I didn't really know. He said that in the lead you do so-and-so. I did the lead and brought it up to him and he said, 'Now you need a second paragraph.' He took me through this article. . . . When he finished that, I really understood more about how to write newspaper articles."

Caro began gaining confidence after getting sent to the Federal Aviation Administration office in New York City on a Saturday to examine documents an editor had heard might yield a good story. Apprehensively, he summarized the documents in a memo for mercurial editor Alan Hathway, one of those who had been displeased about the hiring of a tweedy Princeton graduate. On Monday, Caro's day off, he received a call at home from Hathway's secretary, asking Caro to report to the newsroom. Fearing he would be fired, Caro instead experienced one of his most gratifying moments in journalism when Hathway looked up from the memo to say, "I didn't know someone from Princeton could do digging like this. From now on, you do investigative work."

As Keeler notes, "Once he attained that status, Caro was not always a popular figure in the newsroom. Some considered him a prima donna who seemed to prefer dealing with no editor below the level of Hathway and Al Marlens, the city editor. But no one could deny that he brought to his work a high level of talent and a searing intensity. For Caro, journalism was a mission, an outlet for his sense of outrage at the world's injustices." His intensity led him to fight with editors about receiving enough time and space for his heavily researched articles.

Caro's first investigative series, "Misery Acres," dealt with fraudulent land sales in Arizona's desert. The first part, January 7, 1963, included a photograph of Caro sitting at a table, sipping wine, in the barren desert. After publication of the series, dozens of indictments resulted. Alicia Patterson, *Newsday*'s publisher, told Caro to lobby in Albany for a tighter state law on out-of-state land fraud. When Nelson Rockefeller signed the resulting bill into law, a photographer snapped Caro with the governor.

The next investigative efforts by Caro showed both his penchant for research that other reporters found boring and his missionary zeal. The subject of the September–October 1963 series and its January 1964 follow-up was the unplanned growth in Suffolk County, Long Island. Lee Koppelman, county planning director at that time, recalled to Keeler how Caro began the interview over lunch by smiling and asking soft questions. "I'm waxing poetic about how this new administration is going to guide the future," Koppelman said. "I'm into it for about a half hour, and finally Caro cuts in and . . . reels off a bunch of statistics. Southold was a disaster area. The population was aging. The young people couldn't stay there. The unemployment rate was going up . . . he caught me up short."

At Caro's urging, *Newsday* began a campaign to establish a regional planning board, which eventually came to pass. While doing the planning series, Caro realized how much more he had to learn about the topic, so he applied for and won a Nieman fellowship at Harvard University, where he studied urban and regional planning in 1965–1966. It was there that he decided to research a biography of Robert Moses, the New York planning czar. "His decision to leave the paper, after *Newsday* had supplemented the stipend that he received from the Nieman program, nearly ended that supplement for future Niemans from *Newsday*," Keeler wrote. "But Caro was too committed to the Moses project to stay at *Newsday*, even though it had been the training ground where he had acquired much of his now-legendary persistence and attention to detail."

Caro planned to return to *Newsday* in a year. Instead, he took seven years to complete the Moses book, finally published as *The Power Broker: Robert Moses and the Fall of New York*. He never returned to daily journalism.

Go Tell Moses

The controversy surrounding Caro's portrait of Moses set the stage for the far more widespread and virulent controversy over the multi-volume Johnson biography. Although Caro took a great deal of time to research and write the Moses book, he did it with very little money. As a result, it is not nearly as apt an example of his search for truth as the Johnson project, for which Caro received sizable advances. Furthermore, the Moses book attracted a smaller readership because the subject was a regional figure rather than an international household word; that limited the debate about truth to a relatively small circle of lay readers, public officials, academics, book reviewers, and fellow biographers. Nonetheless, it is important to give at least brief attention to the Moses debate, because it became a harbinger of the controversy over the Johnson biography—and because the Moses book, even more than the Johnson volumes, influenced the course of contemporary biography in America.

Caro's advance to write the Moses book for Simon and Schuster was just $5,000. He eventually sold his house to keep going, while his wife, Ina, turned to teaching to help pay the bills for the family, which included a young son. When Simon and Schuster failed to provide additional support after seeing a partial manuscript five years into the project, Caro went to Bob Gottlieb at Knopf, who agreed to publish the book.[4]

The Power Broker was assured more attention than the usual first biography by an obscure author about a relatively obscure person when *The New Yorker* magazine published excerpts. Not surprisingly, Moses (who had cooperated briefly with Caro before slamming the door) reacted angrily on the basis of those excerpts, writing a twenty-three-page rebuttal that the *New York Times* summarized. The book, Moses said, "is full of mistakes, unsupported charges, nasty, baseless personalities and random haymakers thrown at just about everybody in public life." But, as is almost always the case with Caro's critics, specifics were lacking. Caro responded: "One aspect of Robert Moses, which my book attempts to portray, is that of the smearer of reputations, the purveyor of baseless innuendo and outright falsehood, the wholesaler of defamation. I am not displeased that the commissioner has furnished this additional up-to-date documentation. . . . It is slightly absurd, but typical of Robert Moses, to label as without documentation a book that has 83 solid pages of single-space small type notes and that is based on seven years of research, including 522 separate interviews."[5]

When the completed book reached the stores, most of the reaction was undiluted praise for the writing, for the reliance on primary sources rather than hearsay and newspaper accounts. From the first page, it was obvious the book would be exciting to read, even without a prior interest in Moses's life. The introduction recounted an incident from Moses's young adulthood that seemed to say worlds about his character. It was written compellingly and sourced about as well as any recounting could be. There was a hint, too, of Caro's controversial practices, as he placed a recalled conversation from about sixty-five years earlier in direct quotation marks.

The Society of American Historians awarded Caro its Francis Parkman Prize for the book it said "best represents the union of the historian and the artist." Gore Vidal, no slouch as a writer himself, recognized the artistry, commenting that despite the book's length, "not once—uniquely—did I find myself glumly rifling the pages still to be read at the back." Caro also won the Pulitzer Prize for biography. Not bad for a first-time author.[6]

The Power Broker has endured, unlike most biographies, which tend to have a shelf life of less than a year. It is still in print, used as a text in many college courses, read regularly by journalists and biographers who want to study one of the best-reported, best-written nonfiction books ever. Its success encouraged daily newspaper journalists to risk their careers by trying to write biographies and encouraged publishers to offer contracts to those journalists.

But some criticism seeped into the overall acclaim, criticism that would be echoed, much more loudly, in the reviews of the Johnson books. *New York Times* reviewer Christopher Lehmann-Haupt worried about Caro's reductionism in trying to explain Moses, the "superficial but insistently repeated explanation that 'the shadow flickering in the depths of Moses' character was the arrogance he inherited from his mother.'"[7]

Dick Netzer, an urban economics professor, disliked the book. Netzer used his review in the *New Republic* to accuse Caro of "readily imputing motives for actions, imputations that only occasionally reflect his evidence." In addition, Netzer criticized Caro for believing human sources with scores to settle. Netzer cited an episode "in which I was a direct participant, John Lindsay's effort in early 1966 to merge New York City's transportation agencies. Caro relies heavily on self-serving reminiscences by the two city officials who were most responsible for turning the inevitable defeat (due to Governor Rockefeller's lack of support) into a humiliating debacle. They, not surprisingly, depict the rest of us as bumbling fools. We are in good company, for Caro in his late chapters portrays most prominent public officials (Rockefeller, Lindsay, Wagner, Ronan) as knaves or fools."[8]

Reducing a complex person to a caricature driven by a single trait. Imputing motives for that person's actions that overreach the available evidence. Relying too heavily on biased sources. Those three criticisms would surface again during the controversy following publication of each Johnson volume. But are those criticisms valid? And, if they are at least partially valid, do they finally undermine Caro's belief that he has come closer than any other writer to the truth about Moses and Johnson, about the abuse of power on the path to power?

Unearthing the truth about uses and abuses of power was, after all, Caro's objective from the beginning of his book-writing career. He made that clear in the opening of his book, stating that Moses's life "has been a drama of the interplay of power and personality." Moses's own testimony was not to be trusted: "It was very important to him that no one be able to find out how it was that he was able to build. . . . Because what Robert Moses built on was a lie. The lie had to do with the nature both of the man and of the public authority. . . . Moses said that he was the antithesis of the politician. . . . Public authorities are also outside and above politics, Moses said. . . . These statements were believed almost implicitly for almost 40 years by the public to which they were made. . . . Moses repeated his contentions a thousand times and for four decades they were repeated, amplified and embellished by a press that believed them, too."

Caro's introduction, in which he summarized the themes he would be pursuing, almost certainly caused some of the strong reaction to his work. Moses's supporters girded themselves for a form of negative biography recently termed "pathography." Caro did not write a pathography, but the undiluted starkness of his introduction, the assertions at that point put baldly instead of within a factual context, could easily have caused a negative mind-set in certain readers.

That said, biographers are supposed to make choices, to form opinions. That is what readers pay biographers to do. By serving as a skilled, responsible seeker of truth, Caro had entered a grand tradition. Leon Edel, probably the most prolific writer about biography as a genre, once noted, "The biographer needs to discover human self-deceptions. . . . Such deceptions may become a covert life-myth out of which lives, and biographies, are fashioned."9

Caro made his ultimate goal unarguably clear:

> I was never interested in writing biographies merely to tell the lives of famous men. I never had the slightest interest in doing that. From the first time I thought of becoming a biographer, I conceived of biography as a means of illuminating the times and great forces that shape the times—particularly political power. A biography will only do that, of course, if the biography is of the right man. Why am I so interested in political power? Because in a democracy, political power shapes all our lives.
>
> You can see this in simple, relatively insignificant things. Robert Moses . . . agreed to put the Manhattan terminus of his Triborough Bridge at 125th Street instead of 96th Street, as had been planned and as was more convenient and logical, because William Randolph Hearst owned real estate on 125th Street and wanted it condemned for the bridge. Every time you drive 29 blocks out of your way to get to the Triborough Bridge, your life is being affected . . . by political power as exercised by Robert Moses. . . . What I was aiming at was to show how urban political power worked in America in the middle of the 20th century. . . . I selected Moses because he was never elected to anything. But for 44 years he exercised more power in New York City and State than any official who was elected.

Caro's focus on the anatomy of power provided him with his lens for viewing Moses, and with his theme for writing about Moses, as shown by the successive section headings in the table of contents: "The Rise to Power," "The Use of Power," "The Love of Power," "The Loss of Power."

In the afterword to his Moses biography, Caro admitted that, as a newspaperman, he had thought he understood the nature of power, but had been mistaken: "If his monologues, shying from the sensitive as they did, were in a sense lectures on the philosophy and art of Getting Things Done in a democratic society, they were nonetheless the lectures of a genius. Having been an investigative and political reporter for some years, I naively believed that I knew something about the innermost fabric of decisionmaking in New York City and New York State, and not a little about government and politics in general. All that I knew was as nothing besides what I learned from this unique Gamaliel."

In other words, daily reporters have only the illusion of being insiders; in fact, they are outsiders in too much of a hurry. Time can unearth the facts to approximate truth, and daily reporters just do not have enough time. That is why a book about Moses seemed necessary. When it was finished, the next step was obvious to Caro— telling the story of one of the most powerful Americans in our century.

All the Way with LBJ

"I selected Lyndon Johnson as my next subject because I wanted to attempt to do the same thing with national political power, to show through his life the times and how he shaped them," Caro likes to explain. "What first attracted me to Johnson as a subject was not his presidency but his time as Senate majority leader. When he was leader it was said of him that no leader in history ever controlled, dominated, the Senate as he did. So I felt, if I could show how he did that, I would be showing the essence, the heart, of national political power."[10]

In an era of virtually anonymous biographers, the publicity and expectations surrounding Caro's prepublication research were unusual. Caro signed the contract with Knopf for a multivolume LBJ biography in 1976. By the time the *Atlantic Monthly* published excerpts, in 1981, the book had become an Event; Caro's name was a household word among the literary and political sets. Magazines ranging from *Publishers Weekly* to *People* ran profiles of him. He had achieved the same kind of recognition that painters in times past achieved—we speak of Rembrandt or Van Gogh, not of the people they painted. His fans believed Caro would accomplish with the LBJ book what Leon Edel says biographers, like painters, ought to accomplish: "Both portrait painters and biographers are permitted few liberties. The demand is for a studied likeness, no prettying up, no retouchings, softenings or hardenings, no pastiche. The artistic statement is most powerful when it is asserted with clarity, lucidity and no vestige of ambiguity."[11]

The hoopla over Caro's findings was especially poignant when contrasted with the publication just several months earlier of another Johnson biography, by Ronnie Dugger. Dugger, a longtime Texan, unlike Caro, had been a Johnson watcher for decades and had interviewed his subject before Johnson's death, also unlike Caro. For years, Dugger had edited a respected small magazine called the *Texas Observer*, which many readers relied upon for its inside scoop on politics. Yet Dugger's book received scant attention compared to Caro's, and certainly did not shoot to the top of the best-seller lists like Caro's.[12]

The attention given to Caro's first volume, however remarkable, was nothing compared to the interest in the long-anticipated second volume, published in 1990 and covering just seven years of Johnson's life (1941–1948). *The New Yorker* excerpted the second volume in 1989, leading to hundreds of news articles and commentaries about Caro's findings. After publication, the praise flowed as the book reached the top of the best-seller list quickly.[13]

The most glowing account came from the usually acerbic Nicholas von Hoffman, writing in *Vanity Fair* magazine. He said volume two seemed to contain so much new, unflattering truth "not because it was so deeply hidden but because journalists didn't look for it, or when they did look . . . the more influential political public was disposed to chalk it up to the quaint way they did politics down there in Texas." Terming Caro "the super-reporter of his time," von Hoffman said, "The crimes and misdemeanors laid out . . . are not merely confessed but explained and analyzed by the men who committed them . . . Caro . . . gets interviews from people who never, ever talk. Compare *Means of Ascent* with Lincoln Steffens' early twentieth century classic *The Shame of the Cities*. The political malefactors in Steffens' pioneering book told him little and elaborated on that little with the scantest details. Contrast that with what Caro found out about Brown

& Root [a construction company with ties to LBJ]. . . . Bagging the big interview doesn't suffice to explain how Robert Caro has changed the art of political biography. . . . Caro has tracked down every living member of Johnson's grammar-school class, and sniffed out every connection to the third, fourth and even fifth degree." Von Hoffman offered the best explanation for the success. Caro, von Hoffman wrote, combined two elements "which seldom go together, sensationalism and immaculate scholarship."[14]

Stephen Harrigan, profiling Caro for *Texas Monthly*, harked back to volume one, telling how Caro took "what should have been the most boring subject on earth—the advent of rural electrification—and turned it into a single chapter called 'The Sad Irons' which may be the most brilliant single passage of prose ever written about Texas."[15]

Amid the praise for volumes one and two, the same criticisms arose as had arisen about the Moses book, only to be largely drowned out in the din: Reducing a complex character to a caricature whose behavior could be explained easily by harking back, over and over, to a few root causes. Imputing motives for various actions beyond what the facts could sustain. Relying too heavily on biased sources. Making the biography too long, with Caro seeming to dump the contents of his note-pads into the books' pages. Paying too much attention to LBJ's times, with Caro losing sight of the protagonist for many pages at a stretch. Probably worst of all, being much too negative, creating a book maybe justifiable if marketed as investigative journalism, but certainly not good biography.

Much of the criticism has been general and ill-informed. The charge of excessive negativism is especially easy to counter. Those who make that charge either failed to read the two volumes carefully or brought personal blind spots to their analyses, or both. One reviewer, Henry C. Fleisher in *Dissent* magazine, summarized the phenomenon well: "Because the book concentrates so heavily on detail, a casual reader may get the impression that it centers only on Johnson's ego, his crassness, his relentless ambition for popularity, wealth and power. But in fact Caro pays tribute to Johnson's dedication and hard work, and to his genius for the art of politics."[16]

David Herbert Donald, a Pulitzer Prize–winning historian who did not come out of a journalism background, was perhaps the most precise of the critics. Writing about volume one in the *New York Times Book Review,* Donald said Caro had "studied his sources. It is not always clear, however, that he knows how to evaluate those sources." Donald raised the specter of reductionism, saying the book is "more like a caricature than a portrait" because of its reliance on Johnson's lust for power to explain everything he did. On Caro's practice of imputing motives to Johnson's actions, Donald found the author unconvincing when passing judgment: how, after all, could Caro reasonably surmise what Johnson—whom he never interviewed—was thinking at a specific moment? As for the supposed use of biased sources, Donald said Caro had "a tendency to believe sources that he himself ferreted out rather than those that are a matter of public record. . . . For instance, his sharply hostile version of Johnson's college years minimizes the favorable testimony of classmates, collected in oral histories at the Johnson Library, and relies mainly on the belated recollections of two disgruntled San Marcos graduates who had for half a century been nursing a grievance."[17]

Although Donald raised some valid questions about Caro's work, like most of the other critics he failed to examine the other side of the coin. Take the oral histories at the Johnson Library, for example. Many were recorded while LBJ was alive. Why does Donald believe that persons who knew and loved or feared LBJ would be candid? Merle Miller, whose generally laudatory oral history/biography of Johnson sold well several years before Caro's first volume, said he used 276 oral histories from the library, but rejected others because of their suspect nature: "Many persons taped before Lyndon's death apparently thought he would get up the morning after the interview was transcribed and rush to the library to read it." In addition, many oral histories are conducted by unskilled interviewers who fail to ask the right questions in the first place, or fail to ask follow-up questions to answers pregnant with significance.[18]

Much of the rest of the criticism, unhappily for public understanding, was clever, but less precise than Donald's, and generally more wrongheaded. Tom Dunkel, writing in the *Washington Times* magazine *Insight,* said, "If this book were the Mona Lisa, there would be an arrow pointing to her enigmatic smile."[19]

In an article that promised a great deal (the headline said "The

Years of Robert Caro / Getting It All Wrong"), Sidney Blumenthal, writing the cover piece in the *New Republic* after the publication of volume two, did manage to raise the right questions about the author's quest for truth: "The heart of the Caro legend is his 'genius' for finding and delivering the complete truth. . . . What does Caro mean by 'truth'? He appears to mean the unparalleled and comprehensive accumulation of facts. . . . The swarm of particulars in his possession are what invests him with powers of mythic explanation and moral judgment. And the sheer quantity of his facts is what gives his work its aura of unassailable authority. . . . But Caro's legend poses a danger to his work. For he has staked everything on his encyclopedic mastery of his sources, on having penetrated every corner. . . . But what if there are corners Caro has not penetrated? What if there are sources he does not know, particulars that rearrange the light and the shadows on all his subjects?"[20]

Despite Blumenthal's determination to show that truth had eluded Caro, his essay proved nothing on that score. Blumenthal indeed identified a few sources whom Caro either never interviewed or interviewed briefly, but utterly failed to convince that such sources were more reliable or insightful than the hundreds Caro did rely on. In the end, Blumenthal's indictment of Caro—while promising so much at the beginning—is like almost all the others: at bottom emotional, based almost entirely on arguable opinion, almost never on facts.

Caro himself anticipated, or reacted to, many of his critics in his introductions to the books, in his speeches, and in interviews. Occasionally, he swept the criticisms away with broadsides aimed at the reviewers, broadsides that relied on his belief that his research techniques, combined with the time he took, had yielded truth. In one interview, Caro said the criticisms "are not fair. In fact, they're not true, they're lies. The documentation is so thorough and complete that no real questions can exist in the mind of a truthful person." Later, responding to one eminent and virulent critic, David Broder of the *Washington Post,* Caro said, "I heard the same thing Mr. Broder was told and by many of the same people I suspect he talked to. And then I did the thing he didn't do. I did the work." In the trade paperback edition for the second volume of the LBJ biography, Caro added a fifteen-page essay refuting certain critics in detail on certain points (that essay is reprinted at the end of his chapter, along with Caro's notes on sources).[21]

Perhaps Caro brought on some of the extracritical examination of his work by making statements about having found truth where other journalists and historians had failed. Writing in *L.A. Weekly*, reviewer Tom Carson said Caro sometimes came across as "a self-righteous prig." Robert Sherrill, longtime chronicler of Texas politics, was the most open in resenting what he perceived as Caro's claim to the throne, wondering why such an outsider came "to us in the guise of the divinely-appointed biographer carrying The Torch of Truth and pretending that the major points of the Lyndon Johnson story haven't been told before by expert and eloquent biographers."[22]

A careful reading of previous Johnson biographies shows Sherrill's haymaker to be misguided. No previous Johnson biographer is Caro's equal as a stylist. As for research expertise, it is unquestionable that a few previous biographers had exposed particular episodes before Caro arrived on the scene. But, again, a careful reading of those biographies shows beyond a shadow of a doubt that none approached Caro's comprehensiveness in telling Johnson's life through 1948.

Approaching the Throne of Truth

What about Caro's claims to truth so angered Sherrill and a vocal minority of other reviewers? A sampler of Caro's own statements will provide a logical lead-in to a closer examination of specific passages. That examination will determine whether Caro practiced what he preached, and whether other journalists turned biographers can benefit from emulating his practices.

When biographer Joseph Lash died in 1987, Caro spoke at the memorial service. He praised Lash's books for a "truly rare sincerity . . . an unshakable determination, rare in its purity, to find and tell the truth." Caro could have been talking about himself. When he set out to tell the saga of LBJ, it was partly because he believed nobody had told it thoroughly and truthfully. As Elizabeth Bennett wrote in the *Houston Post* after interviewing Caro, "Seventeen biographies of Johnson had already been published, all covering his early years, but

Caro's painstaking, exhaustive research soon convinced him that most of what had been written about the former president 'wasn't correct.'"[23]

In a lecture at the New York Public Library, Caro set out his motivation: "Lyndon Johnson was a great storyteller, vivid and persuasive, and he told stories that were repeated over and over again, in books and articles, thousands of times. He really created his own legend. And the legend isn't true."[24]

As Caro began his interviewing around Johnson's boyhood home, he said he would "repeat the stories that had become the legend of Lyndon Johnson's youth, the legend he had created. At this point I really had no idea that they weren't true. But the people would say, 'Well, some of that didn't really happen, you know,' or 'Well, there's more to it than that, but I don't want to tell you what it is—you shouldn't tell bad things about a president.' I began to get the feeling that something was drastically and basically wrong with the legend, but I didn't really pick up on what they were trying to tell me."[25]

The epiphany arrived when Caro interviewed LBJ's brother, Sam Houston, for probably the sixth time, after he had stopped drinking and had suffered through cancer. He seemed changed—calmer, more reliable. Caro convinced Sam Houston to meet with him in the Johnson family home, re-created by the National Park Service. Sam started talking at length. Caro broke in: "Now, Sam Houston, I want you to tell me all the stories about your brother's boyhood that you told me before, the stories that your brother told all those years, only give me more details." There was a long pause, Caro said, after which Sam Houston replied, "I can't." Caro asked why not. "Because," Sam Houston said, "they never happened." Caro said that on the basis of Sam Houston's revised accounts, he reinterviewed numerous sources: "And this time, when I went back to the people who were involved in these incidents, they remembered and confirmed them."[26]

Using the pages of his two Johnson volumes, Caro explains again and again how journalists and biographers coming before him had been mistaken. In his first volume, for example, Caro relates one of the ways he began learning the truth about LBJ's college years. At first Caro had no reason to doubt the conventional wisdom of Johnson as a popular, charismatic campus politician. Certainly the oral histories of his classmates, on file at the Johnson Library in Austin, were unanimously in that vein. When Caro first heard a contrary view, he wrote it off as "a prejudiced account by an embittered man." But Caro took the time to seek out other classmates who had never been interviewed, who had never provided what he says turned out to be whitewashed oral histories. Caro's discovery was to him another example of time helping an author approach truth. The result, Caro said, was a portrait "substantially different from all previous portraits."

Concerning Johnson's college romance with Carol Davis, it had "been told repeatedly in biographies of Lyndon Johnson," Caro commented. "But none of the authors who repeated it had interviewed Carol Davis. She was there to be interviewed; she still lives in San Marcos."

About Johnson's home life, Caro said, "Before they died, his sister Rebekah and his brother Sam Houston both told me that [Lyndon's] picture was all but unrecognizable to them. But it is not necessary to accept their word. One can ask others who spent time in the Johnson home—not only daily visitors such as his parents' friend Stella Gliddon and Lyndon's cousin Ava, but three more disinterested witnesses, three women who worked or lived in that home as housekeepers. None of these three had ever been interviewed. . . . The true relationship is also fascinating, but it is not the one that has been analyzed." Elsewhere in volume one, Caro quotes his previously untapped sources as agreeing "that the attempts of some biographers to portray the Johnson home as one of unending and bitter conflict between husband and wife are incorrect."

While developing evidence of Johnson's physical cowardice, Caro noted that the whippings Lyndon's father administered almost surely hurt much less than the boy let on as he howled in apparent pain. Lyndon's playmates knew this, Caro said, "but not all adults understood—and many, ready to believe the worst of a man who 'drank,' would tell biographers years later that Sam had been physically brutal to Lyndon."

In relating what Caro believed to be the true story of LBJ's pseudo-runaway trip to California as a teenager, the author commented, "Johnson's description of the trip . . . no matter how enthralling to biographers—a passage in a typical biography reads 'Johnson was barely able to survive on the grapes he picked, the dishes he washed and the cars he fixed. . . . [He] lived the vagabond life'—is no more accurate than the reason he gave for taking it." In fact, Caro shows the trip was mostly undramatic, that Johnson found an undemanding job, and that he was not ever starving.

Concerning Johnson's relationship with the company Brown & Root, Caro said it "has been until now largely a matter not only of speculation and gossip, but of incorrect speculation and gossip." In his second volume, Caro made similar statements. For example, concerning LBJ's accumulation of wealth during the 1940s, Caro said, "Here we can pursue in detail and without complication a subject that has been endlessly discussed but little understood, at least partly because of the dearth of detailed information—the role and significance of favoritism and influence in a democratic government. The birth and early years of the Johnson financial empire illuminate very clearly the subtle means by which favoritism and influence are exercised, and their effect on other individuals and on the body politic."

Caro said he would portray LBJ's six months of Navy service as far more complex than ever portrayed before. He said his explanation of vote stealing in the 1948 U.S. Senate race would change a "previously bewildering picture" into a "blindingly clear" one. About whether Johnson had used political clout to obtain a lucrative CBS network affiliation for his Austin radio station, Caro said, "Journalists may have regarded this story [Johnson's version] skeptically, but they felt they could not disprove it. In fact, however, it is possible to know what would have happened if a non-Congressional station owner had applied." Caro then explained how he found the answer.

Some Doubts about Whether Truth Is Attainable

For all Caro's success at revealing LBJ's falsehoods, sometimes the author conceded that finding truth was tough. In volume one, he tells how Lyndon was whipped in a fight after high school. Caro asks half a page of questions about the youth's reaction, ending the section with these words: "Is it possible to read into his 'That's enough' a surrender not just in a dance-hall fight but in the larger fight he had been waging for years, the fight to be somebody without following the course his parents wanted him to take? No one can say. No one knows what Lyndon Johnson thought that night, on the way home and lying in bed, and no one will ever know. But the next morning, he told his parents he would go to college."

Again, in volume one, after recounting Lyndon's mastery at manipulating adults, Caro shows his uncertainty by resorting to questions, a few of which are: "What was the reason he acted this way? That he screamed and sobbed over spankings that didn't hurt and cried hunger when he wasn't hungry, and made public complaint about the sloppiness of his sisters' bedroom? . . . What was it he wanted—attention? sympathy? respect? dominance? Whatever it was, he was desperate to have it."

In volume two, discussing charges of vote stealing in a Senate election, Caro says, "Because of the manner in which votes were falsified in San Antonio . . . and because . . . no testimony was ever taken under oath from any San Antonio election official, it has been impossible, forty years after the election, to determine the number of votes illegally cast for Lyndon Johnson . . . or to determine if the 10,000 figure is correct. But that figure does not appear to be greatly exaggerated."

When a seemingly responsible source has cast doubt on what Caro believed to be the true version, Caro warns the reader. Concerning a news leak about Johnson to journalist Paul Bolton, Caro says his sources are a letter in the private papers of an LBJ mentor, plus an interview with one of LBJ's political colleagues, both of whom the author names. Caro has no reason to doubt his dual sourcing, but responsibly points out, "Bolton says he does not recall the incident."

Occasionally, when Caro anticipates readers' questions about the reliability of a source, he addresses the doubts head-on. David Votaw, a teacher at Southwest Texas State Teachers College when Lyndon registered there as a freshman in 1927, clearly recalled seeing Lyndon on registration day—four decades later. How many college professors can remember one student out of hundreds or thousands so vividly, so many years after the event? Knowing Votaw's account might strain credulity, Caro says, "If he appears to remember too well, to have recreated a conversation in light of the boy's later fame, other faculty members remember [Votaw] telling them that same day in 1927, 'I've just met a boy who's going places.'"

In a later section, Caro believes it necessary to explain why his dark portrayal of Johnson's college years should be accepted as truer than previous versions, should become the new conventional wisdom: "The hostility that many of his fellow students felt for Lyndon Johnson is striking in its depth and passion. It does not surface immediately, for not only is it deep, it lies deep—deep and hidden. The researcher begins his interviews on Johnson's college years expecting to hear about a popular campus leader—because the LBJ Library has collected oral histories only from students who describe him in this way. The researcher's initial round of interviews confirms, in general, this expectation. If, when he interviews men who were not interviewed by the library—an Edward Puls or a Henry Kyle—he gets a different picture, he dismisses it as a biased view, the view of men who lost to Lyndon Johnson and were embittered by the experience. But there are enough puzzling hints even in the interviews with men and women who praise Johnson to make the researcher go back and re-interview them, and when he does, other feelings begin to surface. They surface slowly—because of fear. In some cases, they never surface. . . . But when at last the picture comes clear, it is far from a picture of a popular campus hero." Another persuasive indication came when Caro interviewed a classmate of Johnson's whose yearbook was missing pages damaging to LBJ's reputation, pages carefully cut out with a razor blade. Caro learned that Johnson had supervised the razor-blade brigade.

In general, Caro appears to be confident that his assiduous research over the first sixteen years of his LBJ project allowed him to capture Johnson about as accurately as is humanly possible. Other professional biographers, however, are less certain that truth, about LBJ or anybody else, is attainable in any precise way.

The difficulty of finding truth is a common theme not only among historians and biographers, but also among philosophers and theologians. There is certainly ample evidence that time does not always unearth facts that can lead to truth, per Caro's equation. Many books that take years to research and write are wrong. When two books on the same subject are published simultaneously, a close reading always points up discrepancies. A recent example involves two books on Panamanian dictator Manuel Noriega. The authors, John Dinges and

Frederick Kempe, are respected journalists. The books are both well-researched, well-written, responsible tomes. Yet they differ on a number of crucial points. That means that on each point at least one of the journalists, despite taking time, missed the truth.[27]

All that said, Caro is quite within bounds to believe that truth is attainable in some fashion. He is working well within journalistic and historical traditions in his quest. Caro set out to answer the open-ended question of what made Johnson the way he was. If Caro could find the answer, it might explain a lot about contemporary American and international history. The overriding question remains, did Caro succeed? And, if so, how did he do it?

Volume One of the Johnson Biography

Caro tells the Johnson saga chronologically. As he explains, "I think it's absolutely vital to stick to strict chronology because they [Moses and Johnson] were so devious. Things they did that you can't understand if you try to take them as isolated decisions suddenly become very clear if you just make yourself take one thing after another. Then you can see what the person was doing."[28]

The chronology starts before LBJ's birth, which is not chronicled until page 56. Background about Johnson's ancestors and about the place where he grew up helps to achieve truth by providing context. To learn about the ancestors, Caro relied on Johnson relatives and their scrapbooks, on county historical societies and their clippings from local publications unavailable anywhere else, and on amateur and professional genealogies.

To learn about the land that helped shape Johnson, the Texas Hill Country, Caro supplemented numerous interviews by reading municipal, county, and state histories; located unpublished master's theses and doctoral dissertations; and found government publications such as a 1904 bulletin from the U.S. Department of Agriculture titled "Forest Resources of Texas."

All such sources have their limitations. The memories of longtime area residents and LBJ relatives (as is true of all human sources) are selective, screening out either the bad memories or the good memories, depending on the disposition of the particular person. Furthermore, their recollections might be contaminated by all they have read about their famous relative over the decades. (It would be that way with almost any family: how much accurate information would a biographer learn from a first cousin the subject saw only occasionally, or from a grandfather who never thought the subject could do any wrong and whose memory is failing besides?)

Scrapbooks are by nature somewhat unreliable, too. Many newspaper articles from a century earlier were written by hacks or housewives whose standards of proof for what they included were low or nonexistent; that meant hearsay and gossip might masquerade as fact. Local histories written in the nineteenth and early twentieth centuries often cannot stand close scrutiny; many of them lack endnotes, bibliographies, and even indexes. Yet such sources might be the best available information. They may not be truth incarnate, but they can aid in the quest.

To help overcome the necessary use of such iffy sources, Caro and his wife moved to the edge of the Hill Country and lived there for about three years. He was aware from the start that his background (as he put it, "an entire life spent in a city filled with museums and concerts, a life spent on crowded streets and sidewalks") might hinder his understanding of Johnson growing up in the unpopulated Hill Country.

Despite his noble purpose in moving to Texas, Caro's attempt to absorb the culture by living there received criticism later—for being insincere or condescending or useless, or all of these. As one Johnson loyalist told a reporter writing about the Caro method, "Anyone who arrives in Texas from New York City with a poodle dog in one hand and a tennis racket in the other and tries to tell us what Lyndon Johnson was all about, well, that really chaps my hide." Another journalist writing about the Caro-Johnson controversies transmitted the rejoinder: "Caro pleads guilty to being a New Yorker and an avid tennis player, but took exception to something else. 'My dog, now deceased, was a Shetland sheepdog and would be very insulted to be called a poodle.'" It was one of the few light moments in what was generally a deadly serious debate.

Living in the Hill Country not only helped Caro absorb the culture, but also helped him develop specific, valuable human sources. "When Ina and I moved up to the Hill Country and people realized that I was there to stay—that I wasn't just one more reporter coming through for a month and then going back to write the definitive work on what the Hill Country was like—they started talking more frankly." They showed the city boy what it had been like to live without electricity, without running water, without so many of the conveniences taken for granted in New York City. The demonstrations gave Caro vivid impressions, and helped him understand why LBJ as a congressman became a hero for bringing electricity to the Hill Country.

Despite Caro's obvious skill at finding information, a page-by-page examination of his sources and conclusions sometimes gives pause to an experienced researcher. On balance, however, volume one is a superbly documented book. Without question, it approaches truth more closely than anything previously written about the first four decades of Johnson's life.

Nonetheless, I will begin the page-by-page examination with a sampler of hesitancies. Sometimes the generalizations Caro draws about LBJ's ancestors make one wonder. On page 3, Caro mentions how the eyes of LBJ's Grandmother Bunton "talked. They spit fire . . . the Bunton eye was famed throughout the Hill Country." Can eyes be so expressive as to be famous?

On page 8, Caro discusses the effects of the Bunton blood and the Johnson blood mingling: "It was only when, in Lyndon Johnson's father, the Bunton strain became mixed with the Johnson strain that the Bunton temper and pride, ambition and dreams, and interest in ideas and abstractions brought disaster, for the Johnsons were not only also dreamers, romantics and idealists, not only had a fierce pride and flaring temper of their own, and physical characteristics which greatly resembled those of the Buntons, they also resembled the Buntons in their passion for ideas and abstractions—without resembling them at all in shrewdness and toughness." Is such generalizing fair and apt across the board, covering so many disparate members of the same clan? Could Caro in all honesty write a similarly general passage about every one of his relatives?

The answer is probably yes for some clans, no for others. Such generalizations ought to be treated with caution by journalists and their audiences. But an author like Caro who has steeped himself in a subject has the right—and maybe the obligation—to make judgments, to draw conclusions, in the quest for truth. Caro's judgments are certainly within the realm of acceptable biographical practice. A skilled biographer need not be invisible. As Leon Edel has noted, "The integrity and intensity of the biographer's process, and his ways of proceeding, usually shine through his work. He is far from anonymous. He is present in his work as the portrait painter is present in his. And he stands or falls by the amount of confidence or of distrust he creates in the reader. If he is absent from the work, his book is usually a flabby performance, lacking force and heart."[29]

Another hesitancy stems from Caro's use of secondary sources. On page 61, for example, Caro seems to rely solely on a newspaper clipping as his source of information, a dangerous practice in many instances; on page 75, he also seems to rely on a clipping, but one that has greater authority. The distinction between those two clippings is important.

Most journalists know that other journalists get things wrong a lot—sometimes the facts themselves, sometimes the words in a direct quotation, sometimes the shadings of meaning. Clippings are an important starting point for background, but everything should be rechecked whenever possible. As a result, it is puzzling that, on page 61, Caro cites an article from a 1919 issue of the *Fredericksburg (Tex.) Standard* as his only source for a passage on LBJ's father buying and selling ranches. Why not go to the land records themselves at the county courthouse? Caro's seemingly unnecessary reliance on a secondary source does not promote truth.

The citation on page 75 is to a 1968 article in the *San Angelo (Tex.) Standard-Times*. Caro uses that article to relate how August Benner, opposing LBJ's father for the state legislature in 1918, charged election fraud. Examination of the actual article, obtained from the librarian in the San Angelo newsroom, shows it was written by an Associated Press correspondent named Jack Keever, who checked election returns in three of the four counties making up the district (by 1968, the records had been destroyed in the fourth county), as well as checking the certification report by the Texas legislature. Given the inevitable limits on Caro's time, money, and energy, relying on what appears to be such a well-researched article probably made sense and did no harm to the quest for truth.

Overall, Caro uses secondary sources too much, to the detriment of total confidence in some of the details. When he relates how Johnson vomited after coaching a high-school debate team to the championship and then losing, his only stated source is a *Time* magazine article from 1965. An independent examination of that article shows the anecdote to be unattributed. Why rely on *Time* magazine? But the use of secondary sources never shakes confidence in Caro's overall picture.

On page 104, Caro describes LBJ's father as he aged and lived a troubled life: "His mouth, day by day, pulled tighter and grimmer; his eyes, which had always been so piercing, now, often, glared defiantly back at the world." Such a passage provides great color, and makes the reader seem part of Sam Johnson's world. But how could Caro know about day-to-day changes? Is this truth telling, or authorial license? It may be that Caro has impeccable sources for such a passage, including a series of photographs. Then again, maybe not. An author, no matter how much he has won our trust through accumulated research, ought to retain our trust by sourcing everything, either in the text or in the endnotes. For this passage, Caro, unfortunately, does neither clearly.

Happily, Caro's successes at truth telling far outweigh the shaky passages. For example, on page 154, Caro ends previous speculation about Johnson's college grades by reporting that his average was a B–, with eight A's out of fifty-six courses. He was able to see a handwritten record of Johnson's grades kept by a former dean. Overall, the sources for this chapter are a model for all journalists: a master's thesis from 1930 about the college's history; much of LBJ's correspondence with his mother during the college years; interviews with twenty-seven fellow students, two faculty members, four administrators, and three townspeople; oral histories from five faculty members; articles by and about Johnson from two college newspapers published during his time on campus; plus a tape recording of Johnson back on campus in 1970, reminiscing with professors and students from the 1920s. Out of such variety, truth often emerges.

One enlightening piece of truth that emerged from Caro's digging into Johnson's years on campus was the meaning of his college nickname, "Bull." Probably the leading piece of conventional wisdom had been endorsed by *Time* magazine, in its 1965 profile of LBJ as the education president, when it quoted a classmate as saying LBJ "was always promoting something and had such drive," making the nickname sound like a compliment. In his biography, Ronnie Dugger placed emphasis on Johnson's hard-charging, bull-like nature. Caro, however, determined that "Bull" was short for "Bullshit." His sources are convincing—in the 1928 college yearbook, Johnson is pictured as a jackass with the caption, "As he looks to us on the campus everyday." The campus newspaper humor column defined "Bull" as "Greek philosophy in which Lyndon Johnson has an M.B. degree." Three of Johnson's classmates told Caro that the M.B. stood for master of bullshit, or otherwise referred somehow to bullshit.

Caro's portrait of Texas Congressman Sam Rayburn, eventually speaker of the House of Representatives, has received some criticism for appearing idealized. Not so. It is a full-blooded portrait based on first-rate research—with a necessary emphasis on the Rayburn-LBJ relationship. How Johnson twisted that relationship for his own ends came to Caro as a surprise, as he explained: "I'll never forget learning about his betrayal of Rayburn. You never learn a thing like that from just one document. But when you're sitting there in the Johnson Library, which has 32 million documents, if you keep reading enough of them you'll eventually come across almost everything. And gradually, as I was going through the intra-office memos, and the telephone calls and the telegrams from many different files, I began to see unfolding what was happening between Roosevelt and Rayburn and the role Lyndon Johnson had played in it. I can still remember my feeling, which was 'God, I hope this doesn't mean what I think it does' . . . [but] the story was just as sordid as I had feared it would be."[30]

Plowing through what seemed to be endless documents also paid off when Caro was able to illustrate Johnson's central role in the successful last-ditch fund-raising for the 1940 Democratic congressional candidates, a role that left many legislative colleagues owing him a great debt. Caro said for years during his research that he thought he would be unable to prove the insider wisdom that Johnson gained power so fast because of money. "But then one day," Caro said in a talk, "while I was sitting in the Johnson Library looking through files that supposedly dealt with some totally unrelated subject, suddenly there it was, the intra-office memos—Congressman so-and-so needs $1500. . . . The frantic telegrams from the congressmen themselves. . . . And in the margins, next to the congressman's requests, Lyndon Johnson would write 'O.K.' or 'Give 500" or 'none.' That sort of thing. So it really is necessary to look at as much material as you can."

When documents do not exist to fill in the blanks, hard work might be a substitute. Caro went to great lengths, profitably for truth telling, to reconstruct Johnson's "basic impromptu speech" during his first race for Congress. Caro began by taking paragraphs and phrases from descriptions of the speech printed in daily and weekly newspapers. Then he contacted about a dozen Hill Country residents who had heard the speeches and were also familiar with Johnson's way of talking. Caro asked them to recollect what Johnson had said, recalling as specifically as possible the phrases he had used. "Those phrases which recurred most often were combined with the written material to reconstruct the speech," Caro explained.

Interviewing and reinterviewing. Prodigious documents research. Informed reconstructions. Another strength is Caro's use of perspective. He says, for example, that as a U.S. representative, Johnson introduced only five national pieces of legislation and almost never gave floor speeches. Some reviewers criticized Caro for naïveté, noting that any expert on Congress knows most of the work is done in committees. But Caro's truth meant something, because he did his homework; he showed that other members of Congress, Johnson's contemporaries, introduced far more national legislation, gave far more speeches, while also doing their committee work. Caro's portrayal of an indifferent Congressman Johnson appears to approximate the truth. The supposedly low-profile Johnson, so active behind the scenes in the House that he had no time for introducing legislation or speaking on the floor, appears to have been a fiction unintentionally created by previous chroniclers, with Johnson's connivance. Those chroniclers perhaps failed to understand the relationship between taking time and finding truth.

Perhaps the most telling controversy embedded in the debate over

Caro's claim to truth focused on LBJ's relationship with Alice Glass, the mistress and later the wife of Charles Marsh, a Texas newspaper magnate and enthusiastic Johnson supporter. Before Caro came along, the possibility of a long-term Glass-Johnson sexual relationship had been all but ignored. Sam Houston Johnson, Doris Kearns, and Merle Miller, authors of best-selling books about LBJ pre-Caro, never even mention Alice Glass. Ronnie Dugger, whose biography appeared just months before Caro's, mentions Glass on one page; he accepts that LBJ flirted with Glass, but hints at nothing more.

Caro, on the other hand, mentions Glass prominently. He says he received evidence of the affair from Alice's sister, Alice's best female friend, two male confidants (one of whom later became Alice's brother-in-law), Alice's daughter, and a Texas politico who knew her well. Caro names all six of those sources, plus refers to a seventh source who received a grant of anonymity.

Despite Caro's evidence, David Donald, reviewing volume one, was dubious: "The evidence for the alleged affair is so thin that the verdict for a professional historian should be, at most, 'not proved.'" Paul Conkin, author of a little-noticed post-Caro biography of LBJ, tried to evaluate the evidence used by Caro. Conkin concedes that Glass was "an important woman" in Johnson's life, and that there was at least an infatuation. He also raises some useful cautions—there are few references to Glass in LBJ's surviving correspondence, Glass apparently took other lovers, she may have had reason to boast falsely of being intimate with a man who became president, and her letters to LBJ in his retirement "suggest a very special and enduring friendship, not any more than this. Intense affairs of passion rarely wind down so smoothly."[31]

Maybe rarely, but sometimes it does happen. Donald's deep skepticism seems to be based, at least in part, on Caro's lack of academic credentials; Conkin's caution seems, well, too cautious. Caro appears to be on the mark, revealing truth about as fully as is humanly possible under the circumstances.

Volume Two of the Johnson Biography

Caro received criticism from some reviewers for what they considered an unrelievedly negative second volume. But Caro warned in his introduction that what he had previously termed "the bright thread" of Johnson's career would be missing from volume two, which "is about a seven-year period . . . in which his headlong race for power was halted." That summary of Caro's turns out to be confusing, because the largest chunk of the book chronicles the 1948 race for the U.S. Senate—a race barely won (or stolen) by Johnson amid charges of vote fraud on both sides. The victory put Johnson on the fast track to power, as it turned out.

The most troublesome criticism for an essayist trying to determine if Caro achieved truth to a greater extent than any journalist before him is the treatment of Coke Stevenson in volume two. Stevenson, a former Texas governor, was Johnson's 1948 Senate opponent. Most reviewers believe Caro destroyed his previously well-deserved credibility by turning Stevenson into a saint, unfairly using him as a foil to a totally evil Johnson.

Dugger's 1982 biography of LBJ introduced Stevenson like this: "A right-wing Texas rancher, Stevenson had served in Austin quietly through the war. He appointed reactionaries as regents to the state university. When [Homer] Rainey, the liberal president of the school, was fired and ran for governor, Stevenson joined the gang-up against him. The governor's emblems were his pipe and his taciturnity. Announcing for the Senate, he advocated less government, lower taxes, segregated schools, 'the complete destruction of the communist movement in this country.'" If Dugger's description is accurate, how could Caro portray Stevenson as a hero?[32]

David Broder, the respected political columnist for the *Washington Post*, savaged Caro for his treatment of Stevenson. Broder says the saga of the 1948 U.S. Senate election is "a story that needs no hyping, but Caro isn't satisfied just to uncover and recount how one politician outfoxed another. Instead, he makes Johnson's opponent, Coke Stevenson, a saintly figure of surpassing virtue and innocence, ravaged by the Predator of the Pedernales. There was something of this in the first volume, when Caro sought to strip Sam Rayburn of the wiliness that made him such a great Speaker of the House in order to portray him as the hapless victim of Johnson's favor-seeking with FDR. But with Coke Stevenson, he pulls out all the stops—and distorts history in a way no serious biographer should do."[33]

Caro does no such thing. Caro does portray Stevenson as unyield-ing in his principles, even when his principles seem downright ridic-ulous. Caro does not dissect Stevenson's mixed record as governor in detail, but never was that the intention of his book—no biographer can be all things to all readers. When the paperback edition of volume two appeared in March 1991, Caro had added a fifteen-page note on sources, opening like this: "After this book was published in March 1990, a number of articles about it that appeared in magazines and newspapers made statements about Coke Stevenson for which I be-lieve there is no factual basis. Some of these articles, no doubt inad-vertently, repeated allegations and rumors circulated in 1948 by Lyn-don Johnson and his followers in their campaign to undermine Coke Stevenson's reputation—allegations and rumors I also believe to be without factual basis. I am adding this note . . . to expand and clarify the record in these areas, and to explain the process by which I learned about Coke Stevenson."

Most biographers never explain the processes they used to dig out information and draw conclusions. Caro explains his processes admi-rably, while not pretending omniscience: "No writer can be certain that he knows all the facts about private financial affairs dating back fifty years and more. But I tried to ascertain as many of those facts as possible, and after doing so I was convinced—and am convinced—that Coke Robert Stevenson was a public official of extraordinary personal integrity."

Calling Stevenson a politician with integrity did not mean Caro was placing him on a pedestal. As Caro explained:

This is not to say that I approve of Coke Stevenson's record as gover-nor. Indeed, aspects of that record—his refusal to intervene in the Beaumont race riots or to investigate the Texarkana lynching (his seg-regationist views in general, in fact), and his stance in the [University of Texas] Rainey affair—are indefensible. These episodes—and the un-compromising conservative philosophy that ran through his Admin-istration as a whole—made him a symbol of all that Austin's liberal academics, intellectuals and journalists opposed, and if I had been in Texas in the 1940s, I would have been on their side.

In the era about which I am writing, however, Texas was not a liberal state, but an extremely conservative state. The views of the Austin liberals were not the views of the majority of the Texas electorate, and it is important to realize that the 1948 election was not, as several articles published in 1990 would have it, a campaign between a liberal and a conservative.

Caro understood that his critics were basing much of their brief on hindsight: "I try to make the reader see events as they unfolded, to make the reader feel as if he were present at the scene when the events described were taking place. If the reader had been in Texas during that hot summer of 1948, watching Lyndon Johnson and Coke Stevenson campaign, he would have heard very little about race or Rainey, and for that reason he will read little about those matters here."

Sidney Blumenthal of the *New Republic* found Caro's additional explanations unconvincing. In a lengthy letter, Blumenthal expressed his dismay: "Robert Caro has a reverence for facts, which is admirable. He suggests that his encyclopedic thoroughness is unmatched, and must therefore be accepted as canon. In political history, however, Mr. Caro's narrow, positivistic cult of the fact will take you only so far. In this field there are many kinds of facts—reputations, images and prejudices are as much facts as vote counts, dates and place names." Blumenthal's letter addresses specifics to an extent, raising legitimate questions about Caro's renderings of a few episodes. But I found Blumenthal's sources no better than—and in most instances inferior to—Caro's.[34]

In my opinion, Caro's addendum on Coke Stevenson demolishes his critics, and I have reprinted the full text of the addendum at the end of this chapter. To reiterate: Did Caro violate truth with his portrayal of Stevenson? No. In the context of the 1948 Senate campaign, Johnson and Stevenson were indeed foils for each other: the young against the aging; the new-wave, heavily financed media campaigner against the low-budget old plodder; the more-or-less unprincipled win-at-all-costs politician with his career on the line against the more-or-less principled politician who has come out of retirement reluctantly for one last try at elective office.

Most journalists, most biographers, do a lousy job of presenting the supporting cast three-dimensionally—of showing how a spouse, a lifelong friend, or a political opponent changes as the main character changes. Caro is actually one of the best at this, especially in his portrayals of LBJ's wife, Lady Bird, and of Stevenson. Rather than suffering criticism for his portrayal of Stevenson, Caro ought to receive praise for one of the most detailed portraits of a supporting character in the annals of modern-day journalism.

As for the remainder of volume two, Caro takes us a long way down the trail of truth in his examination of how LBJ acquired and ran Austin radio station KTBC. It was not solely Lady Bird's management skill, as LBJ always maintained. Ronnie Dugger had helped blaze that trail, but neither his research nor his writing could match Caro's. (An aside on Caro the writer: Virtually every reviewer notes Caro's powerful narrative skill, but some scold him for his repetition. That repetition exists, but it usually serves a purpose. Caro is following the formula of good daily journalists—tell them what you are going to say, say it, then tell them what you have said.)

On page 88, Caro sets the stage for his radio station revelations: "During the Johnson presidency, a number of reporters attempted to probe the Johnson empire. But their efforts were hamstrung by inadequate access to Johnson family financial records (which continues today), and by the reticence of KTBC employees, Johnson political aides, FCC commissioners and staff members and Austin businessmen; members of these groups have become dramatically more candid in recent years. Moreover, during the 1960s journalists did not have access to memoranda and letters that can be found today scattered through a score of different files in the LBJ Library." Caro credits reporters at the *Wall Street Journal*, the *Washington Star*, and *Life* magazine with significant breakthroughs at the time, but notes LBJ neutralized them from his presidential perch, so that the revelations "became blurred in the public consciousness."

To learn whether Johnson's political clout contributed to his station being awarded a CBS network affiliation, Caro went through the back door, since direct proof seemed unlikely. He decided to explore whether other Austin radio station owners at the time also had sought a CBS affiliation—owners who were not members of Congress. The answer was that one had, and that owner had been rejected by CBS more than once.

Caro used another usually ignored source judiciously—a self-published book about LBJ by J. Evetts Haley. Caro termed the book an "anti-Johnson polemic which could not be confirmed on many points," but decided to rely on parts of it during his radio station research because Haley had been directly involved in negotiations for the radio station on behalf of somebody other than Johnson.

Studying the text and endnotes of books by a super-reporter and biographer like Caro is instructive. For those rare (and rarely talented) journalists turned biographers like him, time does help achieve truth because time provides the opportunity to use and interpret more and different sources, some of them brilliant in their originality. The remainder of this chapter presents Caro at length, in his own words, as he explains how he unearthed information for the Moses and Johnson biographies.

From *The Power Broker: Robert Moses and the Fall of New York*, by Robert A. Caro. Copyright © 1974 by Robert A. Caro. Reprinted by permission of Alfred A. Knopf, Inc.

A Note on Sources

From its inception, Robert Moses did his best to try to keep this book from being written—as he had done, successfully, with so many previous, stillborn, biographies.

After I had been researching it for more than a year, however, he apparently realized that it would be written despite him. He agreed to sit for a series of interviews with me, and, over a period of some months, seven interviews—long hours in length; one lasted from 9:30 A.M. until evening—took place in his summer cottage at Oak Beach, on the far end of the "Jones Beach" portion of the Long Island barrier beach, where Robert Moses sat talking, framed, through a picture window, by the Robert Moses Causeway and Robert Moses State Park. "Interviews" is a less appropriate term than "monologues," for Moses permitted few questions, none on sensitive subjects, and when the time came that I had no choice but to ask some (for, having interviewed others involved in the subjects in question and having examined the records—many of them secret—dealing with them, it was necessary to reconcile the sometimes striking disparity between what he told me and what they told me), the series of interviews was abruptly terminated. Nonetheless, the long hours alone with Robert Moses have enriched the book immensely, not only in the many incidents and anecdotes he related that turned out to be accurate, and in the masterful word pictures he drew of all but forgotten eras (to hear Robert Moses talk about the Legislature's "Black Horse Cavalry" of the 1920's is to *see* the Black Horse Cavalry), but because, as is always the case when a reporter can spend enough time with a subject, the subject reveals more of himself than he knows. All unknowing, Moses told me, I believe, much that he didn't realize he was telling me. The subject of this book is, therefore, the first source that I must cite.

I must thank him as well. If his monologues, shying from the sensitive as they did, were in a sense lectures on the philosophy and art of Getting Things Done in a democratic society, they were nonetheless the lectures of a genius. Having been an investigative and political reporter for some years, I have naïvely believed that I knew something about the innermost fabric of decision-making in New York City and New York State, and not a little about government and politics in general. All that I knew was as nothing besides what I learned from this unique Gamaliel.

During the era of cooperation, moreover, Moses relaxed the rule, hitherto rigid throughout his empire, that no one was to talk to me, and allowed certain of his aides to do so. Most importantly, he allowed Michael J. (Jack) Madigan and Sidney M. Shapiro to do so. Madigan worked hand in glove with Moses for thirty-five years. Although an engineer who headed the engineering firm most closely identified with Moses in the public mind, his real importance to Moses was in his secret role as architect of the intricately crafted bond issues that made Moses' public works possible. If the Moses empire had a treasurer, Madigan was the man. Shapiro was even more important to me. If the empire had a prime minister, it was he. General manager and chief engineer of the Long Island State Park Commission, he worked for Moses for more than forty years, the last twenty or so as his closest and most trusted aide. With Shapiro, I spent more than a hundred hours. Besides showing me what the "royal tour" for a Moses guest meant—and I am grateful for, if still somewhat incredulous at, that experience—he talked to me freely, having obtained my promise not to quote him directly or indirectly. He agreed, however, that his death would void that promise, and he died on July 20, 1972. It is thanks to Shapiro more than to any other single source that I came to understand Moses' attitude toward Negroes, toward "that scum floating up from Puerto Rico" that was befouling his parks, toward what "RM" called the "lower classes"—as well as Moses' reasoning on such questions as mass transit vs. highways. As to why Shapiro spoke so openly, promise or no promise, I have, after much speculation over intriguing possibilities, concluded that perhaps the primary reason was that he did so simply because he believed what Moses believed—believed it so fervently that he could see nothing wrong with it, and could not understand how anyone of "real intelligence" could see anything wrong with it. Forty years in the insulation of the Moses inner circle had taken its toll.

One further note of detailed explanation on a particular source may be of interest to some readers. When, in the Notes that follow, I cite the "Secret TBTA Files," I refer to the secret files of the Triborough Bridge and Tunnel Authority, kept under lock and key to this day on Randall's Island, barred for forty years to inspection by public or press, none of whose contents has, to the best of my knowledge, ever been revealed. It was some of those files, made available to me, that became the primary source of the information in this book on such political payoffs as insurance premium commissions to selected legislators. In those files—the legendary Moses dossiers—are the frankest of memos on who's getting what, and why.

Several other collections of documents which, so far as I can determine, have never been consulted before by any writer, have been of use in my research.

The voluminous personal files of W. Kingsland Macy, State Republican Chairman from 1930 to 1934, Suffolk County Republican Chairman from 1927 to 1960, and a power in New York State politics for thirty years, were discovered by the author in the cellar of the Macy mansion in West Islip, Long Island. They are referred to in the Notes that follow as the "Macy Papers."

Other perhaps virgin collections of documents consulted include the internal memoranda of the New York City Park Department during the twenty-six years of Robert Moses' commissionership. These files, made available to the author through the cooperation of Mary Perot Nichols, are stored in the dank recesses below the Seventy-ninth Street boat basin near the West Side Highway. They are referred to as the "Park Department Files." Other collections include the letters, memos and informal diaries of reformer William Exton, which detail his battles during the 1930's against the West Side Highway and such other Moses projects as the remodeling of Washington Square Park. The "Exton Papers" are kept at his family's home in Millbrook, Dutchess County. The internal memoranda and draft reports of the State Reconstruction Commission, of which Moses was chief of staff in 1919, were preserved for half a century by commission staffer John M. Gaus at his home in Utica, together with a vast collection of forty years of unpublished reports on Moses projects by planning and reform organizations. This huge compilation—the result of Gaus's enduring fascination with his first boss long after he himself became a Harvard professor and respected political scientist—is referred to as the "Gaus Papers."

The memos on the Title I scandals of the 1950's written by Gene Gleason and other New York *World-Telegram* reporters to rewriteman Fred J. Cook and various editors and kept by Cook in his home in Interlaken, New Jersey, were given to the author by Cook. These are referred to as the "Cook Papers." Various other documents relating to Title I given to the author by Stephen G. Thompson, then on the staff of the New York *Herald Tribune,* are referred to as the "Thompson Papers." Letters, memos and secret internal documents relating to Moses' 1964–65 World's Fair—obtained, and painstakingly filed and cross-referenced, by New York *Post* reporter Joseph Kahn—were given to the author by Kahn. These are referred to as the "Kahn Files."

In 1966, 1967 and 1968 audits were made of the Triborough Authority and of Moses' Long Island State Park Commission, Bethpage State Park Authority and Jones Beach State Park Authority by auditors on the staff of State Comptroller Arthur Levitt. In addition to the published "audit reports," there were made available to the author some of the unpublished—and, since the published reports were heavily edited at Moses' insistence, far more revealing—work sheets of the auditors. These are referred to as the "Levitt TBTA Audit" and the "Levitt LISPC Audit."

Of the manuscript collections cited, the following mayoral papers are at the Municipal Archives and Reference Center, 23 Park Row, New York City: La Guardia Papers, O'Dwyer Papers, Impellitteri Papers and Wagner Papers. The Alfred E. Smith Papers are at the New York State Library in Albany. The Franklin D. Roosevelt Papers and the Henry Morgenthau, Jr., Diary are at the Roosevelt Library in New Hyde Park. The Henry L. Stimson Papers are at the Sterling Library, Yale University.

The "Black Papers" refer to the vast collection of questionnaires and reports on displaced tenants on Moses' Title I sites compiled by Mrs. Elinor Black in her capacity as chairman of the housing committee of the Women's City Club. The "Edelstein Papers" refer to the documents collected by Mrs. Lilian Edelstein during her fight against the Cross-Bronx Expressway. They are now back in her possession at her new home near Boston. The "Gabel Papers" refer to a few documents Hortense Gabel gave the author from her tenure as Deputy State Housing Rent Administrator, the "Kopple Papers" to a collection of memoranda and files given the author by Robert Kopple, the true creator of the 1964–65 World's Fair, the "Zeckendorf Papers" to copies of letters and memos relating to the creation of the United Nations Headquarters given the author by William Zeckendorf.

The Joseph M. Price Papers are at Butler Library, Columbia University. The Maurice P. Davidson Papers are in the possession of the Davidson family.

The Oral History Project is at Columbia University.

More than one hundred brochures written or edited during a period of more than forty years by Robert Moses and published by one of his public authorities or the Mayor's Slum Clearance Committee or the New York City Park Department were given to the author by Sidney M. Shapiro. There is no one location in which the numerous other Moses brochures can be found, but most are located in the New York Public Library or the La Guardia, O'Dwyer, Impellitteri or Wagner Mayoral Papers.

A Note on Sources

Because Lyndon Johnson would have been only sixty-seven years old when, in 1975, I began my research on his life, most of his contemporaries were still alive. This made it possible to find out what he was like while he was growing up from the best possible sources: those who grew up with him. And it also makes it possible to clear away in this book the misinformation that has surrounded the early life of Lyndon Johnson.

The extent of this misinformation, the reason it exists, and the importance of clearing it away, so that the character of our thirty-sixth President will become clear, became evident to me while researching his years at college. The articles and biographies which have dealt with these years have in general portrayed Johnson as a popular, even charismatic, campus figure. The oral histories of his classmates collected by the Lyndon Johnson Library portray him in the same light. In the early stages of my research, I had no reason to think there was anything more to the story. Indeed, when one of the first of his classmates whom I interviewed, Henry Kyle, told me a very different story, I believed that because Kyle had been defeated by Johnson in a number of campus encounters, I was hearing only a prejudiced account by an embittered man, and did not even bother typing up my notes of the interview.

Then, however, I began to interview other classmates.

Finding them was not easy. For years, Johnson's college, Southwest Texas State Teachers College at San Marcos, had not had an actively functioning alumni association and had lost track of many of its former students, who seemed to be scattered, on lonely farms and ranches, all across Texas, and, indeed, the United States. When I found them, I was told the old anecdotes that had become part of the Lyndon Johnson myth. But over and over again, the man or woman I was interviewing would tell me that these anecdotes were not the whole story. When I asked for the rest of it, they wouldn't tell it. A man named Vernon Whiteside could have told me, they said, but, they said, they had heard that Whiteside was dead.

One day, however, I phoned Horace Richards, a Johnson classmate who lived in Corpus Christi, to arrange to drive down from Austin to see him. Richards said that there was indeed a great deal more to the story of Lyndon Johnson at college than had been told, but that he wouldn't tell me unless Vernon Whiteside would too. But Whiteside was dead, I said. "Hell, no," Richards said. "He's not dead. He was here visiting me just last week."

Whiteside, it turned out, had moved from his hometown and was traveling in a mobile home. He had been heading for Florida, where he was planning to buy a condominium, Richards said, but Richards didn't know which city in Florida Whiteside was heading for. All he knew was that the city was north of Miami, and had "beach" in its name.

I traced Mr. Whiteside to a mobile home court in Highland Beach, Florida (he had, in fact, arrived there only a few hours before I telephoned), flew there to see him, and from him heard for the first time many of the character-revealing episodes of Lyndon Johnson's career at San Marcos at which the other classmates had hinted. And when I returned to these classmates, they confirmed Whiteside's account; Richards himself added many details. And they now told additional stories, not at all like the ones they had told before. I managed to locate still other classmates who had never been interviewed. Mylton (Babe) Kennedy, a key figure in many of these stories, was found in Denver: I interviewed him in a lounge at the airport there. And the portrait of Lyndon Johnson at San Marcos that finally emerged was very different from the one previously sketched.

This experience was repeated again and again during the seven years spent on this book. Of the hundreds of persons interviewed, scores had never been interviewed before, and the information these persons have provided—in some cases even though they were quite worried about providing it—has helped form a portrait of Lyndon Johnson substantially different from all previous portraits.

This is true of virtually every stage and significant episode in his life. Lyndon Johnson was fond of talking about the young woman he courted in college, Carol Davis, now Carol Davis Smith. He told at length how, stung by criticism of his family from her father (who he said was a member of the Ku Klux Klan), he vowed (despite her tears and pleading) not to marry her; how he had gotten married (to Lady Bird) before Carol married; how, during his first campaign for Congress he attacked Carol's father before taking pity on her "agony" as she listened to his speech; how, when he was hospitalized with appendicitis at the climax of his campaign, he awoke to find her standing in the doorway of his hospital room; how she had proven her love for him by telling him she had voted for him. His version of this thwarted romance—a version furnished with vivid details—has been retold repeatedly in biographies of Lyndon Johnson. But none of the authors who repeated it had interviewed Carol Davis. She was there to be interviewed; she still lives in San Marcos. Two of her sisters and several of her friends, and several of Lyndon Johnson's friends who observed the courtship, were there to be interviewed. When they are, a story emerges that, while indeed poignant and revealing, bears little resemblance to the one Johnson told. (Apart from the central story told in this book, the following minor details in Lyndon Johnson's own account do not appear to have been correct: that her father was a member of the Ku Klux Klan; that it was Lyndon who decided not to get married; that she pleaded with him to marry her; that he got married first; that she visited him in the hospital; that she voted for him.)

Similarly, Lyndon Johnson gave a vivid and fascinating picture of his family and home life. Before they died, his sister Rebekah and his brother Sam Houston both told me that this picture was all but unrecognizable to them. But it is not necessary to accept their word. One can ask others who spent time in the Johnson home—not only daily visitors such as his parents' friend Stella Gliddon and Lyndon's cousin Ava, but three more disinterested witnesses: three women who worked or lived in that home as housekeepers. None of these three had ever been interviewed. Lyndon Johnson's supposed relationship with his mother and father has served as the basis for extensive analysis. The true relationship is also fascinating, but it is not the one that has been analyzed.

Because Lyndon Johnson's contemporaries were alive, I could walk the same dusty streets that Lyndon Johnson walked as a boy, with the same people he had walked with. During his boyhood and teenage years in Johnson City, his playmates and schoolmates were his cousin Ava and Truman Fawcett and Milton Barnwell and Bob Edwards and Louise Casparis and Cynthia Crider and John Dollahite and Clayton Stribling. Many of these people—and a dozen more companions of Lyndon Johnson's youth—are still there in Johnson City, and the rest live on nearby farms and ranches, or in Austin. Together, their stories, and the stories of their parents, who observed gangling young Lyndon through the eyes of adults, add up to a fascinating story—but one which has never been told.

In revealing Lyndon Johnson's life after boyhood—his years as a congressional assistant, as the Texas State Director of the National Youth Administration and as a Congressman—interviews are only one basis of the portrait. A rich mine of materials exists in the Lyndon Baines Johnson Library and Museum in Austin, Texas. But although the information is there—in the Library's collection of 34,000,000 documents which, encased in thousands of boxes, four stories high behind a glass wall, loom somewhat dauntingly over the researcher as he enters the building—this mine, too, has gone largely untapped. Because of this source, however, it is not necessary to speculate or generalize about how the young Congressman rose to national power and influence; one can trace precisely how he did it. In this tracing, too, the fact that when Johnson died, on

January 22, 1973, his age was sixty-four, and that many of those who knew
him were still alive, is significant. Upon first coming to Washington, he
became part of a quite remarkable group of young men: Benjamin V.
Cohen, Thomas G. Corcoran, Abe Fortas, James H. Rowe, Eliot Janeway
and the lesser-known Arthur (Tex) Goldschmidt. These men—once the
bright young New Dealers—gave me their time with varying degrees of
generosity, but some of them were very generous indeed, and when the
meaning of documents in the Library was not clear, they often made it
clear. For these men watched Lyndon Johnson rise to power. Perceptive
as they are, they understood what they were watching, and they can
explain it.

George Rufus Brown, of Brown & Root, Inc., had never previously
talked at length to interviewers or historians, but finally agreed to talk
with me, out of deep affection for his remarkable brother Herman—an
affection which had led George to attempt in several ways, among them
the building of the Herman Brown Memorial Library in Burnet, to per-
petuate Herman's name. After two years of refusing to respond to my
letters and telephone calls, he decided that although Herman's name
might be engraved on buildings, in a few years no one would know who
Herman Brown *was* unless he was portrayed in a book, and that he could
not *be* portrayed because no one knew enough about him. I told him that
I could not say that my portrait of his brother would be favorable, but that
if he discussed Herman with me in depth, the portrait would at least be
full. He told me stories which he said had never been told outside the
Brown & Root circle, and told me still more at a subsequent interview,
which also lasted an entire day. Taken together, these stories add very
substantially indeed to knowledge of the relationship between Lyndon
Johnson and Brown & Root, a relationship that has been until now largely
a matter not only of speculation and gossip, but of incorrect speculation
and gossip. Mr. Brown's account has, moreover, been verified in every
substantial detail by others; to cite one example, his account of the extraordinary story behind the construction of the Marshall Ford Dam, and of
Lyndon Johnson's role in it, was corroborated by Abe Fortas and Tommy
Corcoran, who handled the Washington end of the matter, and by the
Bureau of Reclamation official involved on the site, Howard P. Bunger.

The persons who knew Lyndon Johnson most intimately during his
years as a congressional secretary were the assistants who worked in the

same room with him: Estelle Harbin, Luther E. (L. E.) Jones and Gene Latimer. (Jones and Latimer also lived in the same room with Johnson.) They had been interviewed before, but never in depth. For a while, Carroll Keach worked with him in the same office; later, Keach became his chauffeur. Still later, in 1939, Walter Jenkins became Johnson's assistant. These persons gave generously of their time, although some of these interviews—particularly those with Latimer and Jenkins—were difficult for both sides, because of the emotional wounds which were reopened. I should mention here that John Connally, who became a secretary to Mr. Johnson in 1939, refused during the entire period of research on this book to respond to requests for an interview.

Lady Bird Johnson prepared carefully for our nine interviews, reading her diaries for the years involved, so that she could provide a month by month, detailed description of the Johnsons' life. Some of these were lengthy interviews, particularly one in the living room of the Johnson Ranch that as I recall it lasted most of a day. These interviews were immensely valuable in providing a picture of Lyndon Johnson's personal and social life, and of his associates, for Mrs. Johnson is an extremely acute observer, and has the gift of making her observations, no matter how quietly understated, quite clear. The interviews were less valuable in regard to her husband's political life. In later years, Mrs. Johnson would become familiar with her husband's work, indeed perhaps his most trusted confidante. This was not the case during the period covered by this first volume. (The change began in 1942—shortly after this volume's conclusion—when Mrs. Johnson, with her husband away during the war, took over his congressional office, and proved, to her surprise as well as his, that she could run it with competence and skill.) During this earlier period, Mrs. Johnson was not familiar with much of the political maneuvering in which her husband was engaged, as she herself points out. Once, when I asked if she had been present at various political strategy sessions, she replied, "Well, I didn't always want to be a part of everything, because I was never. . . . I elected to be out a lot. I wasn't confident in that field. I didn't want to be a party to absolutely everything."

Although from the first I made it clear to Mrs. Johnson that I would conduct my own independent research into anything I was told by anyone, for some time she very helpfully advised members of the semi-official "Johnson Circle" in Texas that she would have no objection if they talked with me. At a certain point, however—sometime after the interviews with Mrs. Johnson had been completed—that cooperation abruptly and totally ceased.

One further note of detailed explanation on a particular source may be of interest to some readers. When, in the Notes that follow, I refer to the "Werner File," I refer to a collection of papers written by Elmer C. Werner, a Special Agent of the Internal Revenue Service, who in the years 1942, 1943 and 1944 was in effective day-by-day charge of the IRS investigation of Brown & Root, Inc.'s political financing, largely of Lyndon Johnson's 1941 campaign for the United States Senate.

These papers fall generally into three categories. The first is summaries of the investigation: a 14-page "Chronological History of the Investigation of the Case SI–19267-F and Related Companies" and a five-page report, "In re: Brown and Root, Inc. et al," which Mr. Werner wrote for his superiors and which summarizes the conclusions reached by the team of IRS agents on the case. The second is his office desk calendar, for the year 1943, with brief notes jotted down by day to show his activities. The third is 94 pages of his handwritten, detailed, sometimes verbatim transcriptions of the sworn testimony given by Brown & Root officials and others before IRS agents.

The Werner File was given to the author by Mr. Werner's daughter, Julia Gary.

The papers dealing with the period covered in this volume are found in a number of collections at the Lyndon Baines Johnson Library and Museum in Austin, Texas. They are:

House of Representatives Papers: The memoranda (both intra-office and with others), casework, speech drafts and texts, and other papers kept in the files of Johnson's congressional office from 1937 through 1948, when he was Congressman from Texas. These papers also include records pertaining to his other activities during this period, records which were originally compiled by his staff in other offices, such as the records compiled in an office he temporarily rented in Washington's Munsey Office Building when he was raising money for scores of Democratic Congressmen in 1940, and records kept in his Austin campaign headquarters during his first campaign for Congress in 1937 and his first campaign for Senate in 1941. These papers, of which there are 140 linear feet, contained in 349 boxes, are abbreviated in the notes as "JHP."

Lyndon Baines Johnson Archives: These files were created about 1958, and consist of material taken both from the House of Representatives Papers and from Johnson's Senate Papers. It consists of material considered historically valuable or of correspondence with persons with whom he was closely associated, such as Sam Rayburn, Abe Fortas, James Rowe, George and Herman Brown, Edward Clark and Alvin Wirtz; or of correspondence with national figures of that era. These files, of which there are 34 linear feet in 61 boxes, are abbreviated as "LBJA" and are divided into four main categories:

1. Selected Names (LBJA SN): Correspondence with close associates.
2. Famous Names (LBJA FN): Correspondence with national figures.
3. Congressional File (LBJA CF): Correspondence with fellow Congressmen and Senators.
4. Subject File (LBJA SF): This contains a Biographic Information File, with material relating to Johnson's year as a schoolteacher in Cotulla and Houston; to his work as a secretary to Congressman Richard M. Kleberg; to his activities with the Little Congress; and to his naval service during World War II.

Pre-Presidential Confidential File: This contains material taken from other files because it dealt with potentially sensitive areas. It is abbreviated as PPCF.

Family Correspondence (LBJ FC): Correspondence between the President and his mother and brother, Sam Houston Johnson.

Personal Papers of Rebekah Baines Johnson (RBL PP): This is material found in her garage after she died. It includes correspondence with her children (including Lyndon) and other members of her family, and material collected by her during her research into the genealogy of the Johnson family. It includes 27 boxes, as well as scrapbooks.

Papers of the Lower Colorado River Authority (LCRAP): 60 linear feet contained in approximately 165 boxes (the material is currently being refiled), this material, invaluable in tracing the early political careers of both Lyndon Johnson and Alvin Wirtz, consists of the office files of the LCRA from 1935 through 1975, as well as material dealing with the authority's two predecessor private companies, Emory Peck and Rockwood Development Company and Central Texas Hydro-Electric Company, which throws great light on Wirtz, and was associated with both of them.

Personal Papers of Alvin Wirtz (AW PP): 25 boxes.

White House Central File (WHCF): The only files in this category used to a substantial extent in this volume were the Subject Files labeled

"President Personal" (WHCF PP). They contain material about the President or his family, mainly articles written after he became President about episodes in his early life.

White House Famous Names File (WHFN): This includes correspondence with former Presidents and their families, including Johnson correspondence when he was a Congressman with Franklin D. Roosevelt.

Record Group 48, Secretary of the Interior, Central Classified Files (RG 48): Microfilm from the National Archives containing documents relating to Lyndon Johnson found in the files of the Department of the Interior.

Documents Concerning Lyndon B. Johnson from the Papers of Franklin D. Roosevelt, Eleanor Roosevelt, John M. Carmody, Harry L. Hopkins, and Aubrey Williams (FDR-LBJ MF): This microfilm reel was compiled at the Franklin D. Roosevelt Library at Hyde Park and consists of correspondence to and from Johnson found in various PPF and OF files at the Roosevelt Library. Whenever possible, the author has included the file number, by which the original documents can be located at the Roosevelt Library.

Johnson House Scrapbooks (JHS): 21 scrapbooks of newspaper clippings compiled by members of his staff between 1935 and 1941.

Each document from the LBJ Library is cited in the Notes by collection in the Library, by box number within that collection, and by the folder title within that box. If no folder title is included in the citation, the folder is either the name of the correspondent in the letter or, in the case of files kept alphabetically, the appropriate letter (a letter from Corcoran, for example, in the folder labeled C).

A Note on Sources

The research for these first two volumes of my life of Lyndon Johnson, two volumes which together cover what I consider the "Texas part" of the work since in the volumes to come the focus will shift to Washington, has taken place over the past fourteen years. A portion of it has taken place at a single location: a desk—two and a half feet by four feet—in the Reading Room on the eighth floor of the Lyndon Baines Johnson Library and Museum in Austin, Texas, where, on periodic visits to the Library, I sat while the Library's archivists wheeled in to me on large wooden carts the document cases, some plain red or gray cardboard, most covered in red buckram (and stamped with a gold replica of the presidential seal), which contain the written materials—letters, memoranda, scribbled notes, transcripts of telephone conversations, speech texts—relating to my subject's boyhood, his early years as a schoolteacher, congressional aide, and Texas State Director of the National Youth Administration, his eleven and a half years as a Congressman from Texas' Tenth Congressional District and his 1948 campaign to become one of the state's two United States Senators. Other boxes contain his Senate Papers, which I have studied primarily for my third volume, but which of course contained more than a little information that helped illuminate that earlier period. In all, during those fourteen years, a total of 787 boxes were delivered to my desk. They contained, by the Library's estimate, 629,000 pages of documents. How many of those pages I read I don't know, but I read a lot of them.

The time I have spent at that desk has been a wonderful time—thrilling, in fact. From the first time I thought of becoming a biographer, I never conceived of my biographies as merely telling the lives of famous men but rather as a means of illuminating their times and the great forces that shaped their times—particularly political power, since in a democracy political power has so great a role in shaping the lives of the citizens of that democracy. What I set out to try to do was to examine the way power works in America in the middle of the twentieth century. I have been fascinated by political power ever since I was a reporter and realized how little I knew about it—and you can learn quite a bit about that subject if you just sit there and read enough documents in the Lyndon Johnson Library.

A single example—one of a hundred that could be given—will perhaps illustrate what I mean. When I was beginning the research, one of my first interviews was with Thomas G. ("Tommy the Cork") Corcoran, Franklin Roosevelt's political man-of-all-work and a Johnson intimate during his early rise to power. By this time I had found that the crucial time in which young Johnson was elevated from the mass of congressmen to a congressman with influence over other congressmen—a congressman with at least his first toehold on national power—occurred during a single month: October, 1940. When I asked Corcoran how Johnson had attained this power, Corcoran replied, in his gruff, cryptical way: "Money, kid. Money. But you're never going to be able to write about that." When I asked him why I would never be able to write about that, he replied, "Because you're never going to find anything in writing." For some years thereafter—perhaps three or four years—I felt that Corcoran was correct, but then, among those hundreds of boxes in the Johnson Library, there before me suddenly—in Boxes 6, 7, 8 and 9 of the Johnson House Papers, to be exact, was the written documentation of what Corcoran had meant, and I was able to understand, and, I hope, to explain (in Chapter 32 of Volume I) Lyndon Johnson's leap to national power through the campaign contributions he obtained from Texas oilmen and contractors to whom he alone had access and that he distributed, at his sole discretion, to other congressmen.

Here is a description of the papers in the Johnson Library that form part of the foundation of these first two volumes—and an explanation of how they are identified in the Notes that follow. [I have condensed this section, to avoid word-for-word repetition from "A Note on Sources" to volume one, reprinted above.]

House of Representatives Papers (JHP): . . . More than 70 boxes of documents contain about 56,000 pages of material on his 1948 senatorial campaign. These include letters and memoranda from campaign headquarters in Austin to district leaders and campaign aides in the field; confidential intraoffice memoranda; communications between the Austin headquarters and Johnson's congressional office in Washington, and reports from local campaign managers on Johnson's activities and behavior in their districts. These boxes also contain memoranda sent back to Austin from Horace Busby, who traveled with Johnson during part of the campaign. Also in these boxes are Busby's "suggested releases" and speech drafts, including releases to be issued and speeches to be given by others. These boxes also contain poll tax lists, lists of the candidate's supporters, "contacts" and potential financial contributors (with notes about them), briefing papers for the candidate, newspaper clippings, schedules, and expense accounts. They include scribbled notes from one headquarters worker to another. . . .

Pre-Presidential Memo File (PPMF): This file consists of memos taken from the House of Representatives Papers, the Johnson Senate Papers, and the Vice Presidential Papers. While these memos begin in 1939 and continue through 1963, there are relatively few prior to 1946. While most are from the staff, some are from Johnson to the staff. The subject matter of the memos falls in numerous categories, ranging from specific issues, the 1948 Senate campaign, liberal versus conservative factions in Texas, phone messages and constituent relations. . . .

Senate Papers (JSP): The scope is similar to that of the House Papers. However, these files are far more extensive than the House Papers. These papers include "Committee files" dealing with specific committees on which Johnson served and the papers collected when he was Democratic Leader during the years 1951–60.

Senate Political Files (SPF): These files cover a time period from 1949 to 1960. They concern the consolidation of Johnson's position in Texas following the 1948 campaign, the 1954 Senate campaign, and Johnson's 1956 bid for the presidency, as well as numerous county files. They were made into a separate file by the Library staff. . . .

Written documents can never tell the whole story, of course, and, as in the first volume, I have also relied heavily on interviews with the men and women closest to Lyndon Johnson during the seven years covered by this volume. Thirteen of the men and women who were, during these years, particularly close to Lyndon Johnson were alive when I began work on this book, and I have interviewed all of them, most of them in repeated, lengthy interviews. They are George R. Brown, Horace Busby, Edward A. Clark, John B. Connally, Thomas G. Corcoran, Helen Gahagan Douglas, Abe Fortas, Welly K. Hopkins, Walter Jenkins, Gene Latimer, Mary Rather, James H. Rowe, Jr., and Warren G. Woodward. (Busby and Woodward came to Johnson's staff later than the rest of this group—only during the last year of this period—but were quickly put on an intimate footing with him.)

During this time, Johnson's two principal assistants in his congressional office were Connally and Jenkins, both of whom joined his staff in 1939. Jenkins, who succeeded Connally as Johnson's administrative aide during this period, had helped me greatly with his recollections on the first volume; for this volume, he continued his detailed assistance until his final illness. He died in November, 1985. Connally refused during the entire period of research on my first volume even to respond to requests for an interview. Some two years after it was published, however, Governor Connally said he had read the book, and now wanted to talk to me at length. He told me that the only way in which he could free the requisite bloc of uninterrupted time would be at his ranch in South Texas. For three days there, we talked, from early in the morning until quite late at night, about his thirty-year association with Lyndon Johnson. Governor Connally had told me that he would answer any question I put to him, without exception. He was true to his word, and discussed with me—as indeed he also did at a subsequent lengthy interview—with considerable, and sometimes startling, frankness, perhaps a score of pivotal events in Lyndon Johnson's life in which he was a key participant. His interviews were especially valuable because, in more than one case, he is the only participant in those events still alive. I am all the more grateful to him because his silence about some of these events that he broke in talking to me was a silence that had lasted for decades.

During his years as a Congressman in Washington, Johnson was part of a quite remarkable group of young men and women: Benjamin V. Cohen, Thomas G. Corcoran, Helen Gahagan Douglas, Abe Fortas, Arthur Goldschmidt, Eliot Janeway, James H. Rowe, Jr., and Elizabeth Wickenden Goldschmidt. These men and women—once the bright young New Dealers—gave me their time with varying degrees of generosity, but some of them were very generous indeed, and when the meaning of documents in the Library was not clear, they often made it clear. These men and women had ringside seats at Lyndon Johnson's rise to power. Perceptive as they are, they understood what they were watching, and they can explain it. The greatest single loss to my research, in my opinion, came with the death of Abe Fortas after I had had only a single interview with him. But even in that one interview, he explained things for which I would otherwise have had no explanation.

If many of the names above are known to readers familiar with American political history, the name of Edward A. Clark is not. The only high public position he ever held was as United States Ambassador to Australia during Lyndon Johnson's presidency. Because I rely on his recollections quite as much as on those of the more famous figures, however, I feel I should identify him. In 1936, this canny politician was already not only Texas Secretary of State but chief political adviser to Governor James V. Allred. Seventeen years later, in 1953, as the most powerful lawyer and lobbyist in Austin, he was named "the Secret Boss of Texas" by the *Reader's Digest*. Thirty years after *that*—in 1982—he was still identified as "one of the twenty most powerful Texans." Of all the men with whom Lyndon Johnson would be allied in Texas, Clark was the one who would, over the long years to come, acquire and hold the most power in that state. More to the point, so far as my work is concerned, he was Brown & Root's lawyer—and, for twenty years, Lyndon Johnson's. When I finished the first volume of this work, I wrote that "over a period of more than three years, Mr. Clark . . . devoted evening after evening to furthering my political education." During these past seven years, the education has continued, to my benefit.

It is necessary, I think, to repeat here the note I made in Volume I about Lady Bird Johnson and my work. Lady Bird Johnson prepared carefully for our ten interviews, reading her daily calendars for the years involved, so that she could provide a month-by-month, detailed description of the Johnsons' life. . . . At a certain point, however—sometime after the interviews with Mrs. Johnson had been completed—that cooperation abruptly and totally ceased.

Learning About Coke Stevenson

[Caro added this section to "A Note on Sources" for the paperbound printing of volume two. Such an addition is unique to book publishing in my experience, and shows Caro's devotion to accuracy and truth. Like the original "Note on Sources," it is reprinted with permission.]

After this book was published in March, 1990, a number of the articles about it that appeared in magazines and newspapers made statements about Coke Stevenson for which I believe there is no factual basis. Some of these articles, no doubt inadvertently, repeated allegations and rumors circulated in 1948 by Lyndon Johnson and his followers in their campaign to undermine Coke Stevenson's reputation—allegations and rumors I also believe to be without factual basis. I am adding this note to the paperback edition of the book (and to all subsequent hardcover editions) to expand and clarify the record in these areas, and to explain the process by which I learned about Coke Stevenson.

A particularly serious and dramatic allegation concerned Stevenson's personal integrity. Nineteen-ninety saw the revival of the rumors circulated in 1948 that Stevenson had accepted large financial payoffs from oil companies, which camouflaged the payments by taking leases on Stevenson's ranch although they never had any intention of drilling there. According to one allegation, these leases were patently "phony" because Stevenson's ranch and indeed Kimble County as a whole were notoriously barren of oil ("the poorest oil prospecting land in the world"); no oil company, it was stated, would ever seriously consider actually drilling for oil out there.

I heard these allegations while I was doing research on this book, and attempted to determine if they were true. On June 21, 1977, I drove to the Coke Stevenson Ranch (which, after his death, in 1975, had been divided between his widow and his son) in Kimble County. I am certain that anyone who had been with me on that day would have no difficulty believing that an oil company would seriously consider drilling for oil on Stevenson's ranch. For as I drove down a dirt road on the ranch, I passed trucks and equipment of the Great Western Petroleum Company—which was drilling for oil on Stevenson's ranch.

On that trip, and on others that I made to Kimble County over the next few years, I interviewed ranchers and studied records and maps in the Kimble County Courthouse in Junction. The records showed that oil companies had been leasing the Coke Stevenson Ranch for exploratory drilling for over six decades, including times when Stevenson had no political office or influence. (One lease, a ten-year lease by the Lewis Gas Products Company, was made in December, 1927, when Coke Stevenson was not in public life; others were made—in 1950, by oil broker W. E. Sultenfuss, and in 1954, by the Ohio Oil Company—after Stevenson had left public life forever; another, made in 1972 by the Wayne Petroleum Company, was renewed annually after Stevenson was dead.) In fact, had anyone taken the trouble to telephone Stevenson's widow, Marguerite King Stevenson, at the time this book was published, he would have learned that oil companies were still leasing the Stevenson ranch—fifteen years after his death; Mrs. Stevenson received her latest annual royalty check (for $4,483) in May, 1990.

Much of the hearsay and gossip about Stevenson's "phony oil leases" focused on alleged "deals" with the Magnolia Petroleum Company, supposedly made in return for his political influence. According to the rumors, these deals involved large sums of money—figures as high as $75,000 or $100,000 were mentioned to me. The Deed Records of Kimble County, in the County Courthouse, show that Magnolia took one lease on the Stevenson Ranch, a ten-year lease registered on May 10, 1939. It wasn't for $75,000. Stevenson received from it a total of $19,571, paid in a single payment at the signing of the lease. His income from the lease therefore averaged $1,957 per year. This lease was one of sixteen leases signed by various oil companies with sixteen ranches that lay in a line running north-south through the county; all sixteen leases were made in that year because a promising geological fault had been discovered along that line (and because in that year a small well came in in Kimble County). By 1939, in fact, scores of Kimble ranchers—none except Stevenson with a political position—had signed leases with various oil companies, including Magnolia. The $1,957 per year rental that Stevenson received was consistent with that paid to ranchers without political influence; in fact, the Kimble Deed Records show that a few months before the Stevenson lease was signed, the Humble Oil and Refining Company leased the Lottie Bolt Ranch some ten miles away—at terms considerably higher than Magnolia gave Stevenson. Ramsey Randolph, Kimble County Clerk in 1939 and 1940, says: "The Humble lease certainly indicates that the Stevenson lease was legitimate." ("Actually," Randolph says, compared with the amounts given other ranchers Stevenson received a "pretty low" rental for his lease.) Every aspect of the Magnolia lease is consistent with the company's other leases in Kimble. There is not the slightest reason to believe it was given to buy Stevenson's political influence; in fact, every piece of documentary evidence that I could find suggests it was not. (Exploratory wells have been drilled on the Stevenson ranch for decades; although, as is the case with Kimble County as a whole, little oil has been discovered on it, enough—together with natural gas deposits—has been discovered to encourage oil companies to continue drilling and paying rent.)

I had been told that "everyone knew" about the "phony oil leases." But over and over again during years of research, I have been taught that things that "everyone knew" often turn out, when investigated, to be without factual basis. Investigating the oil lease rumors, I found this to be the case. Not only could I find no evidence to substantiate these rumors, all the evidence I *could* find contradicted the rumors, and suggested that they were false.

I did further research into Stevenson's financial situation, studying as many of his personal financial records—including his bank statements and income tax returns—as I could obtain, and interviewing members of his family and the few elderly Kimble County neighbors who remembered him. From every one of these sources I received a picture of a man who, despite the years in which he held great power in Texas, never had much money. One fact remembered by several persons was that when, during the late 1930s, Stevenson wanted to pay a local man to make wrought-iron railings for the balconies in his house, he had to have the work done piecemeal because he didn't have enough money to pay for all of it at once. His income tax returns for the 1930s and 1940s, the years during which he was Speaker, Lieutenant Governor and Governor, show that in the 1930s his reported net income, including the income from the Magnolia lease, averaged about $5,200 per year. During the 1940s it averaged about $8,000 per year—and most of this income consisted of his salary from the state; during this decade, in which, according to his opponents, Coke Stevenson's acceptance of huge payoffs was "so well known," the most income he ever reported in one year was $13,139. (The $19,571 Magnolia check, deposited in the Charles Schreiner Bank in Kerrville on May 12, 1939, was more than twice as large as any other deposit I could find during the 1930s and 1940s.) As I note on page 404, Stevenson once said that he wanted to avoid any hint that he was using his influence with state officials. Therefore, he said, when, after his retirement from public life, he practiced law, he took cases only "for fees . . . that I could write on a blackboard in my office for all to see and not be ashamed of a single one of them." This, too, was confirmed from local sources, and from his income tax returns. (Stevenson's family has given me copies of the personal income tax returns of Stevenson and his first wife, Fay Wright Stevenson, for every year between 1927 and 1950.)

Finally, I read the probate records of Stevenson's will, and the tax records of his estate. These show that when he died in 1975, Stevenson left an estate totalling $708,000. But the bulk of this amount—$639,000—consisted of the value the Internal Revenue Service placed on the land of his ranch. Most of this land was purchased before Stevenson entered state government, piece by piece as he earned fees as an attorney. Beginning in 1914, he bought it for prices as low as six or eight dollars per acre—and the increase in its value over the sixty years he owned it accounts for most of the estate's total value. Despite his lifelong frugality—so rigid it was a joke among his friends—and despite the fact that his legal expertise made his services as an attorney eagerly sought, Coke Stevenson, for a decade one of the most powerful men in Texas, died with only $59,000 in the bank. (Mrs. Marguerite Stevenson says that when Stevenson died she had in her name $95,205, $45,000 of which represented money—largely from an insurance policy left by her first husband, who was killed in World War II—which she had at the time she married Stevenson, the balance being money given to her by Stevenson during the twenty-one years they were married, together with the interest it accumulated. Mrs. Stevenson says that when she married Stevenson in 1954—he was sixty-six at the time—"he had less money than I did"—she had the

$45,000—and that he built up his cash reserves thereafter only under her prodding. He didn't build them up very far.) That amount, and the land, together with a few minor items, constituted his total estate. The record of Stevenson's life so far as I could determine it is of a man who never had much money; of a man who, so far as his personal honesty was concerned, is as different as can be conceived from the image of a corrupt politician so vividly pictured in 1948 by the Johnson men—and, after publication of this book, resurrected in some articles. (And, indeed, when, over the years I was doing the research on this book, I got to know these Johnson men better, some of them drew a different picture themselves. I will never forget Paul Bolton, one of Johnson's speechwriters and author of some of the harshest attacks on Stevenson during the campaign, saying to me, in connection with another specific charge but in words describing Stevenson generally: "We knew it wasn't true, and I almost felt ashamed of what I was writing sometimes; Coke was so honest, you know.")

No writer can be certain that he knows all the facts about private financial affairs dating back fifty years and more. But I tried to ascertain as many of those facts as possible, and after doing so was convinced—and am convinced—that Coke Robert Stevenson was a public official of extraordinary personal integrity.

Stevenson has also recently been portrayed anew as merely a "typical," totally unexceptional Texas right-winger, just another in the long line of the state's extremely conservative public officials—unintelligent, narrow-minded, bigoted, a segregationist and an isolationist.

This, as it happened, was the impression of Stevenson I myself received when I began research on my book in 1975, and for some years thereafter I had no reason to doubt it. By 1975 Stevenson was a forgotten figure, a man all but lost to history. Two biographies—one by an aide, Booth Mooney, the other by two of Stevenson's Kimble County neighbors—were both so slight, not only in length but in research, as to provide little insight into the man or his career. The literature on Texas history during the era in which Stevenson served in the state government is, as one writer puts it, "notoriously spotty"; moreover, most of it is written from a point of view antithetical to his. In the few books on the era, he was generally given scanty treatment, and even that concentrated on his gubernatorial record, not on his pre-gubernatorial record in government, or on the story of his life as a whole. Apart from these sources, Coke Stevenson had been described—briefly and harshly—primarily in biographies of Lyndon Johnson. Interviews would normally be helpful in learning about a man, but Stevenson was eighty-seven years old when he died. He was almost the last survivor of his generation in Texas politics; only a very few of his friends and political allies—indeed, only a few handfuls of Texas politicians who knew him more than passingly well— were still alive. When, almost thirty years after the 1948 campaign, I began hearing about it in interviews, the description of Coke Stevenson available to history was very largely a description furnished by a younger generation in Texas politics—the Johnson generation, the bright young Johnson campaign aides who helped him defeat Stevenson in 1948 and thereby rose to power in Texas—as well as by Johnson supporters and allies, and by one-time Texas "Loyalists" and their spiritual descendants in the Texas academic, intellectual and journalistic community, a group to whom Stevenson had been a symbol of much of what they hated. It was they who, in interviews with me, in oral history interviews given to representatives of the Lyndon Johnson Library and in opinions repeated in Johnson biographies and other books, described Stevenson as typical, and it was during my interviews with them that I was told that like so many other Texas public officials, Stevenson was just another office-holder on the take (witness those "phony oil leases": the persons who repeated the oil-lease allegations to me all admitted that none of the allegations had ever been proven; they said they were "rumors" or "scut-tlebutt" or "hearsay." But, they all said, "everyone knew about them"; they were, I was told over and over again, "common knowledge"). As for the allegations of Johnsonian vote-stealing in the 1948 election, these were also dismissed as nothing more than typical Texas politics. If there had been any stealing in the 1948 election—and, I was told repeatedly, no one really knew for sure whether there had been or not—the stealing had been done by both sides. Coke Stevenson, like most Texas politicians, had always stolen votes in his elections, I was told; "everyone knew that." There was, in fact, nothing unusual or significant about the 1948 campaign as a whole, I was told; Johnson had simply made use of the "issues" in the race—these were identified to me as Stevenson's isolationism, his racism, his identification with the ultra-right Texas Regulars—to persuade a majority of the voters to vote for him. That was the accepted image of Coke Stevenson and of his last campaign, and for a long time I had no reason to think the image incomplete or inaccurate. I was planning to make the 1948 campaign only a single long chapter (as I did with Johnson's 1941 campaign in Volume I), and I wasn't doing extensive research on it, or on Johnson's opponent in it. I was learning about Stevenson only incidentally, during the course of interviews about other aspects of Johnson's life. Moreover, since these interviews were almost entirely with people who ridiculed and despised Stevenson, they only reinforced the picture of the man that I had obtained from the history texts. (I never interviewed Stevenson. He died, in June, 1975, just about the time I was making my first trips to Texas; at the time I had no idea that he would be a figure of any particular significance in my work, and I had never tried to contact him.)

After a while, however, my circle of interviews about Johnson's life began expanding so that I was talking to political figures from the 1930s and 1940s who had been outside Johnson's orbit. At the time, I wasn't interviewing these people about Stevenson or the 1948 campaign; the necessity of learning about that campaign in detail had still not sunk in on me. But although my interviews were primarily concerned with other subjects, sometimes the interviewees would bring up Stevenson's name— and slowly (very slowly, I must admit) I was beginning to realize that from these new sources the picture I was being given was quite different from the picture I had been given before.

If there was a single decisive moment in this process—a moment in which I finally understood that there might be much more to Coke Stevenson than I had previously believed—that moment occurred during an interview I conducted in 1977 in Bristol, Tennessee, with Wingate H. Lucas, congressman from Fort Worth in the 1940s.

I wasn't interviewing Mr. Lucas about the 1948 campaign; at that point, I had no idea that he had *had* any connection with the 1948 campaign. I had located Lucas in Bristol (he had left Texas almost twenty years before) and had gone there to interview him because I was trying to talk to as many as possible of the surviving members of the Texas delegation in the House of Representatives who had served with Johnson when he was a member, from 1937 to 1948. At one point during two long days of interviews, however, Lucas began attempting to explain the sources of Johnson's unusual power within the Texas delegation. He said that part of that power was based on Johnson's entree to Franklin Roosevelt's White House, which enabled Johnson to obtain favors for influential Texans. In his own Fort Worth, for example, Lucas said, Johnson had through such favors cemented an alliance with several of Lucas' most influential constituents, notably publisher Amon Carter and oilman Sid Richardson. He himself, Lucas said, was therefore afraid of Johnson's power, although he personally detested him. And then Lucas said, "Why, I even had to support him in 1948. And that was really hard for me. I was a Stevenson man. Coke Stevenson lived by the code of honesty."

During those two days of talking to Mr. Lucas, I had found him to be an extremely pragmatic and cynical politician—as pragmatic and cynical, I think, as any I have ever encountered—and rather bitter about politics and politicians as well. His use of such a phrase about another politician was therefore striking to me. The moment was decisive, moreover, not merely because Lucas used such a phrase but because when he used it I realized that I had heard similar phrases before. At that moment it dawned on me that I had been hearing testimony to Coke Stevenson's honesty and personal integrity for months—ever since I had begun interviewing outside the Johnson-Loyalist circle. The Johnson people said Coke Stevenson was dishonest, a typical venal Texas pol. Others—almost all the others outside that circle, I suddenly realized—had been telling me that Coke Stevenson was a singularly incorruptible public official. It was at this point that I began to do more intensive research into the campaign, and into Johnson's opponent in it.

As for other assertions repeated recently—for example, that Stevenson had often stolen votes in elections, just as so many other Texas politicians had—my education about these matters followed the pattern of my education about the oil lease "deals." The vote-stealing allegations were repeated to me by Johnson aides, and by members of the Loyalist circle and their intellectual and journalistic heirs. I feel that most of these people were not deliberately misleading me, that they had been repeating these stories for so long that they themselves believed them. Listening to them, one hears a convincing case for Coke Stevenson's transgressions in this area, and I was at first convinced. But I subsequently found that while most of the younger members of the Johnson circle claimed that Coke Stevenson had frequently stolen votes in those elections, most of the politicians outside that circle who were old enough to be Stevenson's contemporaries said he had never stolen votes, and considerable research showed, as I state in the "Head Start" chapter, that the allegations about Stevenson's political integrity were, like the allegations about his personal integrity, merely gossip and rumors that supposedly "everyone knew"—but for which I was not able to find any factual support. Stevenson certainly received the bloc vote from the Rio Grande Valley several times, but not by purchase. Rather, as I note on page 190, he received it in most instances because his immense popularity made victory a foregone conclusion, and the border bosses preferred being on the winning side. In this aspect of his career as in others, Coke Stevenson was not the typical Texas politician but what I call him: "the exception." For those who are interested, a rather detailed analysis of the vote stealing in the 1941 Senatorial campaign may be found in my first volume, pages 734–740. And as for the similarly oft-repeated (and convincingly repeated) contention that no one really knew for sure whether votes were stolen for Johnson in 1948 or not, and that no one would ever really know, what I found in regard to that is also in the text of this book. Even if no other evidence were available—and, of course, plenty is—the 1,040 pages of court testimony settle the question once and for all. Moreover, while Johnson and his apologists have always contended that his vote from the Valley was nothing more than normal Texas politics, and while Johnson's younger aides—men such as Horace Busby and Warren Woodward, who had worked for Johnson for only a few months and who were not privy to any of the maneuvering in the week following the 1943 election—may believe that, not one of more than a score of older Texas politicians active in the 1930s and early 1940s whom I interviewed supports that contention, as is shown in the chapter entitled "Lists of Names." (Not even Johnson's older, higher-placed advisers believe that, as is shown on pages 320–322; moreover, Ed Clark, commenting on allegations that Stevenson's aides stole votes in 1948, says flatly: "They didn't know how, and Governor Stevenson didn't know how.") While the limits of Texas politics were indeed notably loose, in 1948 Lyndon Johnson went beyond even those limits.

The dissimilarities between the Coke Stevenson vividly described by Loyalists and Johnson men and the Coke Stevenson I discovered in my research extended to other areas besides his personal and political integrity. There was, for example, the larger question of his place in Texas history. The Johnson-Loyalist circles said he was "typical"—nothing unusual about his career. But, I found, this description did not take into account Stevenson's popularity—or the reason for that popularity. When, belatedly beginning now to research the Coke Stevenson story more thoroughly, I finally looked up the vote totals in Stevenson's previous statewide elections, not only those for Governor but for Lieutenant Governor, I found that he had achieved the unprecedented triumphs detailed in the text of this book: For example, that in both his campaigns for

Governor, he received a higher percentage of the vote in the crucial Democratic primary than any candidate before him in the history of Texas, and once carried every one of the state's 254 counties, the only gubernatorial candidate in the state's history who had ever done so in a contested Democratic primary. Even in his earlier, pre-gubernatorial campaigns, his record was striking. In 1940, for example, he ran for Lieutenant Governor. Liberal journalists assailed his conservative views, and journalists of all political persuasions ridiculed his old-fashioned style of campaigning. He had two opponents. One received 113,000 votes, the other 160,000. Stevenson polled 797,000, carrying all 254 counties. Whatever one's opinion of Stevenson's record as a public official, obviously a man who in running for office had done, and repeated, what no other candidate had ever done could hardly be described with fairness as merely "typical." Even beyond the election victories, his entire career—the fact that he held the governorship longer than any individual before him in the history of Texas, the fact that he was the only Speaker in the state's history ever to succeed himself, the fact that he was the only man in the state's history ever to hold all three of its highest offices—was not only not typical but was, in fact, unique.

His popularity was based on the facts of his life, which held a deep emotional appeal for Texans. By the time I was researching the 1948 election in depth, knowing now that there was far more to it than I had been aware of, I had begun reading weekly and daily newspapers and magazines from the 1930s and '40s, many of which chronicled the life that seemed like a western epic, and contained the physical descriptions of Stevenson that made him seem the archetypal Texan. I couldn't find many individuals personally familiar with his life story (or, indeed, with him as a younger man), but I found a few, and their oral description confirmed the written. Looking through smaller, more obscure publications—*Sheep and Goat Raiser*, *Frontier Times* and *West Texas Today*, for example—I found several long articles written by contemporaries, and they, too, contained the same facts as the newspaper profiles. The "Story of Coke Stevenson," as I call it, was a very dramatic one. But the story— of the young boy who was a great rider, of the teenager starting up the freight line, of the self-education by campfire light, of the founding of the almost mythical ranch, of the reluctance to enter politics, of the unprecedented political triumphs, of the refusal to trim political philosophy to prevailing political winds—was beyond dispute. The drama was rooted in the facts I found.

More important, in reading not later accounts influenced by—or, more often, based wholly upon—an image of Stevenson presented by his opponents but rather those newspapers and magazines contemporaneous with Stevenson's tenure in public life, I found that the Stevenson story had already been transmuted into legend: the legend that I summarize in the book by quoting excerpts from some of these articles. In discussing Stevenson, there was a tone in many newspapers and magazines—not in the liberal *Texas Spectator* or the *Austin American-Statesman*, of course, but in many others—of a near-reverence quite unusual in descriptions of a public official. The man Lyndon Johnson had to defeat in the campaign of 1948 was not merely a public official but a folk hero, not just a typical Governor but one of the most beloved public figures in the history of Texas. I considered it essential to show why Stevenson was a folk hero. The image of Coke Stevenson that had come down to history (to the very limited extent that *any* image of Stevenson had come down to history) was the image the Johnson people painted during the campaign, and that, today, more than forty years later, the Johnson-Loyalist group still paints for biographers and historians. They were able to paint this image during the campaign for many reasons, one of which was that their target disdained to fight back. They have been able in recent years to paint this image virtually without refutation, for there is almost no one left to dispute them. But the image the Johnson people painted and paint is a strikingly incomplete image. They describe Coke Stevenson as a figure scorned and despised. That is certainly what he was to them. To the overwhelming majority of Texans, he was something quite different. No one could hear old men talk—as I have heard many old men talk—about Coke Stevenson, the Cowboy Governor, "*our* Cowboy Governor," riding at the head of a rodeo parade; no one could hear them talk, decades later, about "Mr. Texas" riding by as a memorable moment in their lives, and not *know* he was something quite different.

This is not to say that I approve of Coke Stevenson's record as Governor. Indeed, aspects of that record—his refusal to intervene in the Beaumont race riots or to investigate the Texarkana lynching (his segregationist views in general, in fact), and his stance in the Rainey affair—are indefensible. These episodes—and the uncompromising conservative philosophy that ran through his Administration as a whole—made him a symbol of all that Austin's liberal academics, intellectuals and journalists opposed, and if I had been in Texas in the 1940s, I would have been on their side.

In the era about which I am writing, however, Texas was not a liberal state, but an extremely conservative state. The views of the Austin liberals were not the views of the majority of the Texas electorate, and it is important to realize that the 1948 election was not, as several articles published in 1990 would have it, a campaign between a liberal and a conservative.

Race is an example. Texas was a segregationist state in 1948. In that year, President Truman submitted a civil rights program—including a proposal for a federal law against lynching—to Congress, and a poll conducted in March showed that only 14 percent of white Texans favored that program. Certainly, Stevenson expressed himself on more than one occasion in decidedly racist terms, but those who claim that his segregationist attitude was an issue in the campaign choose not to remember that both candidates—not just Stevenson—opposed Truman's program. Lyndon Johnson used the opening speech of his 1948 campaign to make an all-out attack on that program. "The Civil Rights program is a farce and a sham—an effort to set up a police state," he said.

> I am opposed to that program. I have voted *against* the so-called poll tax repeal bill; the poll tax should be repealed by those states which enacted them. I have voted *against* the so-called anti-lynching bill; the state can, and *does*, enforce the law against murder. I have voted *against* the FEPC; if a man can tell you whom you must hire, he can tell you whom you can't hire.

And, of course, as is noted in the Introduction to this book, for eleven years in Congress Johnson had voted against every civil rights bill, including an anti-lynching bill (as he would, following the 1948 campaign, vote against every civil rights bill for the next nine years). This is not to say that Johnson was a segregationist, just as I do not say that Stevenson was not a segregationist. Stevenson was one. Nor, of course, is it to condone Stevenson's views. What I *am* saying is that since Texas was a segregationist state and the public positions of both candidates were the same, civil rights was not an important issue in the campaign. Nor, sadly, did Stevenson's deplorable record and views ever affect his overwhelming popularity. To have given significant emphasis to race in this book would have been to wrench the campaign out of its historical context, to have looked at a 1948 event through a lens ground in 1990. The Rainey affair, too, despite all the anguish it caused (and still causes) those who love freedom of thought and discussion, was not an important campaign

issue in 1948. Stevenson's Administration as a whole was not an important issue in the campaign; Johnson did not make it an issue, for he was
well aware of the popularity of that Administration—and of the political
philosophy on which it was based—with the great majority of Texans. As
even Stevenson's critics conceded, "He was as liberal as the people." And
since I am writing about Coke Stevenson primarily because of his relationship to Lyndon Johnson and the 1948 campaign, aspects of Stevenson's life which had little to do with the campaign are dealt with in only
summary fashion. (As are aspects of *Johnson's* life that had little to do
with the campaign, such as his stated position on civil rights issues: The
evolution of Johnson's views on civil rights and segregation from his early
days in government to the Civil Rights Acts he championed as Senate
Majority Leader and President will be examined in detail in Volume III,
the point at which civil rights becomes a major theme of his career.)
Moreover, I try to make the reader see events as they unfolded, to make
the reader feel as if he were present at the scene when the events described were taking place. If the reader had been in Texas during that hot
summer of 1948, watching Lyndon Johnson and Coke Stevenson campaign, he would have heard very little about race or Rainey, and for that
reason he will read little about those matters here.

Rather, Stevenson's relation to Johnson and the campaign was as the
folk hero Johnson had to run against, and that is how I portrayed him.
The voters' respect for Stevenson was the main obstacle between Johnson and his goal; it was in effect the main "issue" of the campaign. So the
reputation (and the life story that was its basis) is presented in detail to
show its strength— and to show, as well, the difficulty Johnson faced in
wrecking it.

"Issues," in the conventional sense of the word, had little to do with
the campaign, I found.

This was not at all what I believed during the early stages of my research for this volume. The Loyalists are an issue-oriented group, and
they describe the 1948 campaign as one oriented to issues. In their opinion, Stevenson's views on race were a significant factor in the campaign,
as was the question of United States involvement in the postwar world. In
the Loyalists' opinion, also, Johnson needed them badly, courted them
fervently, and entered into a close alliance with them—an alliance that
they contend was crucial to his victory; they feel that only through understanding the fight between Loyalists and Regulars in the 1944 presi

dential campaign can one understand the Texas senatorial election of 1948. The Johnson adherents in Austin—a group to some degree synonymous with the old Loyalists—feel, in short, that the 1948 campaign was a campaign in which their participation was vital, a campaign that hinged on the issues which were important to them. In oral histories, books and interviews they convey this view quite persuasively—and for some time I shared that view.

Eventually, however, it became impossible for me to continue to share it—or even to remain convinced of any substantial part of it. For one thing, by this time I was reading the approximately 56,000 pages of documents in the Johnson Library relating to the campaign. I was no longer interviewing only pro-Johnson politicians and political observers. And I was now reading—and analyzing—the coverage of the campaign in the daily and weekly newspapers. The more research I did, the more obvious it became that the Loyalists' view of their significance in the campaign was drastically exaggerated. To the extent that the Johnson campaign had a consistent philosophical thrust at all, it was a drive to obtain not the liberal vote but, as this book shows in detail, the *conservative* vote. Although various Loyalists portray Johnson and his top aides as courting them throughout the campaign (and although, of course, *some* courting did in fact take place), talk to the aides—men truly in a position to know, like Edward Clark and George Brown—and read the campaign documents, and it becomes apparent that this portrayal owes more to ego than to reality; the alliance between Johnson's men and the Loyalists became significant to the election's outcome only at the Fort Worth Convention *after* the election.

The Loyalists' view of the significance of their favorite issues also proved exaggerated. Johnson did indeed try out many of these issues, in his constant attempts to "touch" the voters, but most of them were rather quickly discarded.

Perhaps one example, involving a campaign aide, will illustrate. Horace Busby told me at great length that it was Johnson's attacks on Stevenson "as an isolationist" that put Stevenson on the defensive. Stevenson's "isolationism" was a pivotal issue in the campaign, Busby said. "That's why we won," Busby says.

It was Busby who first fashioned a press release for Johnson to use about Stevenson's "isolationism"—the issue is, in a way, *his* issue—and I understand Busby's pride of authorship in that issue. Moreover, I happen to admire Mr. Busby—who was endlessly helpful to me in describing the

Lyndon Johnson he personally witnessed on the 1948 campaign trail—as one of today's most perceptive political analysts. Nonetheless, after talking to as many of Johnson's more senior advisers as I could, and after reading the campaign documents, I am compelled to disagree with his view of the importance of the "isolationist" or foreign policy issue. This issue was part of Johnson's initial "Peace, Preparedness and Progress" campaign theme, and by the first week in June, as I write on page 207, Johnson knew that " 'Peace, Preparedness and Progress' wasn't working." That was a major reason that he began attacking Stevenson personally.

As a matter of fact, while some Johnson men and their Loyalist allies say flatly that Stevenson was a fervent isolationist, that matter becomes somewhat more complicated when one starts reading Stevenson's speeches. In one, for example, Stevenson said: "As I have said before, the time is gone when the United States can isolate itself from the rest of the world. We must be strong enough to face the world without fear. We must be courageous enough to live up fully to our responsibilities to the rest of the world. Our own salvation cannot be separated from theirs." During the campaign, he announced his support for the Marshall Plan, and for President Truman's foreign policy in general. "I know of no changes that I could suggest in our policy. That policy is going to keep us out of war, and I support it."

Unlike many of the other "issues" emphasized by the Johnson-Loyalist group, foreign policy was not discarded as an issue. Johnson continued to make speeches about it. It was certainly a factor in the campaign. But the evidence does not support the view that it was a decisive factor. The overall view of the campaign that had been accepted by history (and that is being repeated to this day by Johnson partisans)—that the campaign revolved around national issues—is a view similarly unsupported by the evidence. What the evidence does show is that the issue which worked for Johnson was the issue identified in this book: the assault on Stevenson's reputation—Johnson's campaign to persuade the voters of Texas that this Governor who was an adamant foe of organized labor had entered into a "secret deal" with "big city labor racketeers" (in other words, to persuade the voters that Stevenson's views on labor and the Taft-Hartley Act were the precise opposite of what these views were in reality); and Johnson's campaign to stand the truth on its head yet again by persuading the voters that this extremely conservative Governor might well be a front man for a Communist conspiracy.

In sum, there was really only one issue in the campaign that played a significant role in its outcome (unless, of course, one includes as an "issue" Johnson's unsuccessful attempt to buy an election, and, when that attempt fell short, his successful attempt to steal it). That issue was Coke Stevenson's reputation—the basis of that reputation, the strength of that reputation, the destruction of that reputation. Lyndon Johnson, as I note in the Introduction to this volume, did not pioneer the techniques by which that destruction was effected—what we would today call "attack politics" or "negative campaigning," complete with the constant scientific polling, the use of advertising, public relations and media experts, and the use of electronic media. But his instinctive genius in the art of politics enabled him to raise these techniques to a new, revolutionary level of effectiveness in Texas. Lyndon Johnson's 1948 campaign for junior United States Senator was, in that sense, the first mature flowering of the new politics in Texas. Since Stevenson was the very embodiment of the old politics, and because Stevenson's campaign was the last campaign of its type ever waged by a major candidate for statewide office in Texas, the 1948 campaign marked the end of an era in politics—as the collision of old and new marked a significant transformation in American politics. By showing the collision between old and new, by exploring in detail the strength of Stevenson's reputation, and the means by which, despite that strength, the reputation was wrecked, I have tried to illustrate the full destructiveness of these techniques on the fundamental concept of free choice by an informed electorate.

CHAPTER THREE
Inquiring Minds

After five years of working together at the *Philadelphia Inquirer*, a daily newspaper, the investigative team of Donald Barlett and James Steele decided to examine the empire of Howard Hughes, one of the world's richest and most mysterious persons. Because of their extraordinary research skills, Barlett and Steele had already won a Pulitzer Prize, newspaper journalism's most prestigious award. Hughes seemed an appropriate challenge for an encore.[1]

Working on the Hughes story, Barlett and Steele, as always, did things differently from other journalists. The *Inquirer* said in a contest entry at the time, "While the personal habits of Hughes, whether in fiction or fact, may often have been more fascinating, it was his business dealings which had a profound impact on the operations of government agencies. The series, we believe, recorded for the first time, with an abundance of detail and documentation, the wide-ranging power and influence of the Hughes organization. The series focused attention on the corrupting influence exercised by businesses not generally subject to monitoring by independent or governmental agencies."[2]

The lead of the series said the average daily take of the Hughes empire from the federal government was $1.7 million, and had been for ten years. Hughes's influence was so far-reaching that after his death in 1976, Barlett and Steele, never before book authors, decided to expand the newspaper series into an investigative biography. They were encouraged by the success of Robert Caro's investigative biography of Robert Moses. After all, Caro had also come from a newspaper background, too, and he had not even won a Pulitzer before taking the plunge into the biography pool.[3]

Barlett and Steele's book eventually appeared with the title *Em-*

pire: The Life, Legend and Madness of Howard Hughes. It begins with Hughes's death, then moves backward to his birth. After that, it is largely chronological. There was nothing particularly innovative about its structure. But plenty was innovative about its underlying research.

Before publication of the Hughes biography, Barlett and Steele were barely known outside Philadelphia. The book's modest commercial success never made them a household name among readers of nonfiction the way Caro became a household name. The book did, however, encourage numerous investigative journalists from newspapers, magazines, and television to think about writing book-length biographies. Caro's success could have been a fluke; the accomplishment of Barlett and Steele seemed to prove it was something else.

The book was available all over the United States, unlike Barlett and Steele's newspaper series. Furthermore, Barlett and Steele, generous to a fault with their time and expertise, spoke regularly to journalism meetings and individual callers about how they had ferreted out previously withheld information. As a result, the duo became an important part of how and why biographers with investigative journalism backgrounds became more and more numerous.

The acknowledgments section of *Empire* is fascinating for what it says, implicitly, about the ways Barlett and Steele operate. First they give their thanks to anonymous sources. Next come librarians at thirty-nine public, private, and university repositories, ranging from the Library of Congress to the Scotland County, Missouri, library. Many of the librarians receive thanks by name, including nine at the *Philadelphia Inquirer*. Then come clerks in twelve courts, public information officers at six federal agencies, and a tax analyst.

In the sources section, Barlett and Steele give special prominence to three cases arising from Hughes's takeover of Air West; documents from two lawsuits involving Robert Maheu, the former Nevada operations chief for Hughes; additional litigation stemming from Hughes's alleged mismanagement of Trans World Airlines; hearings from the U.S. Senate and House of Representatives; and four categories of internal records from the Hughes organization. The remainder of the paper trail followed by Barlett and Steele took them all over the map. Studying the acknowledgments and sources sections can be a comprehensive education for information gatherers.

The preface, reprinted here with permission, captures much of why the Hughes book is such a landmark in contemporary investigative biography.

Few, if any, figures in American history have provoked so many suspicions, stirred so much curiosity, inspired so many images, and been so greatly misunderstood as Howard Robard Hughes, Jr.

Such was the mystery and power surrounding his life that when he was pronounced dead on arrival at Methodist Hospital in Houston, Texas, on April 5, 1976, his fingerprints were lifted by a technician from the Harris County Medical Examiner's Office and forwarded to the Federal Bureau of Investigation in Washington. Secretary of the Treasury William E. Simon, for federal tax purposes, wanted to be sure that the dead man was indeed Howard Hughes. After comparing the fingerprints with those taken from Hughes in 1942, the FBI confirmed the identity.

The public life of Hughes was itself enough to ensure the spinning of a certain mythology. He was a record-setting aviator cut from a heroic mold on the Lindbergh model. His amorous adventures with some of Hollywood's leading ladies and his eccentric lifestyle were the stuff that sold newspapers. His fabulous wealth and his reputed genius at the business of making ever-greater amounts of money only heightened public curiosity.

As the years wore on, Hughes became in the public mind what his public-relations apparatus wanted him to be. In this, the publicists did not lack assistance. All who had known Hughes, and many who only claimed to, had a story to tell about the reclusive industrialist. And so the legend grew, embroidered, indeed made possible by Hughes's pathological obsession with secrecy and seclusion.

So completely was truth distorted that Hughes could lose tens of millions of dollars for more than thirty consecutive years in one of his companies and yet be named one of America's ten greatest businessmen. So impenetrable was the curtain of secrecy that Jean Peters, invariably pictured as a deeply involved Mrs. Howard Hughes, only saw her husband by appointment.

So it is that any serious biography of Howard Hughes must surmount and remold the legend given currency, and all but petrified, by years of repetition. This task is both aided and impeded by the size of the public record, which runs to hundreds of thousands of pages of documents relating to Hughes and his empire. It is clear to the authors, after four years of research, that the record spawned by Hughes is rivaled in size by few men of modern times. Because this material is not found in any central location, but rather is scattered from coast to coast, only bits and pieces have found their way into the public print. As a result, the full story has gone untold. Spanning the whole of Hughes's life, we have compiled the single largest collection of Hughes documents and records outside the Hughes organization itself, the largest and most powerful privately controlled business empire in the country. We examined more than a quarter-million pages of records and documents, from which we reproduced, or in some instances handcopied, some fifty thousand pages. The material was gathered from sources in more than fifty cities in twenty-three states and five foreign countries, from Bayonne, New Jersey, to Santa Ana, California, from Nassau to Tokyo. The papers were drawn from nearly fifty different offices, agencies, and departments of local, state, and federal governments, from the Los Angeles Police Department to the Department of Defense, from the Nevada Gaming Commission to the Quebec Securities Commission.

These papers include thousands of Hughes's handwritten and dictated memoranda, family letters, CIA memoranda, FBI reports, contracts with nearly a dozen departments and agencies of the federal government, loan agreements, hundreds of memoranda and reports prepared by Hughes executives and lawyers, deeds, mortgages, lease agreements, corporate charters, census reports, college records, federal income-tax returns, Oral History transcripts, partnership agreements, autopsy reports, birth and death records, marriage license applications, divorce records, naturaliza-tion petitions, bankruptcy records, corporation annual reports, stock of-fering circulars, real estate assessment records, notary public commis-sions, applications for pilot certificates, powers of attorney, minutes of the board meetings of Hughes's companies, police records, transcripts of Securities and Exchange Commission proceedings, genealogical records, government audit reports, voter registration records, annual assessment work affidavits, transcripts of Civil Aeronautics Board proceedings, the daily logs of Hughes's activities, hearings and reports of committees of the House of Representatives and Senate, transcripts of Federal Communications Commission proceedings, wills, estate records, grand jury testimony, trial transcripts, civil and criminal court records.

None of this is to suggest that all information appearing in an official government document or legal record is the whole truth. Obviously, such is not the case. Long before Clifford Irving appeared with his spurious autobiography of Hughes, forged documents, although uncommon, were not unknown in the Hughes empire. A fake memorandum bearing Hughes's name, submitted to McGraw-Hill by Irving as "evidence" of the authenticity of his manuscript, was not the first—or last—time that Hughes's signature was forged. Nor was it the last time that someone prepared a bogus Hughes memorandum. Moreover, thousands of critical documents once in the possession of the Hughes organization have been destroyed as no longer necessary—or to avoid embarrassment or conceal wrongdoing. Other documents are being withheld from public inspection by United States government agencies for possibly the same reasons. And other Hughes documents have been stolen. The records that are available, however, provide a rich source of new information and enable one to establish what is fraudulent or fiction, substantiate what actually was, and bring one closer to the truth. Because so much misinformation has already been published, we have attempted to reduce speculation to a minimum, to speculate only when the evidence warrants, and to lay out the facts to allow the reader to reach conclusions, to make judgments.

Much of the material presented here, especially covering the last twenty years of Hughes's life, has become available only since his death, and particularly within the past year as courts in Houston, Las Vegas, Los Angeles, and Wilmington have been inundated in an ongoing flood of paperwork growing out of the administration of the Hughes estate. In addition, there has been a series of civil lawsuits involving Hughes companies that have yielded a similar volume of paperwork. Businesses are seldom willing to open their corporate files for historians. But because of the legal actions brought by and against Hughes companies, there now is available an unprecedented accumulation of records and documents that set forth the inner workings of the billion-dollar empire.

For much of his life, everything that Hughes said, everything that he did, was duly recorded in a memorandum, as were many of the actions of his staff and executives. Although he seldom wrote a personal letter—the best estimate is fewer than a dozen over the last half century of his life—he was a prolific memorandum writer, some weeks writing or dictating hundreds of pages, and in the process revealing as much about himself as about his businesses. Indeed, perhaps no other man has poured out so many business communications that told, also, so much about his most personal thoughts and beliefs. These documents, too, have become available in increasing numbers over the past year.

Only this wealth of fresh, inimitable material has made our book possible. But even so, we have not answered each question, explored every road in Howard Hughes's life. No single book could do that. What we have sought to do here is to set down, for the first time, the story of a powerful and curious American who has rightly—if for many of the wrong reasons—fascinated our age.

The Genesis

James Steele and Donald Barlett began work at the *Philadelphia Inquirer* on the same day in September 1970. At the time, nobody thought much of it. Knight Newspapers Inc., now known as Knight-Ridder, had just bought the *Inquirer*. Arguably, it was the worst metropolitan newspaper in the United States under its previous owner. It could claim a reporter sent to prison for shaking down the subjects of news stories; the names of certain prominent individuals were banned from the paper under a blacklist maintained by the publisher. In short, the *Inquirer* had nowhere to go but up. John McMullan, the *Miami Herald*'s editor, received the assignment to clean out the newsroom. He hired Steele, then age twenty-seven, and Barlett, then thirty-four, on the recommendations of editors at other newspapers who knew their work.[4]

Steele had broken into journalism at the *Kansas City Times* while attending junior college. In due course, he attained the rank of reporter, working full-time while attaining a college degree, in English, over six years. While he was weighing offers from other newspapers, he received a call to work for a labor union in Washington, D.C. He accepted, deciding to see a powerful institution from the inside. The experience provided him useful perspective on covering the private sector.

Steele returned to newspapering after two years. When he was hired by the *Inquirer,* his reporting showed promise, but he was mostly an unknown quantity who had done little investigating. His first assignment was to write neighborhood profiles, including urban renewal pieces.

Barlett had been around longer, and bounced around more. After starting at the *Reading Times* in his home state of Pennsylvania, he spent three years in the U.S. Army Counter-Intelligence Corps. Following his discharge, he joined the *Akron Beacon Journal.* Barlett wanted to spend time digging, but there was hardly ever a chance.

Eventually, he did an investigative article on the county prosecutor. "There was one problem," Barlett recalls. "The editor exhibited nervous tics over the publication of investigative pieces. He did, however, promise to print them if they were done along with the regular beat. That translated to very, very occasionally. Those were my first two important lessons: Nothing of any consequence would ever be achieved unless the newspaper's editor was committed to investigative reporting. And, equally important, it was absolutely essential that the job be full time."[5]

Having learned those lessons, Barlett searched for the dream newsroom. In 1965, he moved to the *Cleveland Plain Dealer,* where his first series involved an undercover assignment at the Lima State Hospital for the Criminally Insane. From that experience, he learned a third lesson: investigative reporting generally requires a minimum of a full broadsheet page. Barlett's articles in Cleveland were almost never more than one or two columns in length. Realizing how much better the series could have been with more columns opened up for more detail, he became disillusioned about investigative reporting at the *Plain Dealer.*

So, Barlett returned briefly to the Reading paper, then joined the *Chicago Daily News.* There, he received a commitment for full-page treatments. His most rewarding investigation centered on vote fraud in the 1968 presidential election, resulting in convictions under the new Voting Rights Act.

But Chicago was not investigative Nirvana either. "It became clear that Chicago newspaper investigations tended to focus largely on organized crime, labor corruption and certain limited kinds of political corruption," Barlett recalls.

> Investigations of business activities were out. Investigations of institutional issues like the courts and the local tax system were barred. Certain prominent people were granted a kind of journalistic immunity.
>
> I would hasten to add that those decisions came from the business side, not from the editorial end. I had two major investigations killed. . . . An investigation in which Gov. Otto Kerner figured prominently was terminated. Kerner, I was assured, was a most honorable politician. You may recall he later went to prison. The second investigation involved a justice of the Illinois Supreme Court. He, too, was a thoroughly honorable person, I was assured, who would never do anything improper. Several years later he was forced to resign from the court because of improper activities. In both cases, the investigations were killed not by editors, but by the publisher.

Barlett realized it was probably impossible to figure out who could and who could not be written about. About that time, his former city editor at the *Cleveland Plain Dealer* received a promotion to managing editor. Barlett says the two men shared the same beliefs about what it takes to do quality investigative reporting, and now his former supervisor was in a position to do something authoritative.

After returning to Cleveland, Barlett's first series was on the tax structure of the oil industry, an institutional topic that was a step away from traditional investigative reporting subjects. One of the stories helped push Congress to eliminate an arcane loophole being used by millionaires to become richer still. But Barlett found to his dismay that certain subjects and certain people seemed to be off-limits. A series on a right-wing educational group whose materials were being used in school systems foundered in the publisher's suite. Barlett formulated another axiom that he had begun to understand in Chicago: "It's not sufficient for the top editor alone to support investigative reporting. It must also have the support of the business side. Absent that, the editor must be strong enough to override business-side objections."

About the time the implications of that axiom were dawning on Barlett, McMullan moved to the *Philadelphia Inquirer.* McMullan was a friend of Jim McCartney, Barlett's city editor in Chicago. McMullan mentioned to McCartney that the *Inquirer* wanted an investigative reporter. McCartney suggested Barlett. "Since Pennsylvania was my home and since the *Inquirer* represented one of the real challenges of journalism," Barlett says, he went. As with Steele, Barlett's beginning at the *Inquirer* was inauspicious. He entered as a little-known investigator assigned to write about bank failures and narcotics trafficking.

The Four-Legged Journalist

Barlett and Steele did not meet immediately. They were thrown together one day when McMullan asked them to check into alleged abuses of a Federal Housing Administration program to renovate homes for occupancy by low-income families. By choosing Barlett and Steele, McMullan was exercising perhaps his only sensible option in a newsroom filled with deadwood—if he had any hope of getting the investigation done properly.

It hardly seemed like a match made in heaven. Steele was a midwestern, urbane-looking college graduate, soft-voiced but gregarious, smooth with people. Barlett was from an East Coast state, without a college degree, taciturn, a sometimes standoffish loner, fierce-looking and balding, with an incongruous squeaky voice that no source or editor ever forgot.

It turned out to be a match made in heaven. Within four years, Barlett and Steele won their first Pulitzer Prize. They have now won virtually every other major hard-news or investigative prize, plus a second Pulitzer. Yet when Barlett and Steele won their second Pulitzer Prize in 1989, their names were still pretty much unknown outside the *Inquirer* newsroom and among readers of biography with long memories—even though they are almost certainly the best team in the history of investigative reporting. Woodward and Bernstein included.

In an age of investigative journalist as hero and celebrity, Barlett and Steele tend to have a dry-as-dust image, perhaps the inevitable fate of reporters who look into the genesis of tax loopholes rather than White House wrongdoing. They lack charisma, and they know it. "As two of the more boring people in journalism, little has been written about us," Barlett says. Unlike Woodward and Bernstein, Barlett and Steele never have been portrayed by famous movie actors. As Steele says, "We're not very exciting material, except for the work." That is certainly the perception inside the *Inquirer,* where one long-time quip is that the team's idea of a good time is spending an hour at the copying machine.

To those who have never met them, the duo's identities are not separate, with the names pronounced as "BarlettandSteele," in one breath. At times, they, too, submerge their individuality to think of themselves as a unity. Steele is fond of saying they have stayed together "longer than most marriages last in this country."

Part of the glue is that they both possess the controlled outrage so vital to sustained, quality investigative reporting. Barlett says their foundation is "an old-fashioned brand of idealism." They believe people really should be treated equally, that the playing field should be level, that government should not favor one group over another, that private-sector entities should be watched as closely as the public sector.

They have something else in common: total absorption in their reporting. They have no diversions except their wives and children. Year in and year out, Barlett and Steele happily spend the workdays of their lives together in an office just off the *Inquirer* business news department. A Swedish journalist who visited them described their work area with detached amusement in an article later published in a Swedish magazine: "In Sweden they would be nearly a case for industrial inspection. In a little wretched corner with heavy boxes stacked one on another up to the ceiling, two old gray steel desks are taking up, for the most part, the floor surface. The rest is occupied by a worn document cupboard, crammed bookcases, and computers. Every square millimeter of the floor surface is utilized, except for a narrow entrance for Barlett and Steele to meander toward their cluttered desks. There rise stacks of paper beside powerful calculating machines; [there are] also piles of yellow archive folders to swallow new documents. In front there is a smaller room with yet more document boxes, also up to the ceiling."[6]

From that office they have pursued a range of topics—some assigned by their editors, some of their own choosing, all eventually agreed upon unanimously. The ideas never come to them in plain brown envelopes or during clandestine meetings in parking garages.

Underlying it all is Barlett and Steele's fascination with how businesses, government agencies, and other institutions function or malfunction to the benefit or detriment of society. Institutional biography would be an appropriate term for much of their work. But, good traditional biographers that they are, they rarely lose sight of how those institutions affect individuals. Their newspaper series, as well as their books, contain unforgettable profiles of people.

The Early Series

The body of work that produced those prizes began with the FHA investigation assigned by McMullan. "He asked us to look around Philadelphia for evidence of abuses in the FHA 235 program for the renovation and sale of old houses to low-income families," Steele says. "Philadelphia had been cited in a report by Wright Patman's banking committee in Congress. We spent a few days looking at local real estate records to see what was there. We suggested to the editors that it would take a long time but that the research would be fruitful, so they let us go ahead."

It turned out that the U.S. Department of Housing and Urban Development had a foreclosure problem—low-income buyers would quickly discover the supposedly renovated houses were in lousy shape, so they would walk out. Nobody else would want to buy after that. "It took us six to eight weeks before we were ready to write our first story," Steele says. "We had to go through deeds and mortgages to see what the speculators were doing and who bought houses from them. We went out to see the houses and interview the families living in them. We had to decide how many houses we had to see before we would have enough back-up stuff to prove our thesis." The published series exposed fraud in Philadelphia, showed Barlett and Steele they could work smoothly together, and demonstrated that the *Inquirer* was making a commitment to in-depth journalism.[7]

Barlett began to believe he had reached journalistic Nirvana. At one point during the series, he says, "I received a telephone call from one of the city's real estate brokers who said 'I guess you won't be writing about us any more.' I asked him what he meant and he said the brokers had pulled their ads until publication of the stories was stopped. That was rather significant since the *Inquirer* at the time was only marginally profitable. I will never forget the day that I went in to see McMullan. When I asked him if it was true the ads had been cancelled, McMullan—a man who gave new meaning to the word acerbic—looked up and growled, 'Yes, but that's my problem. Not yours. You just continue to write.' The paper lost several hundred thousand dollars. But the only thing Jim and I were ever told was to keep the stories coming."

The FHA series also led to the now legendary court study. During their research on FHA renovation scams, Barlett and Steele had heard about judges letting the bilkers off easy. So the *Inquirer* duo decided to examine dispositions of those court cases. They ended up doing a lot more than that as other types of cases began to catch their attention. After discussion with *Inquirer* editors, Barlett and Steele decided to look at the handling of a wide range of violent crimes. "There was a lot of debate in Philadelphia at the time about the criminal justice system," Steele says. "How was justice being meted out?" Barlett and Steele set out to find the answer.

In an isolated alcove nestled under one of the domes of Philadelphia's Victorian City Hall were the records of violent crimes for the past quarter-century. Those records were contained in rows of legal-size file folders stacked on dusty metal shelves eight feet high. Using cast-off desks and broken chairs, Barlett and Steele spent the hot summer in a room without air-conditioning, going through thousands of complaints to police, warrants, arrest sheets, bail applications, indictments, court hearings, psychiatric evaluations, and probation reports. From that, they culled the completed cases of 1,034 criminal defendants charged with murder, rape, robbery, or aggravated assault, then methodically recorded forty-two pieces of information about each case—including race of the accused, prior criminal record, length of sentence, and the like. They coded the information onto cards and ran the cards through a computer, something uncharted in American newsrooms at that time. Their guru was Philip Meyer, a Knight Newspapers correspondent who had thought about computer-assisted reporting while on a Nieman Fellowship.

From the resulting four thousand pages of printouts, plus their courtroom visits and interviews with crime victims, prosecutors, defendants, defense lawyers, and judges, Barlett and Steele wrote about criminal courts routinely dispensing unequal justice. As they explained later, "The data we developed on individual judges did not always square with the conventional wisdom around City Hall, which had neatly pigeon-holed judges into 'lenient' or 'tough' categories, often for political reasons. For example, one judge, a political foe of the district attorney, had long been accused of being soft on criminals. If pressed to support their charge, they would eagerly cite a handful of her rulings to buttress their claim. Naturally, this judge was one of those whose cases we studied. As the months passed, a picture of the judge began to unfold that was somewhat different from the one drawn by the court's knowledgeable sources. Far from being lenient, the judge was, if anything, tough. Though slightly more likely to impose probation than a jail term compared with other judges, the jurist imposed much stiffer jail sentences than her counterparts."[8]

Word of the series, and the computer's role in it, spread through investigative reporting ranks. Then Philip Meyer showcased the series in his ground-breaking 1973 book *Precision Journalism: A Reporter's Introduction to Social Science Methods*. The techniques of Barlett and Steele were beginning to trickle down.

A Modicum of Fame

The court series marked a turning point for the *Inquirer* and for Barlett and Steele. After McMullan's broom had swept the newsroom clean, Eugene L. Roberts, Jr., entered from the *New York Times*, hired to build the *Inquirer* into a national model for other newspapers to emulate. Roberts's ascension was the beginning of a shift to subjects of national interest. The oil industry came first, an obvious institutional topic at a time of alleged shortages.

During their preliminary research, Barlett and Steele began noticing the overseas expansion of the multinational oil companies. "By reading the annual report of one company, Mobil, for example, in 1972, covering such operations as refining, sales and exploration abroad, one doesn't learn too much," Steele says. "But if you cull statistics from the previous nine reports, a dramatic picture begins to unfold. In the early 1960s, most of Mobil's operations were based in the United States. By 1972, Mobil was refining and selling more oil abroad than in the United States."[9]

Barlett and Steele inspected shipping records at Lloyd's of London to determine that during the Arab embargo, tanker sailings from Middle East ports to the West increased. They compared oil company advertisements in U.S. and foreign newspapers to document the different lines to different audiences. Their series contradicted the conventional wisdom, concluding the "oil crisis" was more the consequence of oil company manipulations of supply than of the Arab embargo. Members of Congress and other policymakers began citing its conclusions during debates.

For their next project, Barlett and Steele decided to turn to one of the most powerful federal agencies, the Internal Revenue Service. They chose the IRS because during the oil series they had become fascinated with why that bureaucracy was settling claims against huge corporations for much less than what was owed. "Government agencies regularly issue all kinds of information about their operations. You would be astounded at how much information they do in fact release," Steele says. "People have asked us how do you read the annual report of the IRS, and make sense out of it or see the seeds of a story? If you read one report of the IRS, you don't get much out of it. You have to read about 10 or 20 reports covering a long period of time, then chart selected trends within that agency."

The published series focused on the agency's tendency to concentrate its enforcement efforts on low-income taxpayers rather than upper-income individuals and corporations. Barlett and Steele arrived at that conclusion by using the statistics in the annual reports. The data they gathered during their research took on new meaning because they compiled a chronology, standard procedure for them. When pulling together information from different sources, a chronology allows them (and many other journalists who have followed their example) to see the totality of someone's activities in a way scattered notes never allow.

In the IRS series, one of the key figures whom Barlett and Steele profiled was declared bankrupt in Chicago. It seemed he had few assets of interest to the IRS. Yet, the day before declaring bankruptcy he had bought a $200,000 house outside Washington, D.C. They ran across that dramatic juxtaposition because of their chronology of his business life.[10]

The series won the 1975 Pulitzer Prize for national reporting. The award stressed how Barlett and Steele had "exposed the unequal application of federal tax laws."

After winning their first Pulitzer, Barlett and Steele began producing a book-length *Inquirer* series about every two years (and sometimes turning them into books). The next topic was waste and fraud in the spending of U.S. foreign aid. To begin, they compiled briefing books on individual aid projects. They reviewed congressional staff reports and committee hearings, plus executive branch documents at the State Department, World Bank, Export-Import Bank, International Finance Corporation, Asian Development Bank, and Overseas Private Investment Corporation. Then Barlett and Steele split up to travel, visiting sites in Peru, Colombia, Thailand, and South Korea. They found money intended for low-income housing going to luxury homes and apartments. Barlett surprised the director of the Agency for International Development's Thailand office with the extent of his knowledge, thus eliciting an admission that AID had done little to see whether its money was being spent as intended.

During the foreign-aid investigation, Barlett and Steele had a rare experience in a craft where discovery is usually incremental: a dramatic finding jumped out of a document. The team had made a request to the State Department to review the files for a large U.S.-backed housing project in South Korea. After a delay of weeks, they finally got a call to visit Washington. A bureaucrat directed them to a small room piled high with bulging files. "For a week, we sifted through them," Steele says. "Slowly, a picture of waste and mismanagement began to emerge from the bulky record. Then, on our last day, we came across a document tucked into the files which illustrated dramatically just how far the housing program had strayed from the goals set by the U.S. Congress. Supposedly built for Korea's poor, the houses were nearly all occupied by bureaucrats and army officers in the employ of South Korea's dictatorial president, Park Chung Hee. Rather than serving as a symbol of U.S. concern for the downtrodden, the Korean homes had been used by an autocratic ruler to reward those who helped him enforce his anti-democratic rule."[11]

After publication of the Hughes newspaper series and book, Barlett and Steele turned to a topic eventually published in 1980 as the series "Energy Anarchy," the story of a government planning to spend billions of dollars developing synthetic fuel plants even though that same government had been abandoning similar plants for three decades, of a government giving incentives to drill for oil in the wrong locations, of a government working hand-in-hand with multinational corporations to export a dwindling energy resource for less than half the price paid for imported Arab oil.

As they often do, Barlett and Steele provided perspective so that readers could see the whole forest, not just one tree. The first part opened like this:

> The future looked ominous. The nation was running out of energy and, at the president's request, Navy ships steamed at reduced speeds and homeowners and businesses turned down their thermostats to save fuel. Rep. Richard Welch (D-Cal.) expressed a concern shared by many in Washington about the nation's dwindling oil reserves. "The American Petroleum Institute estimates that the oil reserves from known petroleum deposits at the end of the year amounted to approximately 20 billion barrels of crude oil," Welch told his colleagues in the House of Representatives. "Consumption was then at the rate of 1,750,000,000 barrels per year and is steadily increasing. This means our known reserves will be exhausted in less than 12 years."
>
> That was in 1947.
>
> In the years since, the United States has produced 92 billion barrels of oil—nearly five times the oil that the industry said was in the ground in the first place. Today, industry and government alike put this country's oil reserves at 27.1 billion barrels—7.1 billion barrels more than in 1947, not even allowing for the 92 billion barrels pumped out of the ground.
>
> If this seems to suggest that estimates of the nation's oil reserves have little to do with how much oil truly is in the ground, that is precisely the case.[12]

From oil, Barlett and Steele turned to nuclear energy. That series, which appeared in 1983, took eighteen months to complete, involved twenty thousand miles of travel, distilled hundreds of interviews, and assembled a hundred and twenty-five thousand or so pages of documents. Requests for reprints topped forty thousand, from at least forty states and foreign nations. As did other Barlett and Steele series, the nuclear waste articles, while generating praise, also provoked criticism within the affected industry. But critics have never proved any factual errors, nor has the *Inquirer* been compelled to publish any corrections.

The series was the genesis for the book *Forevermore: Nuclear Waste in America.* The book's opening shows how compellingly Barlett and Steele, with help from their main editor, Steve Lovelady, and other *Inquirer* staffers, can explain arcane matters: "The turtles that creep along the banks of the Savannah River, near Aiken, S.C., are radioactive. So is the water in a well that serves the borough of Lodi, N.J. So, too, a drainage ditch that runs along a street in an industrial park in southeast Houston. The turtles, the water, and the soil were once free of radioactivity. They are now contaminated because of the ignorant and careless handling of radioactive materials. More important, they are a symptom of the inability of government and industry to control nuclear waste, a catchall phrase for scores of the most deadly and long-lived toxic substances ever manufactured."

The newspaper series, and the book spin-off, contain a compelling mini-biography of a nuclear waste disposal huckster. This biography is reprinted here, with permission, from the book, which incorporated a few modifications in wording from the newspaper version.

Fred Beierle showed up in tiny Sheffield, Illinois, on a summer day in 1966, a salesman selling an idea. He proposed to convert an abandoned farm into a burial ground for low-level radioactive waste. Although there were skeptics among the townspeople, Beierle soon wore down their resistance. He organized publicity campaigns. He mobilized local business people in behalf of his project. It would, he said, create jobs in a county that was one of the most depressed in the state.

Perhaps more important, he allayed the fears of residents concerned about how radioactive the waste would be and what harm it would cause if anything went wrong. The [radio]activity in a lot of cases is no more than the radium dial of your watch," he told citizens who turned out for a Bureau County zoning-board hearing.

As a further indication of his sincerity, Beierle assured the locals that he would be at the burial ground daily and would personally receive the largest dose of radiation that could be emitted. "In a year's time," he said, "I will absorb about the amount [of] two chest X-rays, and I will be there every day."

Having won the town over, he secured a permit to develop the site, and within a year trucks carrying nuclear waste from around the country began to rumble over the back roads of Illinois. During the next ten years, thousands of fifty-five-gallon drums packed with radioactive waste were dumped into trenches twelve to twenty-six feet deep and covered with dirt. Just as the salesman had said, some of the drums contained no more radiation than the dial of a luminous watch. But others were loaded with lethal materials, such as plutonium in quantities sufficient to build atomic bombs as large as the one that fell on Nagasaki.

Today, the dump is closed. At least one radioactive substance, tritium, is seeping off the property and contaminating adjoining lands. Sheffield must now live with the nuclear cemetery for considerably longer than the 132 years the village has existed. There is little recourse except to wait and watch and monitor the radiation.

For Beierle, who sold Sheffield on the idea of the dump in the first place, the escaping radioactivity poses no problem at all. Soon after the first waste-disposal trucks rolled into Sheffield, he sold out and moved on.

The story of Fredrick P. Beierle, the supersalesman of low-level nuclear waste, is very much a part of the story of radioactive waste in the United States. Beierle set up two of the three commercial burial grounds operating today—in Richland, Washington, and in Barnwell, South Carolina. (The remaining dump, in Beatty, Nevada, was established by a company once headed by a business associate of Beierle.) Taken together, Richland and Barnwell account for 98 percent of the commercial nuclear waste buried annually.

Beierle's activities have made him a pivotal figure in the low-level-waste industry. But he has received little national publicity. He does not testify at Congressional hearings delving into the problems of waste management. Repeated efforts by the authors to interview him in person or by telephone were unsuccessful. On one occasion, in November 1982, when a telephone call was placed to Beierle's Prosser, Washington, office in connection with a series of articles that was being prepared for publication in the *Philadelphia Inquirer,* a woman who identified herself as Mrs. Beierle answered and said her husband would not answer any questions. She explained, "We do not find that publicity with low-level radioactive waste ever comes out the way it is meant to, the way we talk to people, so our policy is no interviews. I am Mr. Beierle's wife. I have gone through all of these things personally. Newspapers per se have such a poor reputation with us that, you know, it is very difficult for me to even be nice to you on the telephone. You people twist the words, you leave out things, just so it comes out the way you want it to come out, not the way the people you are interviewing project it."

Indeed, it is likely that from Beierle's point of view, he has been doing this nation a major favor. The kind of nuclear trash he deals with is piling up at a great rate. It has to be put somewhere. If Beierle and other entrepreneurs don't find the sites, they might ask, who will? Not the federal government, that's for sure. It abandoned that responsibility years ago.

A onetime reactor operator from rural Washington state, Fred Beierle has gone a long way on persuasion and self-promotion. Operating out of Prosser, a small town in the agriculturally rich Yakima Valley, he has made a career out of wooing other small towns, quoting from Scripture and preaching the wonders of nuclear energy. To those who have observed Fred Beierle over the years, the effect has been little short of mesmerizing.

A businessman in a small Texas town where Beierle once tried to establish an atomic landfill says, "If he just walked in this door, and I knew nothing at all about him, I would think he was a preacher. When you talked to him for long, you were just made to feel he was a man of God, that he was standing there right at the foot of the cross."

A state regulatory official who has known Beierle for years says, "Fred really fools people. He's funny-looking, with freckles all over his face. He doesn't seem at first very impressive. But then he starts talking and you listen. Very few people can talk as well as Fred Beierle."

A Kansas man who has seen Beierle in action says, "One part of you says you ought to know better about some of the things he tries to tell you. But he's so convincing you find yourself believing him when you know you shouldn't."

Although Beierle approaches nuclear waste with an evangelical fervor, he is a man of many interests. He is both an inventor and a creationist, a person who eschews Darwin's theory of evolution, believing instead that the earth and all its life forms were created in much the way the Bible says. He has promoted a gasifier that, according to published accounts, runs on a secret material that converts cherry pits, cornstalks, wood chips, rubber tires, paper sacks, and chicken manure into synthetic gas. And he has adapted a pickup truck to run on hay, wood, weeds, and other waste products. To dramatize the truck's potential, Beierle and his brother once drove it from Los Angeles to New York.

The family business in rural Washington state, though, may be the best example of Beierle's knack for juggling different interests. In two small metal buildings on the outskirts of Prosser (pop. 3,000), the B & B Equipment Company has fabricated food-processing equipment and has repackaged liquid radioactive waste from power plants.

That Fred Beierle would become the nation's foremost salesman for nuclear cemeteries is perhaps understandable given his background. Beierle started his career at the sprawling Hanford works of the Atomic Energy Commission, in south central Washington. Covering an area equal to half of Rhode Island, Hanford dates from World War II, when it manufactured the plutonium for the atomic bomb dropped on Nagasaki.

Situated in a desolate area, more than a hundred miles from the nearest city of consequence (Spokane, pop. 175,000), Hanford is a world unto itself, fiercely proud of its role in atomic development. Nearby Pasco boasts a grocery store called Atomic Foods. The sports teams at neighboring Richland High School are called the Bombers. The school's symbol is a mushroom cloud.

It was in this decidedly pronuclear milieu that Fred Beierle (pronounced "buyerly"), born February 2, 1931, in remote Deer Lodge, Montana, broke into the business in 1954. Fresh from a tour of duty as a seaman in the U.S. Coast Guard, Beierle took a job as an assembly-line worker fabricating metal parts for the fuel elements of Hanford's nine reactors.

Within six months, Beierle had been promoted to reactor operator, a job that taught him how to start up, shut down, and refuel reactors. Most important for his future, it also taught him about handling the waste they churned out. At that time, most low-level liquid waste was discharged directly into the ground, on the theory that "natural environmental conditions," as the AEC's 1964 annual report put it, would diffuse the radioactivity to "safe levels." This practice, like others in the waste business, was found to be a bad idea, and was later discontinued.

Beierle parlayed his experience at Hanford into a succession of jobs in the nuclear industry, according to records of state regulatory agencies. In a four-year period, he worked at plants in three states, "starting up," as he once described it, reactors. There were stints at the General Electric test reactor in San Jose, California; at the Hallam sodium reactor in Hallam, Nebraska; and at the AEC's experimental Elk River reactor near Minneapolis. Beierle compiled college credits toward a degree in mechanical engineering from Columbia Basin College, Pasco, Washington; San Jose City College and San Jose State College; and the University of Minnesota. Then, in 1962, a federal decision set the stage for his business.

This was the AEC's announcement that it intended to ban the burial of commercial waste at federal installations in order to encourage private development of nuclear cemeteries. Under this new arrangement, the task of determining where waste would be interred and managed, once a federal responsibility, would be given over to private enterprise. The decision went virtually unnoticed.

Unnoticed, that is, except by those who saw a way to get started in what was bound one day to grow into a booming business. Before the year was out, licenses to bury radioactive waste had been granted to the Nuclear Engineering Company for properties in Beatty, Nevada, and in Maxey Flats, Kentucky. To Beierle, then a shift supervisor at Elk River, the new government policy was an invitation to go into the nuclear waste field. Along with two other men, one a professor of nuclear engineering at Purdue University and the other a health physicist from California, Beierle founded California Nuclear Inc. in April 1963.

The company was incorporated in California, had offices in Indiana, and established its first burial ground in Washington. Although California Nuclear proposed that it would provide a variety of services to the nuclear industry, a primary goal, as papers on file with the state of California spelled out, was to "own or lease, develop, and operate . . . burial grounds for radioactive wastes."

Of all the locations for which Beierle would summon up his superior powers of salesmanship, the site he selected for his first cemetery offered the least challenge. That was the property adjoining the Hanford works, the AEC reservation where Beierle had started out almost ten years earlier. Already committed to atomic development, people around Hanford had few anxieties about nuclear energy or its by-products.

It was not the public that had to be persuaded to buy the idea but rather state and federal officials whose help Beierle needed, for the United

States government owned the land. After months of negotiations, California Nuclear worked out a deal by which the federal government leased the parcel to Washington state, which in turned subleased one hundred acres to California Nuclear.

Thus, at little cost to his company, Beierle managed to get control of land that would prove of inestimable value in years ahead. To help the company get started, the Small Business Administration provided a $147,000 loan, according to California Nuclear's records. And so, with a powerful assist from the federal government, which provided the policy, the land, and the working capital, Fred Beierle was on his way.

He was photographed with county officials when he received a building permit to begin work on what was to be called the Richland Burial Facility. At the start, the company would employ eight people, Beierle told a reporter, but he hoped employment would eventually rise to fifty. He suffered a temporary setback when a state court invalidated the company's lease for technical reasons, but a bill was shepherded through the Washington legislature that enabled California Nuclear to begin operations late in 1965.

Even before the first barrels of radioactive waste were buried at Richland, Beierle was on the lookout for a second site. He settled on rolling farmland three miles southwest of Sheffield, Illinois, a town of 1,000 about 125 miles west of Chicago. Sheffield was ideal for Beierle's purposes. It was strategically located in north central Illinois, only a few miles from Commonwealth Edison Company's Dresden nuclear power station, the nation's first full-scale commercial reactor, and within close range of six other projected nuclear plants, which would soon make Illinois the foremost state in the generation of electricity by atomic power.

The property was in a sparsely populated region where Beierle was not likely to encounter much opposition. He intended to purchase the land, then deed the burial ground to the state. Federal policy encouraged the private development of dumps, but it required that the land be owned by either the federal or the state government.

Beierle moved his wife, Vesta, and the children to Sheffield. He opened an office on Main Street. He joined civic clubs. His wife played bridge with other housewives. He mingled with village leaders and extolled the economic benefits of radioactive-waste burial grounds. "He moved right in like he was here to stay," recalled Jay Langford, the owner of the town's only pharmacy.

Beierle took an option on a sixty-six-acre farm in July 1966 and sought to get the zoning changed from agricultural to light industrial. At a public hearing on July 29, 1966, he told townspeople of his plans for the Sheffield Nuclear Waste Facility. According to a transcript of the meeting found in records of the Bureau County Zoning Board of Appeals, Beierle said the property was "the best possible site in the state of Illinois as far as the geology and the hydrology is concerned." The radioactive particles, he assured residents, would remain in the burial ground, where "the soil in fact acts as a water softener, so this radioactive material can die away and present no hazard because it is contained within that soil. . . ."

When one resident asked whether cattle could graze on the burial ground after it was filled with nuclear trash, Beierle replied, "It is possible." Noting that radioactivity levels in the waste to be buried would be quite low, Beierle declared, "The material we handle is sweeping compound, glassware, rags, clothing, contaminated tools and even chairs. In some cases the rubbish material we put in the drums and bury is less than the radium of an alarm clock."

Years later, after learning that thirty-four pounds of plutonium and seventy pounds of enriched uranium were buried at Sheffield, residents bitterly recalled Beierle's assurances. Both materials are lethal; neither could be buried under regulations that now govern so-called low-level graveyards like Sheffield. Ironically, Sheffield also turned out to be the burial plot for a nuclear reactor that Beierle himself helped start up before he entered the business. About 47,000 cubic feet of debris from the Elk River test reactor was dumped into Sheffield's trenches in the early 1970s.

The only opposition at the 1966 rezoning hearing came from a United Mine Workers representative who arrived from Washington, D.C. The union official spoke against the project because the nuclear industry threatened to take jobs away from mine workers by reducing the demand for coal. With no local resistance, the zoning board unanimously approved Beierle's rezoning request.

Three weeks later, California Nuclear applied to the AEC for a burial license at Sheffield. The company submitted voluminous documents to support its claim that it possessed the necessary expertise. Beierle, whom it described as a man of long experience in the field, would be the company's resident manager. "Mr. Beierle," the application stated, "is now living at Sheffield. . . . All burial operations will be under the direct personal observation of Mr. Fredrick P. Beierle. . . ."

The company also contended that the property was ideal for nuclear-waste burial. A geological report of the company's private consultant said that Sheffield was "adequate on nearly all counts." California Nuclear assured the AEC that "no increase in the natural radioactivity will be measured outside the Sheffield Nuclear Center due to the burial of radioactive wastes."

Although Sheffield received substantial rainfall, which led to major fluctuations in the area water table, no government agency seriously questioned California Nuclear's optimistic assessment of the geology.

The Illinois State Geological Survey said that Sheffield was a "far superior" location, compared with others in the state, and possessed the "appropriate geological and hydrological factors." The U.S. Geological Survey said that company data indicated that conditions "appear to be suitable for burial of low-level solid radioactive wastes." The AEC expressed concern about the "inadequacy" of some data, but after California Nuclear drilled a few more test wells, the federal agency was satisfied. On July 13, 1967, it gave the company permission to begin burials.

Within a year, California Nuclear and Fred Beierle, the man who told Sheffielders that he would be at the cemetery "every day," were gone. The business was sold to the Nuclear Engineering Company, which then owned and operated the Beatty and Maxey Flats dumps. California Nuclear's licenses for Sheffield and Richland were transferred to the new owner.

But that was not the end of the Sheffield story. In 1976 Illinois health inspectors discovered that water was seeping into closed trenches and carrying off radioactive tritium. The Illinois Department of Public Health was disturbed. Up to then, Sheffield's trenches had been considered "impermeable" because the waste was buried in clay. "If tritium could migrate," a state legislative report warned, "so could other contaminates."

Nevertheless, the health department did not acknowledge to the public that the burial ground might be geologically unsuitable. In a letter to a Sheffield resident in 1977, Dr. Allen N. Koplin, the department's acting director, said, "The soils at the site are highly impervious to water. . . . The time required for the waste to migrate from the point where it is buried to the site boundary will be long enough for the radioactivity to decay away."

That assessment proved far too sanguine. By late 1978, tritium leakage was more pronounced. A Bureau County judge determined in March 1979 that "radioactive contamination has reached, or is about to reach, one site boundary." Early in 1982, tritium showed up for the first time in monitoring wells outside the graveyard. This prompted renewed court action against Nuclear Engineering, which by then had changed its name to US Ecology, and led to the drilling of more test wells.

Additional tests in 1983 turned up more evidence that radioactivity was leaking out of the burial plot. According to court papers filed by the Illinois attorney general, tritium had "migrated at least 700 feet away from the site boundary through at least one relatively narrow geologic pathway consisting of coarse, sandy soil extending away from the site in a northeasterly direction toward a strip mine pond." Although Sheffield was shut down in 1978, when the existing twenty-acre burial ground was filled to capacity, the leaks go on.

Just what, if anything, can be done is the subject of considerable debate. A Nuclear Regulatory Commission study commissioned in 1980 offered a variety of bizarre remedies, ranging from the dropping of forty-ton weights on defective trenches to the dynamiting of portions of the burial ground. The Illinois attorney general's office, for its part, came up with more conventional solutions: constructing a barrier wall to prevent further leakage; shoring up the trenches and pumping out those that contain water; constructing a facility to capture and treat all escaping radioactive material; and digging up defective trenches to remove contaminated material. If none of these suggestions are approved, the attorney general's office has a fallback position: it would seek a court order forcing US Ecology to purchase more land to the north and east as a buffer to absorb the steadily moving tritium. In other words, Illinois would create a second nuclear-waste site to trap the radioactive runoff of the first.

Thus, the nuclear burial ground that Beierle opened at Sheffield is likely to be the subject of legal wrangling among Illinois, private landowners, and US Ecology for years.

When Sheffield and Richland were sold to Nuclear Engineering, in 1968, Beierle joined the new owner as manager of sales and promotion, but the association lasted less than six months. By the end of 1968, Beierle was on the road again, in search of another burial ground. His attention soon focused on South Carolina, which, like Washington State, looked favorably on atomic development. South Carolina was the home of the Savannah River plant, the huge AEC installation that manufactures plutonium for nuclear bombs.

Beierle's new company was first called Intercontinental Nuclear Inc.; a few months later the name was changed to ChemNuclear Services Inc., with offices in Richland, Washington, and in Rockville, Maryland. On November 4, 1968, Intercontinental filed a proposal with South Carolina to build and manage a radioactive-waste burial ground. Though no site was mentioned, the company said it intended to work with state officials to locate one. Beierle was identified as its general manager.

The directors included Dr. Robert E. Bergstrom and Dr. Walton A. Rodger. Bergstrom was head of the groundwater section of the Illinois State Geological Survey. Rodger, the application stated, had been general manager for the "construction, start-up, licensing, and operation of the world's first privately-owned nuclear fuel reprocessing plant," at West Valley, New York. Other directors were from Beierle's home state of Washington. Among them were the owner of a drive-in restaurant in Longview, a wheat rancher in Lind, and an apple orchardist in Moses Lake. The company's assets totaled $150,138.

Working closely with state officials, Beierle soon settled on a 200-acre tract near the Savannah River plant, outside the small town of Barnwell, South Carolina. In June of 1969, he unveiled his proposal for the property, but Barnwell residents were given little indication that it was destined to become a graveyard for much of the East Coast's low-level radioactive waste. Instead, they read the following account in the *Barnwell People-Sentinel:*

"Chem-Nuclear Services Inc. announced today that it will build and operate a facility near Barnwell to provide pollution control services to the chemical industry.

"Fred Beierle, president of the Richland, Wash., firm, said Chem-Nuclear hopes to eventually expand the operation to provide burial facilities, materials packaging and other services to the chemical and nuclear industries.

"Beierle said the initial operations would center primarily around the receipt and above-ground storage of materials from chemical plants."

The new entity, Beierle continued, was to "make available to the chemical industry in this region the safe techniques and procedures for pollution control that have been applied so successfully for a number of years in the nuclear field." Beierle praised state officials and legislators for their help. "I know of no state where it is such a pleasure to do business," he said.

For a time, Beierle's new company did indeed engage in the chemical business. But on April 13, 1971, South Carolina granted Chem-Nuclear permission to bury radioactive waste on the property. By then, Beierle had moved on. As soon as the property was selected and the regulatory process under way, he and his partners sold their interest to a company called the Great Columbia Corporation, which soon changed its name to Chem-Nuclear Systems Inc. For several years afterward, Beierle was a director of that publicly held corporation, which emerged as one of the largest handlers of nuclear waste and which has managed the Barnwell burial ground ever since.

Between attempts at setting up nuclear cemeteries, Beierle returned to Washington state. Nestled at the foot of the picturesque Horse Heaven Hills, Prosser—"A Pleasant Place With Pleasant People," as a road sign on the edge of town puts it—is home ground for an extensive clan of Beierle's relatives: brothers, cousins, nieces, nephews, daughters, and grandchildren.

It is also the home of the family business, B & B Equipment. The company's officers include Beierle, his wife, Vesta, his brother, Lenard, and Lenard's wife, Pat, according to state corporation records, and it has provided employment for other family members over the years. Beierle's father was the company's night watchman, living in a trailer adjoining the property until his death in 1981.

Papers on file with the state describe the company's business as the "fabrication of potato-processing equipment." And that is the type of work with which many local business people associate the company. "B & B manufactures agricultural equipment," said Richard Gay, publisher of the *Prosser Record Bulletin*. "Farmers need all kinds of specialized equipment."

B & B has also repackaged radioactive waste—on the same property where it has manufactured food-processing equipment. The waste repackaging has been done for electric utilities with nuclear generating plants. It consists of solidifying liquid low-level nuclear waste so that it can be shipped to a commercial burial ground. Regulations prohibit the burial of liquid nuclear waste. To do the job, B & B was issued a radioactive materials license by Washington State. More recently, work was performed there under a similar license held by the SouthWest Nuclear Company of Pleasanton, California, headed by a business partner of Beierle's, James L. Harvey. Beierle once was president of SouthWest.

On an inspection trip to B & B in September 1979, when one of the waste-solidification jobs was in progress, an inspector for the state Department of Social and Health Services observed violations of radiation-protection regulations. Beierle, his two sons, and other B & B workers were draining liquid from twelve containers of radioactive waste. The drums had originally been shipped to Beatty, Nevada, by the Consumers Power Company from its Palisades nuclear plant, near South Haven, Michigan. When the drums arrived in Nevada, inspectors noticed fluid leaking from four containers and refused to accept them. The containers were taken to SouthWest Nuclear's warehouse in Pleasanton, then trucked to B & B in Prosser, where the liquid was to be solidified.

During the work, in which fifty-seven gallons of radioactive fluid were removed, the inspector observed what he described in his report as a somewhat "lax attitude" toward the decontamination process. Although workers took off their gloves to enjoy soft drinks, they were still clothed in the "overalls and booties" they had worn while extracting the radioactive liquid. The company official who was monitoring radiation levels walked in and out of the restricted area "without checking himself for contamination," the inspection report noted. Moreover, B & B did not use all the required radiation instruments. SouthWest Nuclear was cited for violations on March 3, 1980. When the company told the state that it had implemented "corrective" measures, no further action was taken.

After South Carolina, Fred Beierle put down roots in a different part of rural America in an effort to set up yet another nuclear burial ground. This time it was in Texas, in the dirt-poor county of Delta, about seventy-five miles northeast of Dallas. Spliced into land between the north and south forks of the Sulphur River, Delta County's population had been declining for more than half a century and was down to 4,500 when Beierle arrived in the summer of 1975. To help bankroll his new endeavor, Beierle teamed up with a group of Dallas promoters who were principals in a business called the Enntex Oil & Gas Company. Together they formed the SouthWest Nuclear Company, with the oil company's officers as directors.

Beierle brought his family with him and moved quickly to establish himself as part of the community. He opened accounts at two banks in Cooper, the county seat. He purchased furniture from a local merchant. He opened an office a few doors from the Cooper town square. He and his family attended services at the First Baptist Church. And he bought a new pickup truck. "Everybody here has a pickup truck," said Grace Swenson, a local homemaker, who opposed Beierle's planned dump. "You do everything in your pickup truck. You hunt, you go to church in it. Even the young boys use them on their dates. He did try to fit in."

For his next burial ground, Beierle chose a 268-acre tract of rolling land in eastern Delta County. On this farmed-out parcel, he said in an interview in a local newspaper, he would bury both chemical and "low-grade" radioactive wastes. After taking an option on the land, Beierle put to work his well-honed techniques to win over the county.

He paid a courtesy call on county commissioners. He made the rounds of leading businesses and the chamber of commerce. As one person recalled, he said that he was "going to employ quite a few people at good salaries, and that this would help our economy." He appeared on the "Delta County Hour," a radio program broadcast from Paris, Texas, thirty miles to the north. He bought space in the local weekly newspaper to publish a column entitled "Nuclear News."

"I dare say that if our present environmentally conscious society had been around when initial studies and bomb experiments were being conducted," Beierle wrote in one column, "I sometimes wonder if we would have ever exploded the first device and hence be unable to enjoy the immeasurable nuclear benefits we have today." In another column, he sought to point out the benefits of nuclear energy:

"You all remember the news release about the first atomic bomb which was exploded over Japan and literally wiped out a whole city. Unfortunately this image is still with us today and many people envision the mushroom cloud whenever the word nuclear or atomic is mentioned. There are, however, a lot of benefits we enjoy from nuclear energy, but today I want to share with you some proposed work that will be done by using atomic bombs.

"For those of you who may be familiar with the use of dynamite to dig trenches . . . the same result can be obtained by arranging nuclear devices in a row then exploding them in the right manner. You can dig a very large canal, big enough to float ships over a great distance and through mountainous terrain, in a matter of minutes at relatively low cost."

As for his project to "incarcerate" waste, Beierle wrote that "residue from various sources will be reclaimed for resale or placed in a geological environment that will contain the material for an indefinite time or until future technology will permit reclamation or reuse."

If Beierle's plan sounded inviting to some Delta Countians, it was a call to arms for others. For once, he encountered spirited opposition, at least in part because of growing skepticism across the country over government and industry claims about the safety of radioactive-waste practices. A group calling itself Concerned Citizens for Delta County circulated petitions opposing SouthWest Nuclear's proposal. The group bought space in the local newspaper to rebut Beierle's assertions about nuclear safety. The controversy even found its way into the pulpit, when one minister denounced a Beierle opponent for allegedly slandering "this fine Christian man." Almost overnight, Delta County found itself deeply divided.

"It was a tooth and toenails battle," recalled Hiram Clark, Jr., a county commissioner. "He [Beierle] is a real cool operator. He would be what I would describe as a supersalesman. He had a package to sell, and he almost sold it."

Indeed, although more than half the county's registered voters eventually signed petitions opposing the burial ground and although county commissioners went on record against it, Beierle might still have prevailed and secured a state permit had another event not sealed the project's fate. On November 20, 1975, the Texas attorney general filed a civil complaint in Dallas accusing Enntex Oil & Gas of selling unregistered securities. The state contended that Enntex and its officers had "employed schemes or artifices to defraud or obtain money by means of false pretenses." Three of those officers were also incorporators of SouthWest Nuclear.

When word of the lawsuit reached Delta County, it was enough to finish off Beierle's once-grand design for a nuclear-waste burial ground there. Although Beierle was not involved in the lawsuit, the fact that his business partners in SouthWest Nuclear were accused of securities violations damaged Beierle's campaign to secure public acceptance of the dump proposal, and he formally abandoned his plans in March 1976.

But Beierle did not give up on Texas. He still had hopes of persuading one of the rural counties in the northeast section of the state to provide him land for a nuclear graveyard. A month after he closed SouthWest Nuclear's office in Cooper, Beierle opened a religious book store called Thee Book and Bible Store in nearby Commerce, and from that base he continued the search.

It looked for a while as if he might end up in Lamar County, which borders Delta on the north. Beierle held a series of meetings with local business leaders and politicians in April 1976. He escorted the group to South Carolina to look at the Barnwell burial ground, which prompted one county official to say at the time, "[I] didn't see anything with my own two eyes I was concerned about."

But opposition quickly arose in Lamar County as well, leading the county commissioners to unanimously oppose Beierle's endeavor. And when rumors circulated that Beierle was eyeing nearby Fannin County, the commissioners there also voiced their opposition. For one of the few times in his life, Fred Beierle's ability to sell had failed him.

The Texas period was not a complete loss for Beierle. It brought him close to a meandering, muddy stream known as the Paluxy River, sixty miles southwest of Fort Worth. Winding through flat, uninspiring terrain, the Paluxy is not high on the list of America's most scenic rivers. To Beierle, it had another appeal.

The river has periodically yielded curious fossils—huge tracks thought to have been made by dinosaurs, as well as indentations that resemble human footprints. As a result, the Paluxy has become a mecca for archaeological expeditions by fundamentalist religious groups that see in the tracks hard evidence to refute the theory of evolution. If the tracks had indeed been made by dinosaurs and humans at the same time, they would cast doubt on evolutionary theory, which holds that dinosaurs evolved and died out millions of years before man appeared on earth.

Beierle finds evidence in the Bible to support his creationist beliefs. From the Book of Job, he once cited a reference to a "leviathan," who, "when he raiseth up himself, the mighty are afraid." Beierle wrote, "Here it appears that God is describing a large swimming dinosaur, perhaps a plesiosaur. If these were dinosaurs, they may have either survived the Noahian flood or been transported by Noah aboard the ark. In any event, they appear to have become extinct, except perhaps for the Loch Ness monster which some believe to be a living plesiosaur."

The Valley of the Paluxy, with its rich fossil lore, was thus a logical region for him to explore. During a lull in the Delta County battle in 1976, Beierle led his first expedition. He rented a backhoe and enlisted family members to help him dig along the riverbank. Beierle later wrote and published a book about his Paluxy experiences entitled *Man, Dinosaur and History*, which was distributed by the Bible-Science Association of Minneapolis. In it, Beierle described as follows the method he and his family used in the search for fossil tracks:

"We spent the . . . afternoon wallowing in the Paluxy River. The procedure was to form a human chain with everyone getting into a crawling position, touching hands and searching the riverbed. With five individuals, we could reach halfway across the river. Then everyone got down and began to half crawl and half swim, searching with their fingertips into the various crevices and holes to find the places where [another] track had been excavated; this in turn would locate the general area wherein the tracks could be found."

Although Beierle did not discover human prints on that outing, he and his family returned the following two summers for additional digs. During a dry spell in the summer of 1978, a discovery was made. "Trusting in the Lord," he later wrote, "we began to dig and bail water with shovels, jars and a chocolate milk carton. The water bailing was necessary because here the strata dipped down, and until this year the area had always been covered with three to four feet of water. After about an hour of very tiring and frustrating work over rough but level strata, my wife Vesta thought she had discovered a probable impression. We all began to remove the surrounding sand and loose rock. We then built a dam to hold back the water and bailed out the hole. Sure enough, it was a man track."

Beierle did not doubt that many of the indentations in the river bed had been made by humans. He wrote, "Fossil evidence around the world dictates that giants from the plant and animal kingdom once existed on earth. Newly found geological evidence appears not only to substantiate the presence of such giants, including the dinosaur, but also the concurrent presence of giant humans."

With his hopes for a nuclear-waste dump in Texas dashed, Beierle began to scout for a location in another state. He was backed again by the interests that had bankrolled him in Texas, including the oilmen who had been accused of selling unregistered oil and gas securities in the Enntex case. In the wake of the attorney general's complaint, Enntex was dissolved. Some of its officers founded a new company called the Spindletop Oil & Gas Company, operating out of Enntex's former Dallas offices.

Late in 1976, Beierle teamed up with Spindletop to establish a hazardous-waste burial ground, this time in Louisiana. Court records show he received a $47,000 advance from the company. Once in Louisiana, Beierle lined up powerful political support, retaining the law firm of Nolan Edwards, a brother of Edwin W. Edwards, the governor of Louisiana, to help form a Louisiana corporation. On January 28, 1977, Beierle organized Southwest Environmental Company (SWECO), listing himself and an attorney in Edwards's Crowley, Louisiana, law firm as registered agents.

To help find a piece of land, Beierle called on another brother of the governor, Marion D. Edwards, who owned a real-estate company in Crowley. They decided on a 383-acre tract near the town of Livingston (pop.

1,500), about twenty-five miles east of Baton Rouge, the state capital. Beierle opened an office and had stationery printed carrying the SWECO slogan, "Preserving Our Bountiful Heritage Through Sound Environmental Practices."

With Marion Edwards at his side, he appeared early in 1977 before the Livingston Parish police jury, the Louisiana equivalent of a county council, and outlined his proposal for a chemical-waste installation a mile south of town. Beierle said the project would create jobs and bring business to the parish. Whether his proposal for a chemical dump was a step toward the ultimate burial of nuclear waste is not clear. In South Carolina, Beierle had at first talked about a chemical-waste facility at a site near Barnwell that later was licensed for the burial of low-level radioactive waste.

Nick Erdey, the mayor of Livingston at the time, described in an interview how Beierle secured the support of parish officials. "The police jury met on a Saturday morning," he recalled. "I don't think they knew what the meeting was about until they got there. At the time, Marion Edwards was the brother of the governor and in a position to influence the police jury. And he gave them a real good snow job. The people of Livingston were entitled to a hearing, but by the time they found out about the meeting two weeks had gone by and it was too late."

After the meeting with Beierle and Edwards, Livingston Parish officials sent a letter to the Louisiana Department of Health and Human Resources saying they did not object to SWECO's project. The letter was not an official endorsement but an indication to state officials that the project was not locally opposed. It helped pave the way for state approval in February 1977, and Beierle purchased the land the next month for $596,960, according to Livingston Parish records. Erdey, the former mayor, recalled Beierle's next moves as follows:

"He started attending the local church. He gave the impression he wanted to be part of the community. He invited me to take a tour of the plant [burial site.] They had one hole dug with some barrels in it. He told us how they were going to put a layer of topsoil over it and then plant trees. Make it look just like it used to. He said they were going to reserve the part of the property next to Interstate 12 and Highway 63 for residential development. He painted quite a picture. If you came by that place today, you would ask yourself who would ever want to live next to that dump."

Rather than provide an economic stimulus for Livingston, Beierle's dump created a civic liability. It was built on land that sloped gently toward streams that flowed into Lake Pontchartrain, which borders the northern city limits of New Orleans farther south. The area is one of the nation's wettest, receiving an average of sixty inches of rain a year. Later studies showed that the water table under Beierle's toxic-waste dump was only five to six feet from the surface in some places. The study also disclosed the existence of sand layers running through the property only a few feet from the bottoms of burial pits, meaning that there was a pathway along which contaminates could be carried off to groundwater supplies.

Problems plagued the SWECO dump almost from its opening. Less than two months after burials began, in August 1977, a Louisiana State official found violations during a routine inspection. A state health officer formally reprimanded Beierle by letter on September 27, 1977: "It was reported that rainwater contaminated with various industrial wastes was pumped from a pit containing wastes onto the surface of the ground, from which point it entered surface drainage which ultimately led to Bayou Coyell and the Amite River."

Although the "magnitude of the contamination" is not clear, the letter went on, "the handling of potentially contaminated rainwater in such manner that it can escape from your site constitutes a hazard to public health and the environment and is contrary to your company's operational plan. . . ." The Louisiana Stream Control Commission cited SWECO for water violations on October 12, 1977, and ordered the company to make a full report outlining steps to correct the runoff. Beierle, in a letter to state officials, blamed workers who exercised "poor judgment" for pumping the toxic wastes onto the earth and said they had not received "adequate instruction."

In May 1978, a state health inspector discovered liquid in another pit and ordered it removed. There were also an increasing number of complaints from residents alleging improper burial practices and environmental pollution. On one occasion, according to published reports, a driver whose truck had just pulled out of the dump oozing blue sludge told a deputy sheriff that he was carrying a load of radioactive waste.

Even with its flaws, the Livingston dump was a valuable property, and Beierle and his Dallas partners were soon embroiled in a behind-the-scenes battle over ownership of Southwest Environmental's stock. Whoever controlled the stock would get the lion's share of ever-greater revenues as the volume of waste buried increased.

Spindletop contended that it was entitled to two-thirds of the shares and Beierle to one-third. Beierle countered, according to a court action later filed by Spindletop, by trying to transfer SWECO's stock to "certain third parties, including his brother, Lenard Beierle, and his cousin, Zeke Beierle." Spindletop sought a court order to bar distribution of SWECO's stock in a lawsuit filed in the U.S. District Court in Dallas. The warring forces patched up their feud early in 1978 when they found a buyer for the Livingston dump.

The purchaser was Browning-Ferris Industries Inc., the nation's largest hazardous-waste handler, then managing more than sixty landfills. On May 19, 1978, Browning-Ferris bought the Livingston property for $1.1 million, according to records on file with Livingston Parish. The sale agreement provided that Beierle and Spindletop would receive royalties from Browning-Ferris on the gross revenue generated by future chemical-waste burials. Subsequent court papers showed that the royalties would soon exceed $100,000 a year.

The Livingston dump's assorted failings—especially that of water flowing out of toxic-waste pits following heavy rains—continued after Browning-Ferris acquired the business. Inspectors from the Louisiana Stream Control Commission found "contaminated water outside the waste disposal pits" in October 1978. Browning-Ferris eventually paid a $50,000 fine for violations both at Livingston and at another property the company maintained in Louisiana, according to officials of the state Department of Natural Resources.

Livingston was the subject of a lengthy and controversial licensing proceeding in 1982, as Browning-Ferris sought state approval to keep on managing the facility. After months of hearings and deliberations, the state Environmental Control Commission voted three to two to allow the company to keep the dump open, but only if extensive changes were made, including the construction of an earth levee to try to hold down the off-site flow of rainwater. The company subsequently said it would install polyethylene liners in burial pits and place an inflatable dome over open pits to keep out water.

In 1981, in a lawsuit filed in the U.S. District Court in Dallas, Browning-Ferris contended that the "land farm" Beierle had established was "improperly constructed and could not be brought in compliance with generally accepted land farming principles." After taking over, Browning-Ferris said, it found that several of the pits were "leaking" hazardous wastes. The company demanded that SWECO "repair the leaking cells," but Beierle and his Dallas partners refused to do so, forcing Browning-Ferris to pay for the work.

To the people of Prosser, Washington, Beierle is a curiosity, a charming, engaging figure and imaginative inventor. "Fred's a dreamer," said one businessman. "But I guess it's the dreamers who make the discoveries. They don't always succeed, but sometimes they hit the jackpot."

In recent years, Beierle has been promoting a gasifier that converts agricultural wastes, refuse, and other materials into synthetic gas. The gasifier and the chemical process producing the conversion are the brainchild of Dr. Donald E. Chittick, a former professor of chemistry at George Fox College in Newberg, Oregon. He and Beierle were brought together at a convention of creationists in Minneapolis.

Chittick, according to published reports, believes that oil, coal, and other hydrocarbons were created by a catalyst in the earth that was present at the time of Noah's Flood. After Chittick discovered what he felt was the catalyst, he and Beierle formed a company in 1979 called Pyrenco Inc. to promote and develop the gasifier.

For his part, Beierle is marketing the gasifier with the same zeal he brought to nuclear waste. "Every time you talk to him about the work he is doing in energy," said a Beierle observer in Prosser, "he always manages to link it up with the Lord. To Fred you can't talk about one without mentioning the other."

Beierle eagerly shows off the gasifier to interested parties, saying that it runs a generator that gives him excess electricity to sell back to the local power company. The utility district said that it did purchase power from Beierle's generator, but only rarely. A utility spokesman noted that the generator usually ran only when Beierle was showing it to a visitor. The reason for the infrequent operation, the spokesman said, is that it costs Beierle more to generate a kilowatt-hour of electricity than the utility pays him.

So far, Beierle has managed to get the gasifier placed in a U.S. Forest Service greenhouse at Carson, Washington, for an experimental test run. He was negotiating a contract with a rural Michigan county to build a three-megawatt electric generating plant fueled by scrap wood. The power plant is intended to serve as a focal point of an industrial-development project in the county. Money would come from the U.S. Department of Housing and Urban Development, from the state of Michigan, and from industrial revenue bonds.

Does this mean that Fred Beierle, America's salesman of nuclear burial grounds, has moved on to another calling? Not quite. For as Beierle traveled about the country preaching the benefits of his new gasifier, he was also waiting. He had found a site for another nuclear graveyard and had applied to another state government for a permit to bury radioactive waste. If approval is granted, it could lead to Beierle's most lucrative venture of all.

Screwing the Middle Class

Barlett and Steele won their second Pulitzer Prize for a 1988 series on hidden congressional tax breaks for multimillionaires. At first glance, the topic looked like it would be dry as dust. Even after nearly two decades of investigating complex subjects no other journalists would dare tackle, Barlett and Steele found the tax favors to be their most arcane story yet. "We felt like Egyptologists half the time, just trying to crack the code," Steele says. But through their unflagging doggedness, combined with their techniques that have filtered down to countless journalist-disciples, Barlett and Steele indeed cracked the code.[13]

The duo began their daunting inquiry with a U.S. Senate Finance Committee list naming about 650 beneficiaries of so-called transition rules woven through tax overhaul legislation. The rules exempted certain businesses and individuals from complying with the law. No other investigative reporters looked systematically behind the list's obscure names, like North Pier Terminal and La Isla Virgen Inc. No one else compared the committee's list with the nine-hundred-page law, to see whether it was complete. It wasn't. By the time they were through, Barlett and Steele had found thousands of wealthy individuals and hundreds of well-connected businesses designated to profit from the hush-hush tax favors.

To uncover the identities of those people and businesses, Barlett and Steele deciphered legalistic jargon with no help—indeed, with sometimes open hostility—from the congressional tax-writing committees. A more or less typical provision read like this: "The amendments made by Section 201 shall not apply to a 562-foot passenger cruise ship, which was purchased in 1980 for the purpose of returning the vessel to United States service, the approximate cost of refurbishment of which is approximately $47,000,000." It turned out that paragraph, inserted into the tax code by a member of Congress, gave wealthy investors in the SS *Monterey* an $8 million break. At the beginning, of course, Barlett and Steele had no idea which ship was involved, who the investors were, and why they had succeeded in obtaining special treatment.

To determine the concealed identities, Barlett and Steele searched through records at the U.S. Securities and Exchange Commission, corporation records in state capitols, lawsuits, bankruptcy proceedings, financial disclosure statements of members of Congress, and computer databases covering thousands of newspapers, magazines, newsletters, government reports, and the like. After fifteen months, Barlett and Steele had the pieces in place to write.

Even with all the research, it could have been an important, yet boring, series. It was anything but boring. Part one begins, "Imagine, if you will, that you are a tall, bald father of three living in a Northeast Philadelphia rowhouse and selling aluminum siding door-to-door for a living. Imagine that you go to your congressman and ask him to insert a provision in the federal tax code that exempts tall, bald fathers of three . . . from paying taxes on income from door-to-door sales. Imagine further that your congressman cooperates, writes that exemption and inserts it into pending legislation. And that Congress then actually passes it into law. Lots of luck."[14]

The story then profiled rich, influential person after rich, influential person who had received special treatment. Each case study was a mini-masterpiece, beyond the skills of most journalists. The series reprint—forty-four tabloid pages—drew more than fifty thousand requests for copies. Unlike most investigative efforts, it even changed the world a bit. A newsletter published by the accounting firm of Arthur Andersen & Co. said when the congressional tax writing committees began to think about placing more favors in a later law, they worried about additional Barlett-Steele scrutiny. As a result, not a single tailor-made provision was included the second time around.

Telling the Untold Story

In 1990, Barlett and Steele took a renewed look at Congress's penchant for helping the wealthy. The latest federal budget act was being hailed for its fairness in raising the taxes of the rich. Unlike so many politicians and journalists, Barlett and Steele read the thousand-plus-page legislation, compared it with the Tax Reform Act of 1986, and concluded that in fact it imposed tax increases on the middle class, with the increases at the top being illusory in the longer run.

In October 1991, Barlett and Steele published their most powerful *Inquirer* project ever, "America: What Went Wrong?" The nine-part, book-length series examined how millions of more-or-less middle-class Americans had lost jobs and health and pension benefits and faced other hardships due to government policy and Wall Street maneuverings.

Throughout the series Barlett and Steele wove feature-ish anecdotal mini-biographies with hard statistics and traditional investigative reporting. The mini-biographies read like this one, selected from dozens in the series:

> Rosa Vasquez and Mollie James share a common interest. Vasquez works for the company that once employed Mollie James.
>
> That's where similarities end. James earned $7.91 an hour. Vasquez earns $1.45 an hour.
>
> James lives in a six-room, multi-story house on a paved street in a working-class neighborhood of Paterson, N.J. Vasquez lives in a one-room shack in a Mexican shantytown reachable only by foot along a dirt path.
>
> James' house has electricity and indoor plumbing. Vasquez's house has neither.
>
> When Mollie James wants to watch television, she turns on a set in her living room. When Rosa Vasquez wants to watch television, she connects a car battery to a 13-inch black-and-white set.
>
> For 33 years, Mollie James worked for a company that manufactured electrical components for fluorescent lights. Now Rosa Vasquez works for the same company, making the same kinds of products at a new plant in Mexico.
>
> Mollie James' story is that of many Americans in the 1980s. After decades of working for one employer, they suddenly found themselves out of work—unable to find another job and deprived of benefits they had counted on for their later years. . . .

Given such powerful material, requests for reprints of the series topped four hundred thousand, probably a record for a newspaper. In March

1992, an updated, expanded version appeared as a low-priced commercial book.[15]

Steve Lovelady, who has edited Barlett and Steele's copy at the *Inquirer* almost from the beginning, hopes they go on forever. He marvels at their relentlessness, their understanding that it's a long road to the truth, their acquisition of encyclopedic knowledge about a subject before they conduct key interviews. Their preparation is an example for all journalists to follow. "Like a good lawyer," Lovelady says, "Don and Jim live by the maxim 'never ask a question you don't know the answer to.'"

Happily, Barlett and Steele have decided to ask some of those questions in the service of another full-scale biography. They have signed a contract with the publishing house of Simon and Schuster for a biography of Nelson Rockefeller. He first tugged at their interest during their series on U.S. foreign aid, when they discovered he was conducting his personal foreign aid program to Latin America. As this book went to press, the Rockefeller biography was still in progress. Its publication should be an important milestone in the evolving history of investigative biography.

CHAPTER FOUR
Telling the Untold Story of Armand Hammer

In 1984, I decided to write a biography of Armand Hammer, the elderly but still active industrialist, philanthropist, and citizen-diplomat. It was a near certainty that he would oppose my efforts because of his extraordinarily acute sense of image-making. My approaches to Hammer through his minions confirmed that he had no interest in cooperating. In fact, it appeared he would do a great deal to close off access to his employees, his family, and the documentary record of his long life.

Despite those threatening signs, I decided to proceed. Yes, it is true that most people have considerable claims to privacy. Hammer was not one of those people. He had been in the public eye since the early 1920s. He had relentlessly sought publicity for his accomplishments for decades. It was time to pierce the facade. If I accomplished my mission, it would be the first independent biography of perhaps the most influential private citizen in twentieth-century America.

At that point, I had written two previous books, neither of them a full-scale biography. But I had been inspired by the Robert Moses and Lyndon Johnson biographies of Robert Caro, and by the Howard Hughes biography of Donald Barlett and James Steele. As executive director of an international organization called Investigative Reporters & Editors, I was well aware of how few journalists had used their talents to write ground-breaking biographies of contemporary figures. Caro and Barlett-Steele had paved the way, though, and it was a road I wanted to travel.

It took me eighteen months to prepare a book proposal that might bring me enough money to proceed; after all, it would be an expensive task to document nine decades of activity spread out all over the globe. Fortunately, the proposal attracted interest. Eventually, I signed a contract with Little, Brown and Company. I had obtained something relatively few investigative journalists attain—the time and money to stretch myself, at great length.

Before delving any more deeply into Hammer's life, I worked out some principles with Jennifer Josephy, my editor at Little, Brown. Those principles were outgrowths of my study of biography as a craft. Too many biographers who come from an investigative journalism background jump into the new genre believing that all they need to do is dig out provocative information. They are not reflective enough about how to craft that raw information into a factual, compelling narrative that will hold the reader's attention for days. A biography, after all, is not just a newspaper article writ large. It takes on a life of its own.

I told Jennifer that I planned to tell the life as chronologically as possible. In the end, we violated chronology a bit during the period when Hammer was incredibly active in a huge number of arenas. Trying to help readers follow each activity year by year seemed counterproductive; as a result, a few chapters covered one activity chronologically over the decades. We handled his art collecting that way, as well as his philanthropy.

My list of principles included learning about the context of the times, so I could better explain Hammer's actions in that context. For example, trying to tell the story of Hammer's business and diplomatic successes in the Soviet Union during the 1920s without understanding the shaky state of relations between Washington and Moscow at that time would make little sense.

I was determined to avoid placing Hammer on the psychoanalyst's couch for the most part, despite pressure from friends, my agent, and the reading public (as judged by their book-buying behavior) to do so. I believe that no biographer should presume to accurately represent the thoughts of an uncooperative subject. A related principle was my respect for the complexity of another human being. No one or two motivations can explain anyone's words and deeds; I determined to treat Hammer's life in a nonreductionist way, although I compromised a bit in the end by using an overlay of his quest for respect and respectability to give some shape to his saga. I did, however, hope to delve far deeper than the standard Who's Who, and at least somewhat deeper than an impersonal exterior view. Perhaps I could explain some of the intangibles—Hammer's motives, his emotions, his inner nature.

With my principles more or less enunciated, I had a dilemma familiar to many biographers embarking on a project likely to meet hostility: Do I inform my subject of my inquiries, of my progress, on a regular basis? Or do I operate in relative secrecy as long as possible? My decision contradicted what I believe to be the conventional wisdom among journalists, who fear that early and frequent notification might mean doors prematurely closed and documents fed into shredders.

I have found during my years of investigating that the subject almost always learns quickly, in one way or another, that an author is making inquiries. I prefer to be up-front, if for no other reason than common courtesy. So, I tried contacting Hammer regularly at Occidental Petroleum Corporation. From him, there was total silence. From his minions, there was open hostility.[1] During the five years it took to complete the book, I never received one iota of cooperation from anybody then working at a high level of any Hammer enterprise. His hostility never caused me to become hostile. It was a given to me that any subject has a right to keep his or her life as private as possible from prying outsiders. I found Hammer's life and works endlessly fascinating, so his lack of cooperation was unlikely to discourage me. Most investigative biographers enjoy a challenge; hostility simply makes them more determined to figure out what somebody is hiding, and why.

When researching an individual (or an institution or issue), I like to build a chronology. That device allows me to see a life in a linear way—to understand what came first, what came next, and whether there might be a cause-and-effect relationship. I add to the chronology every week, summarizing the significant information I have collected. I include telling anecdotes and quotations as well as unadorned facts; when it is time to write the first draft, I do it directly from the chronology. If I tried to write the first draft with my piles of files by my desk, I would be paralyzed by the bulk.

There is a caveat. As I winnow and synthesize the information, deciding what goes into the chronology and what does not, I am making choices that might turn out to be wrong. To guard against mistakes, I reread all my documents and notes at various intervals. Information that I set aside at an earlier stage might take on new meaning in light of what I have learned during the interim.

While collecting information, I work from the outside in, beginning with already published primary sources, then concentrating on nonpublished documents. Only after I have learned as much as I can from the paper trail do I move to the people trail. Because so little is completely new in this world, it is a good bet that any biographer will find useful leads in general-circulation newspapers, popular and specialized magazines, newsletters, radio and television broadcasts, doctoral dissertations, master's theses, and books.

I built my Armand Hammer chronology on a foundation of thousands of references from such secondary sources. I summarized every significant article about Hammer from the *New York Times, Washington Post, Wall Street Journal, Christian Science Monitor, Los Angeles Times, Chicago Tribune,* and other dailies. Those papers either have a print index or are available through a computer database vendor, or both. When I wanted information from newspapers that are not indexed or on-line, I worked through a fellow journalist employed there or through the newsroom librarian. Naturally, I promised to return the favors someday, and some of those favors already have been called in.

Never do I trust totally what some other reporter has written. I use no information from secondary sources without verifying it independently. There are questions of art and ethics that arise even when a biographer verifies as accurate something already in print. If, for example, an anecdote already published is compelling, does the biographer appropriate it, giving credit where that credit is due? Or does the biographer find a fresh, unpublished anecdote, although it might be less enlightening? If a well-known anecdote fails to appear, the editor (and readers) might wonder about its omission. If, on the other hand, the anecdote does appear, the editor (and readers) might object to reading it yet again.

In short, reading what is already published presents dilemmas that must be answered on a case-by-case basis. Certainly, every researcher has to start someplace. General-circulation daily newspapers are my favorite beginning point on most in-depth pieces. Some magazines and most newsletters are every bit as valuable, but often harder to locate. We all know about the *Readers Guide to Periodical Literature* from our high school term papers. What too many journalists fail to use are the more specialized print indexes—for legal periodicals, business periodicals, and the like.[2]

Better still, thousands of publications are available through computer databases, which can be searched more creatively than any print index. There are specialized magazines and newsletters covering virtually every industry, every profession, every issue. (Once when I was profiling a congressman who owned a fishing tackle manufacturing firm, I heard that the firm was under investigation by a federal agency. I went to a directory of periodicals, where I found half-a-dozen that write about nothing but fishing tackle. I called the editors at those publications; they provided me with details about the investigation, which was still in progress and unreported outside the industry's specialized press.)[3]

While working on my biography of Hammer, I used specialized publications to help track his career in numerous arcane businesses. The magazines carried names like *Aberdeen-Angus Journal, Arabian Horse Journal, Spirits* (covering the distilling industry), *International Coal Report,* and *Oil and Gas Journal,* to mention just a small percentage of those I consulted.[4]

Hammer's name showed up in hundreds of books that I checked. Some of the most valuable references appeared in memoirs by people who knew Hammer but did not talk to me either because Hammer had asked them not to or because they were dead. Celebrity lawyer Louis Nizer (who represented Hammer and who served on Occidental's board of directors) never responded to my request for an interview. But a chapter about Hammer in Nizer's memoirs was most revealing.

Doctoral dissertations and master's theses (which like periodicals are indexed in hard copy and on computer databases) can contain a great deal of gold. The students who research such tomes are generally thought of as unthreatening, and as a result gain access to private information that a journalist would be denied automatically.[5]

When a subject is hostile, a reporter must find alternate routes to capture that subject in his or her own words. With Hammer, I began by reading his 1932 memoir, his 1975 sponsored biography, and, later, the 1985 coffee-table picture book he subsidized as well as his best-selling 1987 autobiography. I compared and contrasted the books, looking for themes, inconsistencies, and gaps. There were plenty of each that became grist for my version of his life.

I tracked down speeches that he had given around the world by using the twice-monthly publication *Vital Speeches,* by finding reprints of his words in the *Congressional Record* as inserted by his elected admirers, or by calling groups that had invited him to talk and had retained a tape or a printed transcript.

For the first half of the 1940s, Hammer published his own magazine, *The Compleat Collector.* He wrote many of the articles under his own name or used pseudonyms, including Braset Marteau (arm and hammer in literal French). I found the entire run of the magazine in the stacks of the Library of Congress. Again, there was Hammer in his own words. He wrote prefaces for many of the catalogues that explained his various art collections, perhaps never thinking that an investigative reporter would find those words revealing.

Using the Congressional Information Service (CIS) index, I discovered dozens of hearings at which Hammer testified. Then I used the nearby government documents library to find the printed records of those hearings, stretching back to the 1940s. Once more, I had captured Hammer in his own words, sometimes under oath, sometimes answering questions that he could not have anticipated. Weekly and annual compilations of presidential papers by the federal government gave me preliminary insight into Hammer's official dealings with the head of the nation during any given year.

Whenever I located a major magazine or newspaper article about Hammer—concerning his congressional testimony, his White House ties, or whatever—I looked for letters to the editor in later issues. Sometimes Hammer signed the letters himself; sometimes they were written by his friends or his detractors. In many cases, they were highly quotable, providing insight into his character.

Already published primary information was everywhere. To learn about his deceased relatives and his cronies, I located obituaries. Photographs in commercial archives told worlds about relatives and friends, dead and alive. To learn about his donations to controversial cancer

treatment research, I located published proceedings of scientific con-
ferences and transcripts of meetings conducted by the President's
Cancer Panel, which Hammer began chairing in 1981 thanks to an
appointment from Ronald Reagan. Advertisements in trade publications, promotional corporate histories, notices concerning Hammer's
companies in the government's official *Federal Register,* documentation in the newsletters of trade and professional associations to which
Hammer's companies belonged for lobbying purposes—all helped
me understand the tycoon's business ventures.

Almost every in-depth piece benefits from information found in
civil and criminal lawsuits. Because of computer databases that capture decisions from most federal and state courts, learning about lawsuits spread out in courtrooms all over the nation is possible. I began
by searching on a computer terminal at a nearby law school. By tap-
ping into the vendors Lexis and Westlaw, I located three hundred
cases involving Hammer, members of his family, or important associates. After reading the judges' opinions on-line, I decided which cases
were worth pursuing further. I then arranged visits to courthouses
and records repositories (for the older cases). At those sites, I examined trial transcripts (Hammer under oath), depositions, interrogatories, and exhibits.

The search for lawsuits included specialized courts, too—U.S. Tax
Court, federal bankruptcy courts, divorce courts, probate courts, and
the like. Using Lexis, I also searched the court systems of selected
foreign nations, where the multinational Hammer turned up in profitable ways. At the local level, I visited not only courthouses but also
the offices of county and municipal officials. In such places I found
evidence of Hammer's land transactions, tax assessments, personal
property forms, and the like. In state capitals, I found driver's license
information, automobile registrations, renewals of his medical license,
data about secured loans, and numerous filings by his business entities.

When the Internal Revenue Service regional office in California
could not locate the annual tax returns for Hammer's foundation, the
California Registry of Charitable Trusts in Sacramento came through
with admirable efficiency. At the federal level, I found revealing documents everywhere. Unfortunately, I had to invoke the Freedom of
Information Act (FOIA) all too often, which meant huge delays. Many

agencies assume requesters will go away after waiting for months or years. I did not go away. I wrote and called regularly to let the FOIA bureaucrats know that I was serious. I worked through members of Congress when I thought it would help. I traveled to Washington, D.C., to meet the FOIA bureaucrats face-to-face, sometimes walking out the door with documents that weeks earlier I had been told did not exist or probably would not be located for years because of un-avoidable backlogs. Sometimes an agency's regional office helped at the same time the national headquarters delayed. Other times the equation was reversed.

At some agencies, one FOIA officer handled my request for the entire warren of divisions. At other agencies, I had to deal with multiple FOIA bureaucrats, one per division. Within the State Department, the separate FOIA bureaucracy in the Passport Office got me what I had requested with little hassle. But the FOIA team handling diplomatic documents was inefficient and sometimes intransigent for years, until with the help of the Reporters Committee for Freedom of the Press, I found the supervisor who could break the logjam.

It was a much more pleasant experience to work with another arm of the federal government, the National Archives system, including the presidential libraries as well as the main buildings in the Washington, D.C., area. Archivists are trained to be helpful, unlike many FOIA bureaucrats. In most presidential libraries on most days, there were more archivists than there were researchers, so I received lots of attention.

At each library, letters from Hammer to the president or his aides, and letters back to Hammer, resided in abundance. Sometimes correspondence listed in the master index or cross-referenced in documents released to me turned out to be classified for national security reasons. By requesting a straightforward declassification review (a procedure separate from the FOIA), I sometimes gained access to a valuable letter or memorandum. In the main National Archives building, I found federal census records that helped me trace the movements and composition of the Hammer family during the late 1800s and early 1900s; reading books on the techniques of genealogy helped me tremendously in the early going.

Overall, many of my greatest finds were among private papers in semipublic repositories, such as the Socialist Labor Party files at the Historical Society of Wisconsin, the collection of U.S. Senator Styles Bridges (a crony of Hammer's) at New England College, and dozens of other deposits at similar places. Finding where people and organizations dead and alive donated their papers can be easy or difficult, but is almost always possible. For current and former members of Congress, there are more or less thorough lists available from House and Senate historians employed by the federal government. As for finding and using other unpublished primary documents, I always assumed I could find them legally. When it seemed appropriate, I sought and located high school and college yearbooks, academic transcripts, fraternity records, cemetery records, news releases and employee newsletters from Hammer's businesses, and dinner programs from his private clubs. Too many reporters assume such records are unavailable and never try.

Because I was working on long deadlines, I usually contacted potential human sources first by letter instead of calling. Telephone calls are too easy to avoid; nearly everybody opens mail. Telephone calls too often come at inopportune times; most people read their mail when in the mood to do so.

I routinely promised nervous sources that they would be able to review any portions of the manuscript in which they were mentioned. If they could prove to me that something I wrote was inaccurate or out of context, I would make the necessary changes. Most journalists shy away from such a procedure, for reasons I fail to understand. I never lost control; if I did not want to make a change because I knew I was correct, I retained my own phrasing. Because I have confidence in my carefulness, I expect few demands for revisions or deletions. I sent manuscript pages to about three hundred sources. About half responded. Of those hundred and fifty or so, only three pointed out inaccuracies. I fixed those inaccuracies. Another ten asked for changes to save face; in the majority of instances, I said no. But—and here is the advantage to my practice—fully fifty of those responding provided additional useful information when their memories were jogged by the manuscript pages.

Along the people trail, one of the most important distinctions is between the currents and the formers—the current spouse and the former spouse, the current neighbor and the former neighbor, the current minister and the former minister, the current accountant and the former accountant, the current lawyer and the former lawyer, and so on. The formers sometimes have axes to grind. But they generally can talk more freely than the currents. Sometimes the formers had spirited away documents that were revealing.

During my research, I contacted hundreds of sources who refused to talk without permission from Hammer, permission he was withholding. But hundreds more did talk. They fell into the categories of relatives, social friends, neighbors, school classmates, teachers, employees, providers of manual labor, business competitors and suppliers, competing art collectors and philanthropists, recipients of philanthropy, politicians, academic experts, fellow hobbyists, club members, religious leaders, and journalists who had viewed and interviewed Hammer.

Because I had conducted so much documentary research before beginning the interviews, I sometimes knew more (or at least remembered more) than my sources. Often, my sources had nothing to feed me but gossip. I always listened. Much of the gossip, despite its tempting nature, I had to reject or refrain from publishing—especially anecdotes about Hammer's sex life that could not be verified because the alleged sex partner was dead and nobody had photographs of the bedroom activity. But in almost every interview I gleaned at least a few tidbits that were the foundation of a sentence or more in the book. By interviewing sources from all phases of his life and by rejecting unverified gossip, I was able to write what I believed to be a balanced biography. Reviewers by the dozens agreed.

Hammer, however, saw it differently. Angry that I had managed to complete the book despite his opposition, and upset at what I had chronicled, he sued in England, where libel laws are heavily favorable to plaintiffs. Because Hammer sued so quickly after the book's publication in 1989, I found myself unable to do much follow-up research during 1990, other than the research of a professional defendant. Then, in December 1990, four months before the scheduled start-up of the libel trial in London, Hammer died at his home. All of a sudden, information previously off-limits to me because of privacy laws and customs became available. I brought his life up-to-date, for the sake of the historical record, in a revised and expanded paperback edition.

Telling the Untold Story

During my years of research and writing and after the publication of the book, many newspapers and magazines chronicled my attempts to write a thorough, accurate biography in the face of Hammer's resistance. The most informative of those chronicles appeared in the View section of the *Los Angeles Times* on November 22, 1989. The main headline read, "Nailing Down Hammer." The sub-headline said, "Author Steve Weinberg spent five years trying to capture on paper the elusive industrialist who made Occidental Petroleum a giant. Now his subject is fighting to banish the book." Written by Bob Sipchen, the article is reprinted here by permission:

When 91-year-old industrialist Armand Hammer popped up in the news recently because he had a pacemaker installed, he needed no introduction. Anyone who turns Occidental Petroleum into a multinational conglomerate, builds an art empire, pumps millions of dollars into cancer research and shuttles around the world as a citizen-diplomat is sure to be a household name.

With two autobiographies, two authorized biographies and tons of newspaper and magazine articles about Hammer on library shelves, his life is an open book.

Or so it seems.

But in late 1984, author Steve Weinberg, an associate journalism professor at the University of Missouri, decided to get to know Hammer better. Over the next five years Weinberg interviewed about 600 of Hammer's friends, enemies and associates and studied "hundreds of thousands" of pages of documents.

The result is the newly released *Armand Hammer: The Untold Story*, a 501-page profile that Weinberg said is far too intricate to boil down into any sort of a capsule summary.

Hammer's attorneys have had no such reluctance.

In an unusual letter urging publisher Little, Brown & Co. to drop the book, they argued that *The Untold Story* portrays Hammer "as the scion of a morally bankrupt family, who from young adulthood has had a propensity for criminal and fraudulent behavior."

"In keeping with such a theme," the letter continued, "the book contains dozens of passages impugning [Hammer's] motives, reflecting adversely on his integrity and inferring that he is, and has been throughout his life, unscrupulous and willing to attain personal goals and ambitions through criminal acts, breaches of fiduciary duty or other unconscionable behavior."

Neither Hammer nor his attorneys would talk to the *Times* about Weinberg's book.

But in their letter, dated last July, the attorneys stated that the book, which Hammer also has moved to keep from being published in Great Britain, is "beyond redemption by corrections."

Weinberg scoffs at that accusation. In his view, the controversy merely raises basic questions facing any biographer: How does one accurately and honestly portray the life of another human?

Even before Hammer's bestselling autobiography hit the stores in 1987, then-Vice President George Bush, former Presidents Jimmy Carter and Gerald Ford, Sen. Edward Kennedy (D-Mass.) and Israeli leader Menachem Begin contributed gushing publicity blurbs. So did Walter Cronkite, Dan Rather and Barbara Walters.

But in an article in *Regardie's* magazine the year before, Weinberg had written that "Hammer has created a persona that sometimes seems to conflict with the facts. Without the facts it is hard to know where myth ends and reality begins. . . . Many journalists have failed to probe behind Hammer's carefully cultivated image. Hammer has preempted the market in information about himself. . . ."

That assessment was underscored as he set out to research the book, Weinberg said. "The Doctor," as everyone calls Hammer, refused to talk; he and his associates told others not to talk either, sources who did speak up told Weinberg.

"Almost everyone who currently draws money from him in any connection said no," Weinberg said.

Weinberg is particularly angry that while he was submitting his book proposal to various publishing houses, someone violated an unwritten, sacred rule of the industry and, he asserts, leaked a copy to Hammer. He also has heard from former Hammer associates that The Doctor disliked the article in *Regardie's*.

"And common sense says it didn't help that I run an organization called Investigative Reporters & Editors," said Weinberg, the executive director of that respected professional group.

But he remains uncertain why Hammer, who by all accounts relishes publicity, was so adamant in attempting to lower a veil of silence on his effort. Still, bolstered by a $160,000 advance, Weinberg set out to piece together a portrait of a man who didn't want to be portrayed.

With or without Hammer's stamp of approval, the basic threads of his life shake out the same in the various biographies.

The differences are in the authors' approach and inclusion of details.

The differences are even reflected in chapter headings. The first chapter of the authorized biography, for instance, is titled "Genesis of Genius." The first chapter of Weinberg's unauthorized biography is "A Bankrupt Family."

For the most part, though, Weinberg is aggressively timid about drawing conclusions.

He is not, for instance, an admirer of the now popular psycho-historical school of biography, as practiced by Gail Sheehy and others: "I don't think a biographer should put his subject on the couch any more than necessary. . . . We have trouble knowing what our own wife is thinking at any time. What presumption would lead me to tell people what Armand Hammer is thinking?"

Such protestations aside, Weinberg does juxtapose facts and supply a few editorial asides to hint at the psychological forces that shaped Hammer's life and set him on the "quest for respect and respectability."

In Weinberg's portrayal, Hammer's father, Julius, was a man who believed sincerely in socialism, yet worked hard to support his family as a capitalist, managing eight drugstores at one time.

At one point in his investigation, Weinberg unearthed documentation that in 1906 Julius Hammer declared bankruptcy, apparently, the book suggests, to illegally evade creditors.

A long battle ensued. But Weinberg concludes that "the relative painlessness with which Julius and Rose [Armand's mother] escaped from bankruptcy court, despite the untruthfulness of their testimony, almost surely impressed upon everybody that cover-ups and convenient memory lapses could be useful tactics."

At age 10, Armand was sent by his parents to live with a socialist colleague of his father's in Connecticut and stayed there five years—". . . it seems not to have done any lasting harm to his psyche, unless a possible feeling of abandonment should be regarded as causing his lifelong quest for public adulation," Weinberg writes.

Armand Hammer

Hammer took over as the head of his family at age 21, when his father was arrested and eventually convicted of first-degree manslaughter in connection with the death of a woman on whom he had performed an abortion. Many observers at the time contended that the 2$^1/_2$ years Hammer's father spent in Sing Sing prison stemmed from his leftist beliefs more than any lapse in medical judgment.

Hammer's fight to free his father became a personal crusade, and Weinberg traces a similar tenacity—and what the author sees as a similar willingness to bend the rules—through some of Hammer's many other quests, including his thus-far unsuccessful attempt to drill for oil in the Pacific Palisades and his successful bid to receive a presidential pardon for making illegal campaign contributions to former President Richard Nixon.

Hammer first made his fortune selling medicine with a high dose of alcohol during Prohibition and quickly became, in Weinberg's words, "a deal junkie." On a trip to Moscow in 1921, Hammer met, and impressed, Soviet premier Vladimir Ilyich Lenin. Unexpectedly, he settled for nine years in the Soviet Union, where he operated an asbestos mine, established a pencil factory and began dealing in Czarist art, among other enterprises.

Hammer and his third wife, Frances, didn't invest in Occidental Petroleum until 1956, when it was a tiny company with $79,000 in assets. They thought several new wells Oxy planned to drill at the time would be losers and that those financial losses would make a nice tax shelter for their already substantial wealth, Weinberg writes.

Instead, the drillers hit oil.

Other successes followed, and in 1957, Hammer, who had been briefly reluctant to get into the industry, became president of Occidental Petroleum, which then had a full-time staff of three. Quickly, Weinberg writes, Hammer began "reshaping Occidental's board of directors in his image."

Hammer has never been a majority shareholder in Occidental. Rather, Weinberg writes, he controlled the company then and now with "his forceful personality, keen mind, capacity for work and incessant salesmanship."

And cunning. For example, Hammer demanded that many Oxy board members submit signed, undated letters of resignation, which kept the members effectively under his thumb, Weinberg writes.

As the company grew and diversified, it ran into the sort of problems any multinational conglomerate might. Allegations of illegal payoffs to government officials have haunted Hammer for years, for instance. As has labor unrest.

One issue that receives Weinberg's attention is whether Hammer has, at times, put Occidental's bottom line ahead of the greater public good, as when Occidental inherited the toxic mess at Love Canal, and, critics have said, dragged its corporate feet in settling claims.

Similarly, Weinberg's book suggests that Hammer's oil dealings with Libya "set in train the oil price rises of the 1970s" and eventually "without question . . . changed the balance of power in the world."

On the other hand, the book also raises the issue of whether Hammer sometimes puts his own ego—and, some say, capricious goals—ahead of the interests of Occidental, as suggested by the class-action lawsuits that have been filed against him by shareholders over the years.

Weinberg asserts that out of respect for the intelligence of readers, his book leaves such subjective issues open to debate. Besides, he's not sure of his own conclusions, he said. At no point in the writing or research did he ever have the sort of epiphany some biographers experience—a moment when the sea of facts and anecdotes parts miraculously and the True Nature of the person under scrutiny reveals itself.

"I have a great deal of respect for some of what he's done; a great deal of abhorrence for some of what he's done. He's very complex. Maybe that was my epiphany—how complex he is. . . . Some think he walks on water. Some think he is the devil incarnate."

In an essay on the art of biography he wrote for the *Missouri Review,* Weinberg quoted Thomas Carlyle: "A well-written life is almost as rare as a well-spent one."

He rewrote this one six times, from beginning to end. But he remains unconvinced that anyone ever fully captures a person's life in print. "I'm very humble about the biographer's job," he said.

The reviews of *The Untold Story,* however, have been generally favorable. If anything, they accuse Weinberg of letting Hammer off easy. *Fortune* magazine reviewer Irwin Ross called it "a good book, iconoclastic by necessity but judicious in tone, skeptical rather than hostile."

The *New York Times* said that "Mr. Weinberg, in spite of his careful detachment, appears to be too easily won over by Mr. Hammer."

The only review that makes Weinberg bristle appeared in *Business Week.* In it, Stewart Toy wrote that "the most striking thing about this book is how little the facts vary from those in Hammer's 1987 autobiography."

Weinberg argues that while both books *are* basically accurate in the facts they present, his book is packed with new information.

For instance, none of Hammer's four major run-ins with the U.S. Securities and Exchange Commission are mentioned in Hammer's 1987 autobiography. By filing Freedom of Information Act requests with the SEC, Weinberg turned up reams of previously unavailable information, he said.

Hammer continues to fight him in federal court on the release of documents detailing the last two SEC investigations of Occidental, contending those files, which pertain, in part, to Hammer's negotiations in Libya and Latin America, "involve supposed national security issues," Weinberg said.

"Hammer and his lawyers went crazy to stop me. They spent a lot of time and I presume a lot of money to convince the SEC not to release the files," he said. For the book, Weinberg had to rely on now-available public records to discuss those later investigations.

He said he hopes to include the information that will come from further release of documents in subsequent editions.

That is, if a Hammer lawsuit doesn't somehow push the book out of print.

In his biography, Weinberg quotes Hammer attorney Louis Nizer as saying that Hammer is "unabashedly litigious. . . . When principle is involved, he rejects compromise. . . . It does not matter how great the gamble."

So at first, Weinberg thought Hammer was simply trying to quash a book that contained more information than Hammer wanted the public to have. After all, he said, virtually everyone he talked to agrees that "The Doctor likes to control his own image and his own fate."

But lately Hammerologists have suggested to Weinberg that The Doctor may actually be cooking up the controversy as a convoluted way to feed his own fame.

"Enough people who know Hammer have suggested that that I'm beginning to believe it—especially considering that he hasn't pressed things," Weinberg said. "I'm more and more convinced that he's just wily enough to have done all this to boost sales of the book."

CHAPTER FIVE

Short-Form Biography
The Art of the Periodical Profile

A rich literature exists chronicling the histories of magazines and newspapers in America. But none of the histories I have read contains anything substantive about an important development—the rise of the personality profile.[1]

Profiles, or what could rightly be called short-form biographies, have appeared occasionally in magazines and newspapers for centuries. But only in the last fifty years have in-depth, artfully written profiles, often with an investigative bent, begun appearing with any regularity in a few quality periodicals. Only in the last twenty-five years have they become something of a trend.

The New Yorker magazine, founded in 1925, took a big step in 1938 in the evolution of short-form biography by hiring Joseph Mitchell away from the New York City newspaper world. As Norman Sims described in a rare commentary on the nearly forgotten Mitchell, "He wrote profiles for *The New Yorker* of waterfront workers, people on the Bowery, Mohawk Indians who work on high structural steel, and characters from the Fulton Fish Market in the southeast corner of Manhattan near the Brooklyn Bridge."[2]

Perhaps even more obscure today than Mitchell, Lincoln Barnett at *Life* magazine skillfully advanced short-form biography in periodicals. Barnett is the only practitioner I have found who wrote about the similarities of, and differences between, short-form and book-length biography.

Barnett began his journalism career at the *New York Herald Tribune* in the early 1930s, moving to *Life* in 1937 and then beginning a freelancing career in 1946. The remarkable nature of his work elicits little mention today—even a full-length history of *Life* devotes less than a paragraph to him, saying, "The graceful and versatile Barnett would become one of the country's best-known profile writers and win awards as the author of *The Universe and Dr. Einstein* and a book that grew out of a long and very popular *Life* science series, 'The World We Live In.'"[3]

Fortunately, Barnett left behind a legacy, a 1951 book called *Writing on Life: Sixteen Close-ups*, in which he not only reprinted profiles of sixteen famous people but also provided commentary on why and how he wrote each piece. It is in this book that Barnett compares and contrasts short-form and book-length biography. The book-length biographer, Barnett says, "deals with individuals on whom the evidence is mostly complete—the dead—and sublimates his doubts in footnotes. The newspaper writer concerns himself primarily with transitory or exterior qualities like acts or words. But no such limitations restrict the biographical form that has evolved in American magazines in recent years under the generic term 'profile' or 'close-up.' These trade names, suggesting as they do line drawings or snapshots, are misleading. For what they attempt in the space of a few thousand words is qualitatively no less ambitious than what a conventional biography undertakes in the wide galloping ranges of a book."

In the book's first chapter, Barnett discusses the qualities of good short-form biography, which are remarkably similar to what I believe to be the qualities of book-length biography. (I should stop to mention that every chapter of this book was already completed in manuscript form when I serendipitously discovered Barnett's collection of profiles. Immediately I was struck by our agreement on what makes a first-rate biography, even though we were working in different forms and setting down our thoughts forty-one years apart.)

Barnett tended to profile "important" subjects. He recognized, giving a bow toward Joseph Mitchell, that "a few writers are endowed with a degree of craftsmanship that enables them to create luminous and absorbing studies of humble people. Among these in particular one thinks of *The New Yorker*'s gifted, painstaking reporter, Joseph Mitchell, whose many brilliant studies of inconspicuous individuals on the fringes of metropolitan life have an artistic and literary value unique in contemporary journalism. But I have been lucky in having to face no such challenge."

As he chose his topics, Barnett came to realize "that a character sketch might originate out of an editor's or writer's interest in a general subject rather than in the specific individual who plays the title role in the finished article. For every occasion when an editor announces flatly, 'We ought to have a piece about Dr. Blank, the helminthologist,' there will be another time when he says, 'We ought to have a piece about helminthology. Whom shall we hang it on?' This explains why readers will often find themselves deeply interested in a sketch of a man whose name is completely unfamiliar to them; for every good close-up reveals its protagonist in the perspective of his calling and offers a store of wider information that transcends the pivotal facts of his life and personality."

Barnett also learned that short-form biography can work even when the author never meets the subject—just as is true in book-length biography. In his book, Barnett's profile of George C. Marshall falls into that realm.

Short-form biography took another leap forward during the 1960s, thanks in large part to Gay Talese's profiles in *Esquire* magazine, expanded upon by Tom Wolfe in *New York* magazine. In his 1973 essay about "The New Journalism," Wolfe identified four devices of what was then a new kind of profile: scene-by-scene construction, recording of dialogue in full, presenting every scene through the eyes of a particular character, and the recording of everyday gestures, habits, and other symbolic details.[4]

By the 1990s, dozens of newspaper and magazine journalists could be considered regular practitioners of first-rate short-form biography. Among the most notable are Walt Harrington of the *Washington Post* magazine and Madeleine Blais, who gained a measure of fame by winning a Pulitzer Prize for feature writing at the *Miami Herald* before turning to a career of freelancing and teaching.[5]

The two short-form biographies reprinted on the following pages exhibit great, and often contrasting, virtues. One is by a big-name journalist, Calvin Trillin. The other is by an equally talented but lesser-known journalist, Gerri Hirshey. Trillin worked closely with his subject after winning her full cooperation. Hirshey received no cooperation and, in fact, had to overcome formidable hostility. Trillin's style is chatty; he treats the subject at times as a new friend. Hirshey's style is more formal; she treats the subject at times as an enemy. The profiles do have one important thing in common, though: both are about writers who practice hard-edged short-form and long-form biography—Edna Buchanan and Kitty Kelley. Thus, in addition to providing examples of short-form biography, both are valuable for what they reveal about the practice of the craft of biography.

─────────────────
─────────────────

The first profile, by Gerri Hirshey, appeared in the *Washington Post Magazine* of October 30, 1988, and is reprinted with permission. This is the first of three installments. Parts two and three, which appeared in the broadsheet editions of the *Post* the next two days, are not reprinted here.

Oh Kitty!

Washington author Kitty Kelley has made a fortune uncovering the secrets of celebrities such as Jacqueline Onassis, Frank Sinatra and Elizabeth Taylor. So why wouldn't she talk when a reporter tried to ask questions about her life?

"I do unauthorized biographies. It's the best approach because it's accurate. It's not a whitewash job."

—Kitty Kelley

Author's Note: Beginning in February of this year, I tried to interview Kitty Kelley for this article. I called her home in Georgetown and left messages on her answering machine, which played Sinatra singing "My Way" and ended with Kelley saying, "Now, do it your way."

A week later, she called, and politely demurred. "Tell your editor I'm not sanguine towards it," she said.

Shortly thereafter, she appeared on Larry King's television show and did several other interviews. She announced that her next subject would be Nancy Reagan. The advance is believed to be about $3.5 million. I called again. And again. Finally, an answer, on shocking pink stationery: She was still busy. But perhaps we could talk in June. In June, I tried yet again, by letter and phone. The taped message had changed; now Sinatra sang, "If you asked me, I could write a book."

Still no response. Though she was in Washington—society pages ran photos of her attending parties here—certified mail requesting an interview was returned. A hand-delivered request elicited a phone call from an assistant, who stated that Kelley "has just left town." When I requested an interview through her attorney, he wrote back: "We doubt that Ms. Kelley would refuse to be interviewed. Probably, she was out of Washington or about to leave when you contacted her in the past."

It seemed plain enough: Like her famous subjects, Kitty Kelley wasn't talking. This, then, is the unauthorized biography of Kitty Kelley, "celebrated investigative journalist," as one of her book jackets touts, author of *The Glamour Spas; Jackie Oh!; Elizabeth Taylor, The Last Star;* and *His Way: The Unauthorized Biography of Frank Sinatra.*

The Girl Can't Help It

"I hope she gets hit by a truck."

—Nancy Sinatra on Kitty Kelley

Katherine (Kitty) Kelley was 9 when she heard the adults talking about *that woman.* Everyone in Spokane, Wash., knew about Virginia Hill. They called her a gangster moll. A babe. She'd made headlines worldwide, and when she moved to Spokane in 1951, folks gossiped that mob money had bought the handsome $35,000 house two blocks from the Kelleys.

"Glamorous Ginny" Hill had been the consort of Bugsy Siegel, gunned down in 1947 while reading the paper in Hill's Hollywood mansion. Hill would likely have been executed with him if she hadn't fought with Bugsy over his dirty sports shirt. He refused to change it, so Hill flew off to Paris in a fine ermine huff. And on her return, she was subpoenaed by the Kefauver crime hearings.

She took her oath with a mink stole tossed over her shoulders, gestured toward the press gallery and told Estes Kefauver, "I hate those people. You don't know what I've been through with those bums."

Tabloid bums, newsprint maggots—she despised the lot with scorching intensity. Ginny Hill cursed them, pummeled them, took off her spike-heel shoe and tattooed a few skulls with it. Her attitude toward nosy reporters was summed up in one neat wish, precociously Sinatraesque: "I hope an atom bomb falls on every one of you."

And so it was that Virginia Hill didn't exactly exude sociability when she settled in Spokane with her new ski-pro husband. Curious folks would cruise by the house peering from humpback '50 Chevys, but none would approach it.

Except for Kitty Kelley. As her uncle John Kelley remembers it, little Kitty, who had braids down to her waist, slipped into a pair of her mother's high heels one day and followed the whiff of scandal toward the house at S3905 Skyview Dr. She knocked. The scarlet woman opened her door to find a pretty, smiling child who wanted to be friends and who welcomed her to Spokane.

"She was ushered in and treated very hospitably," says Kitty's father, William V. Kelley, a lawyer in Spokane. Afterward, he says, little Kitty got quite a scolding from her mother. Imagine. The child calling on *that woman*. Adds her uncle John: "She was always a high-spirited investigative reporter. Even then."

Digging for Dollars

"Yes [I am] very rich. And I'm going to get even richer. I don't mind saying it. I worked damn hard for it."

—Kitty Kelley, 1978

"Hell, for a million dollars, I'd write about Donald Duck."

—Kitty Kelley, 1981

"Money has never been a motivating factor in my life, ever."

—Kitty Kelley, 1986

That woman. Kitty Kelley has been called the pit bull of the unauthorized biography, the doyenne of dirt, a scalp-hunting biographer. Hers are the books few admit to reading—yet they debut at No. 1 on the *New York Times* Best-Seller List. There's gold in them thar celebrity undies, and no one does a better job of mining it. With her advance for the Nancy Reagan book, Kitty Kelley is the capital's best paid writer—No. 6, in fact, among Washington's top 100 breadwinners, according to estimates by *Washingtonian* magazine. In 1987, she is said to have earned $3.5 million—an amount she subsequently characterized as too low. She made more than Ted Koppel, Bob Woodward, Tip O'Neill. More than Henry Kissinger, Willard Scott, George Will, Donald Regan, Cal Ripken Jr. Asked about objections from those she's written about, Kelley told one interviewer, "I say, 'I'm sorry, I'm on my way to the bank.'"

Stalking celebrities has made her one of them. Her very name defines a genre, as in "doing a Kitty Kelley" on someone. Witty, articulate and ever ready with the juiciest tidbits, she is boffo with talent coordinators and talk-show hosts. She faces criticism with hard facts—and a healthy dose of cute. When Donahue badgers, Kelley leans forward in pink satin with a prim black bow tied at her throat, smiles and fires off a favorite expression.

"Oh, Phil," she scolds. "Ca ca ca!"

The audience roars for the petite blonde who has dared to ask interviewees questions like: What was Liz Taylor like in bed? More times than not, she gets answers to her audacious queries, which lead to scoops like these:

- Jacqueline Kennedy had shock treatments.
- JFK's sister Rosemary was lobotomized.
- Ava Gardner aborted Sinatra's baby.
- Liz Taylor aborted Sinatra's baby.
- Sinatra's mother was an abortionist.
- Sinatra once called Nancy Reagan "a dope with fat ankles."
- Senator John Warner wore a black sleep mask to bed.

For her scoops, Kitty Kelley works very, very hard. As testimony, she always counts up her interviews: She said she did 857 interviews for the Sinatra book, more than 300 for the Taylor book, 350 for *Jackie Oh!* Most at-home interviews with Kelley feature a walking tour of her Sinatra archives. She maintained a file folder for every month of Sinatra's life, reviewed FBI wiretaps, Senate crime committee testimony. She hires researchers and private detectives, will interview a single source up to 17 times. Parsing a famous life, she's said, she always gets "obsessed," if not a little possessed. She has said that she found herself talking in a Jacqueline Onassis whisper and shopping a lot; she ate too much while researching Liz Taylor. And with the Sinatra book? "I started kicking ass."

Booting famous derrières has afforded Kitty Kelley a historic 1807 manse atop a hill in Georgetown, where she stores all that celebrity dirt and collects dainty teacups. She can be seen jogging through Rock Creek Park frequently, a short, busty, bleached blonde in bright red sweats. She dresses conservatively, and expensively, carries Chanel purses that sell for upward of $1,000 each, wears Hermes scarves and pert Adolfo suits just like Nancy Reagan. She drives a $60,000 cherry-red Mercedes 560, reportedly part of her advance for the Reagan book. She calls herself an outsider, but more and more she shows up at Washington power parties, embassy soirees, benefits and awards dinners.

After years of derisive and dismissive reviews, being taken seriously is very important to Kitty Kelley, according to those who know her. "There's something fragile about Kitty," says Washington novelist Barbara Raskin, who has known Kelley for nearly 15 years. "The thing which is most important to Kitty is her good name. If you took away her money or her house, it couldn't bother her as much as negative things being said about her. Or written about her. She wants respectability more than anything."

At 46, she seems on the verge of earning it. Her Sinatra effort has been praised by William Safire. Bob Woodward attended the Sinatra book party and got an autographed copy. Last year, Kelley was given the Outstanding Author Award by the American Society of Journalists and Authors. Critics have finally begun to review her as a writer, instead of as a paste-up artist. Wrote *Washington Post* book critic Jonathan Yardley, "The first two books were star biographies in the manner of the *National Enquirer . . . His Way*, by contrast, contains a large amount of original research, avoids conclusions or insinuations that the evidence does not support, and is written, with only occasional lapses, in what seems a deliberately deadpan style."

Yet at this juncture, she is flirting with the ultimate ostracism. Having taken on a national monument—Sinatra—and impressively reduced him to raving, paranoiac rubble, Kelley dares to invade the Republican holy of holies. She is investigating the wife of one of the most popular presidents, a woman who has endured a mastectomy, her husband's cancer, her husband's shooting and Donald Regan's venomous memoirs.

"It takes a real pushy pants to do it," Kelley has said of her métier. She has been working for nearly a year now, with two more to go. Is Mrs. Reagan worried? The White House has chosen not to comment, but already Kitty Kelley is flinging impolite but quotable adverbs at the First Lady. Recently, Kelley told a national magazine, "I understand she [Mrs. Reagan] has very stupidly written to a lot of people warning them not to talk to me. Why would she write all those letters saying, 'Don't talk'? What does that tell a biographer?"

Because of her position, asserted Kelley, Mrs. Reagan is "fair game."

Fair game. It's an expression Kitty Kelley uses often when describing her quarry. All public figures are fair game, as she was reminded when a caller to the Larry King TV show asked: If someone pulled a skeleton out of your closet, how would you feel?

"I'd feel awful," she answered. "I'd feel just terrible."

The Teflon Biographer

"There's a general paranoia when it comes to discussing that woman. People who know Jackie all share a caution that borders on fear about discussing her."

—Kitty Kelley on Jacqueline Onassis

Little is known of the private life of public figure Kitty Kelley. Interviews have concentrated on the juicy stuff of Kelley's scoops; friends of a decade and more will admit they know very little about her family and her background.

Says syndicated gossip columnist Liz Smith, "I've known her since the mid '70s, and I've always seen her alone, for dinner or something. I don't even know where she's from. There's never any talk of family, husband. Just work. And gossip, of course."

Ask around. In her home town of Spokane, in D.C., in New York publishing circles, many people want to talk about Kitty Kelley—but not necessarily for attribution. Check with friends, interviewees, relatives, and the responses are swift, emotional—and sharply divided. One set is laudatory; Kitty Kelley is charming, a fine reporter and a loyal friend. The other set is cautious, even fearful: *No way. I don't think it wise. I still have to live in this town. I don't want to talk about* that woman.

More than 90 interviews confirmed this much: *That woman* appears to be two women—one a bright, vivacious, fun-loving friend who gives huge Christmas parties and labors tirelessly with writers' organizations on tax and First Amendment issues, and whose worst vices are workaholism and diet cola. The other Kitty Kelley has even more private enemies than she does public ones. She flies into rages, uses foul language, litigates fiercely and is genuinely feared. The first woman can breezily, brilliantly dissect the subplots of *The Brothers Karamazov*; the second is a zealous inquisitor on celebrity sex, abortion and alcoholism. And as the two vastly different images emerge, other fragments clutter the field.

Shortly after I'd begun my research—and shortly after I'd informed Kelley by mail that I was proceeding with the story, interview or not—anonymous mail began to arrive. The mail wasn't threatening, just strange. And eerily predictable.

"Oh, you can expect about 90 days' mayhem by mail," said an attorney who has worked with Kelley. Four journalists who have written about Kelley had also talked about receiving mysterious mail: untraceable names signed to letters with no return address, containing both true and false information about Kitty Kelley, the journalists or their employers. Most often the letters were impassioned defenses of Kelley and her work, and intensely specific. Some were unsigned, with no return address. Sometimes the letters were on corporate stationery, from Time Inc., *Fortune*, *The Washington Post*. Some were mildly obscene and vaguely threatening. During and after reporting on Kelley, some journalists have gotten strange phone calls and lots of hang-ups.

The postal barrages are a joke to some recipients, rankling to others. After printing an item about an unauthorized biography of Kelley in the works (a book to be called *Bimbo: The Kitty Kelley Story*), Liz Smith says she got a stinging letter signed "Disgustedly" from one Barbara Regenstein—no return address—haranguing her for betraying her longtime friend Kitty. It mentioned material that Kelley had, but did *not* publish in *His Way*, concerning derogatory remarks Ol' Blue Eyes made about Smith. Smith wondered who could know this bit of trivia.

"I suspected that Kitty or someone close to her might be involved," says Smith. "So I sent her [Kelley] the letter and said this woman must be a friend of yours. She denied knowing the woman, wrote me a very curt note on the letter and sent it back. It was one of the rudest things I've ever received in the mail."

Could Kitty Kelley be involved in the letter campaigns? Her lawyer says no, Kelley would not "engage in such actions directly or indirectly."

And it hardly makes sense. Why would a bestselling author hunch over a typewriter, pecking out weird notes on a variety of stationery? Could a tough celebrity biographer be that thin-skinned when it came to her own life? Would a longtime beneficiary of First Amendment protection interfere with another journalist's investigations? This is a woman who publicly castigates her star subjects for thwarting her efforts to get at the truth. Finally, why would a top reporter resort to such amateur tactics?

Jonathan Yardley, who panned the Liz Taylor book in 1981 and got a gilded Gucci box of fishheads signed "From the friends of Kitty Kelley," says he was puzzled and amused by this coven of Kelley loyalists. "I've heard that she still vigorously denies it was her, and I can believe that," he says. "But the question persists: Who is behind these campaigns?"

Person or persons do keep up a lively correspondence. My Kelley doppelgängers are tricky and bicoastal. They followed my investigations from Spokane to Georgetown to New York and wrote me several times along the way. They praised Kitty Kelley, limned her accomplishments, her kindnesses to small and crippled children. They used various typewriters and made up names and anecdotes. Sometimes they phoned me. Posing as a reporter for another publication, a man calling himself Michael Fox harassed one of my sources. One called this magazine, wheedling details on the scope and date of this article. Denied information, she thundered: "Do you DARE tell the truth about one of Washington's most esteemed citizens?"

You will hear from this curious cabal throughout this story, as I did in my research. Hereinafter, their intrusions will be identified as Kitty Litter.

The Lilac Princess

"She has a devastating relationship with her mother. They practically hate each other. When I ended up, I felt kind of sorry for her."

—Kitty Kelley on Jacqueline Onassis

Ask people in Spokane about their most famous citizen since Bing Crosby, and some will invite you in for coffee. Others will hang up on you. Even in childhood, a duality existed, one that provoked wildly opposing impressions. Some Spokanians say Kitty Kelly had "the perfect life, a charmed life" there. Others say that she had a painful childhood and adolescence. Some remember her as the friendliest girl in school; others say she had a dark side. Some agreed to interviews, then canceled or changed their minds about being quoted by name. One woman, who provided old yearbooks and a two-hour interview, called the following day at 7:30 A.M., clearly in distress: "Forget you ever saw me, forget you ever talked to me. My husband forbids me getting involved. We still have to live in this town. And I'm afraid of her."

Why?

"I was scared of her as a child, and I still am. And now she just has so much power."

"Go see Marcia Gallucci" was the advice of several people in Spokane. They said she knew everything, but they doubted she'd talk. She is one of the few childhood friends still in touch with Kelley. She knows the good and the bad and still holds her dear.

"You certainly could do a Kitty Kelley book on Kitty Kelley. There are so many gaps, so many rumors. And the facts are pretty strange." So says Marcia Gallucci. She still lives in Spokane, where she and Kitty Kelley went through grammar school at St. Augustine's together, were Campfire Girls, rode in the same car pool, went to the Catholic girls' high school, Holy Names Academy. They both grew up in large, tumultuous

Irish families. Their mothers were friendly. When Kitty married, Marcia gave her a wedding shower.

Gallucci sits in her living room, gamely subduing the family Airedale, and says that she is a bit uneasy. She knows that some of her friends have refused to discuss Kelley's Spokane years. They have been talking among themselves all week. "Look, there's a reason why Kitty writes this stuff," says Gallucci. "I'm telling you this to understand Kitty better. She had a very rough time."

Kelley's proclivity for exposing others comes, Gallucci thinks, from the childhood miseries Kitty couldn't talk about back then. Spokane knew the Kelleys as prominent and well-to-do. But life was far from idyllic behind the big Tudoresque door of their sprawling hilltop home.

This wide gap between public perception and domestic realities would be the very stuff of Kelley's success as a celebrity biographer. The best and the brightest have dirty secrets. This Kelley has shown us over and over again, yanking back the bed curtains in JFK's Camelot, describing the fat beneath Liz Taylor's gauzy peignoirs. Her old friend Marcia thinks that being so naughty in print may be a hurt little girl's reaction to years of desperately trying to be perfect for an implacable, extremely strict, alcoholic mother.

"The mother is the key," says Gallucci. "It's no secret that she was a longtime alcoholic. It was very important for Kitty to be popular, to please those in authority. I believe it was a love/hate thing with her mother. She admired her mother. But I don't think Kitty ever got her mother's approval. There was nothing she could do."

Gallucci says that Spokanians' feelings toward Adele (Delie) Kelley were as divided as those toward her daughter. Gallucci's mother found her a good and loyal friend. But she often had to defend her to those who didn't like her. "Delie could really get after you," Gallucci says. "[She] had the reputation of being vicious, so she [Kitty] learned from a master."

Adele Kelley died 10 years ago at age 60, following a short, undisclosed illness. She was a heavy smoker, frail and tiny, barely five feet and a Size 3. Before she married in 1940, Delie Martin, a clothing merchant's daughter, was a lively sorority girl—a Pi Beta Phi—at the University of Washington, class of '39.

Her husband was 14 years her senior, from an old Spokane family that could trace its northwest roots back to 1872, when John F. Kelley homesteaded 50 miles south of town in Whitman County. The family still owns wheat and barley ranches there. Kitty's father, William, was one of three sons. According to John Kelley, Kitty's uncle, the three brothers "all went to the same grade school, were Eagle Scouts, all went to Cornell, all members of Beta Theta Pi." All became lawyers. It was not a family for surprises.

The consensus is that Delie Martin married up. Her husband decided to build her a grand home near the spot where they picnicked as sweethearts, high on Spokane's South Hill overlooking a pretty vista unfortunately named Hangman Valley. In late 1942, he moved his wife and infant daughter, Katherine, their first child, into the large brick home at E310 High Dr. They raised seven children in the house—six daughters and a son—and William Kelley still lives there, with his second wife, Janet.

But it was built as Delie's house, and while she lived there, she ruled with an iron hand. And a jangling set of keys. "She religiously padlocked the refrigerator," says Gallucci, "so that no one could eat at will. Nothing was accessible to the kids. It would be absolutely disgusting to be heavy. [Delie] was extremely thin. She didn't eat."

Of Delie's daughters, Gallucci says, Kitty was the only one who tended toward plumpness. And it was bright, headstrong Kitty who had the most friction with her mother. Most often, the conflict was over her exceptionally rigid discipline.

All agree that Delie Kelley could make people laugh, just as her oldest can draw gales of merriment from the most moribund dinner seating. But at home, the life of the party was often inaccessible. Visiting children were instructed to be quiet, Mrs. Kelley was resting. Mrs. Kelley rested a lot in the middle of the day.

"I remember the mother being in the study," says Sally O'Brien, who grew up with Kelley. "And being told not to make any noise around there, being told we were not to disturb her."

O'Brien recalls that Kitty was deputized as little mother. "She had a lot of authority over the children and she used it. 'Pick up your things. Have you done your homework?' She was a typical Irish oldest child."

Nonetheless, it was a life of privilege. The Kelleys enjoyed full-time household help, European vacations, country clubs. Theirs was a lively social set—bridge parties, golf, dinners and cocktails at the private Spokane Club. It is Spokane custom to spend summers at one of the many nearby lakes, and the Kelleys did this, at Hayden Lake in western Idaho. But unlike most families crammed into rustic cottages, they maintained two houses, one for the parents and one below for the children. Visitors there remember that offspring were allowed in the upper house by invitation only.

Despite the household tensions, Kitty is remembered as a buoyant child, energetic, outgoing, with plenty of friends. "My memories are of her being absolutely perfect," says Gallucci. "She'd never lose control publicly."

In fact, says Gallucci, the tougher things got, the shinier, the happier the public Kitty. This was especially true in adolescence.

"When Kitty went to high school, she made a lot of friends," says a classmate who knew her from first grade on. "She made a huge effort to win everyone over. She was peppy, smiley. And she was voted the friendliest every year."

Kitty Litter

It was someone's memory of those perfect, glorious high school years that prompted a strange letter from a person signing herself Mrs. J. L. Grimsby. It was postmarked Spokane and arrived shortly after my visit there. Mrs. Grimsby explained her mission:

"OJ Parsons said that you called her to find out information about Kitty Kelley and OJ couldn't remeber [*sic*] too much about her high school record. She asked me to fill you in." (O. J. Parsons, a retired society columnist I interviewed in Spokane, says she knows of no Mrs. Grimsby, can't find one in the phone directory, and that the only person she told of our meeting was her husband. I told only Kelley's father. "Darn it," says Parsons. "Who's using my name in vain?")

Mrs. Grimsby continues: "She was a Lilac Princess which is the highest honor a high school senior can receive . . . Kitty was also a Gonzaga cheerleader. She was . . . Queen of Gonzaga's Senior Prom. She was elected 'Friendliest Girl' for four straight years at Holy Names—the only girl in the history of the school to receive the honor."

All of this is true of the perky girl who collected glossies of her spun-sugar idol, Debbie Reynolds. Holy Names Academy is closed now, but yearbooks and a huge ledger kept by archivist Sister Edwardine Mary show, page after page, that Kitty was perfection. "On paper, it seems to me," says Sister Edwardine, "that this young lady was extremely blessed."

Her grades weren't exceptional but her social life was. She belonged to T'zuma, the best club. As her school's Lilac Princess, Kitty Kelley dressed in a long gown and elbow-length white gloves and rode the Chamber of

Commerce float in Spokane's annual Lilac Festival. Nobody worked harder at being a good girl, a perfect girl, than Kitty Kelley did. She was immaculately groomed, earning her a Gold Stripe insignia to stitch on her forest-green Holy Names jumper. Her saddle shoes shone, her white Peter Pan collars were starched. When she put on the uniform of a Gonzaga Prep cheerleader—the one with the snarling bulldog on the bosom—she shook her crepe-paper pompons for the cutest guy in school.

Kitty Litter

More from the mysterious Mrs. Grimsby letter on Kelley: "Very popular. Went with the handsomest boy at Gonzaga. Perhaps you should call him. Tom Shine. He still lives in Spokane but I8m [*sic*] sure his wife hates Kitty to this day."

"She and I were a very popular couple," says Tom Shine, a Spokane architect who has been married for 20 years and has four daughters. He says he was sweet on Kelley from the time they met in the second grade. Of their high school romance he says, "I probably dated her more than anyone else. We were elected king and queen of the dances, that type of thing."

The teen-queen idyll cracked in Kelley's junior year at Holy Names, when quarrels with her mother resulted in a sentence of a year's boarding at the academy. Anne Driscoll Vigesaa, another Holy Names boarder, describes a late-'50s girl's life in that institution: "We thought it was like prison. We were in little cubicles, like the Army or something. We had to get up at 5 or 6, go off to mass."

Lights out was at 9; there was no dating. Though Kitty was all but cloistered, her mother enjoyed a lively social life. According to Gallucci, there was a nasty shouting match at the Spokane Club between Kitty's parents. If they didn't know it before, the girls at school knew it then: Kitty's petite, sophisticated mother could be a public, nasty drunk. It had to be an agony, but when Kitty spoke of her mother, it was in reverential terms. "She'd brag about her mother," says Gallucci, "this tiny, cute little thing could swing a golf club like any man."

It was the kind of pain-tempered filial piety that surfaces again and again in Kelley's biographies. She has depicted each of her celeb mothers as monstrous—controlling, manipulative, self-absorbed—and alternately feared and adored by their famous children. To wit: Janet Auchincloss made sure that her ex-husband "Black Jack" Bouvier was too drunk to attend their daughter Jacqueline's marriage to John F. Kennedy. Sara Taylor was a stage mother besotted with ambition who allowed Elizabeth's baby teeth to be pulled for her role in "National Velvet" and destroyed her first engagement. Dolly Sinatra was a grasping, foul-mouthed abortionist who browbeat her husband and doted obsessively on her only child. Next on Kelley's agenda is a woman who has already been portrayed in White House tell-alls as manipulative and sharp-tongued, a woman who gave her own children only perfunctory mention in her autobiography, a woman the president of the United States calls "Mommy."

The mommy factor has been widely studied by behaviorists examining the personality traits of adult children of alcoholics. Recent studies suggest that daughters of alcoholic mothers suffer the most devastating effects. Often, they assume classic roles that have come to typify children of alcoholics. One of those roles is that of Family Hero. The hero, the perfect child, does well at school, is a great social and/or academic success. A Lilac Princess. And often, in the case of daughters, she becomes a "junior mom," taking charge of siblings, seeing to it that all appears well. There is a great fear of exposure. No one should *ever* know the family secrets. Marcia Gallucci says this is consistent with what she saw in the friendliest girl at Holy Names Academy:

"I think she was pretty miserable," says Gallucci. "She worked *real* hard at everything."

About his daughter's high school years, William Kelley says, "I always felt she could have gotten better marks than she did. But she had a pretty gay time."

She was allowed to remain at home for her senior year, and it was the gayest, the most triumphant. It was the year she finally made cheerleader, not on looks or athleticism, but on sheer, high-octane P-E-P. In the spring, Shine escorted her to those final senior dances and, in the fall, said goodbye as she headed south to the University of Arizona. And Tom Shine began to understand that the romance was doomed.

It ended, he thinks, because Kitty wanted out of Spokane and out of the quiet, middle-class life a grocer's son would have to offer. "She was privileged, and I was not," he says. "She went away to college, and I went to work. I felt [Kitty] was fairly ambitious and really set on achieving some recognition. She certainly always *wanted* recognition. To prove herself."

On her way, there was a stumble, and some mystery. Kelley withdrew from the University of Arizona in May 1962, with no major declared and no intention to transfer indicated. The ensuing eight months Marcia Gallucci describes as "a gap." She says that she and other friends of

Kitty's did not know for sure where Kelley was or what she was doing until she entered the University of Washington in Seattle in January of '63.

Kitty in Progressland

"As for life in Washington, D.C., Kitty finds it more like that in a small city than in New York for example."

—*Spokane Chronicle,* 1967

In March of 1964, Kelley received her BA in English from the University of Washington, and her teaching certificate. For a few months, she tried to use it in Seattle. "That didn't last very long," she has said, "because I was teaching in what they call a culturally deprived area, a ghetto. I decided I wasn't ready for that yet." Soon after, she headed east. Destination: Progressland.

Kitty Litter

"All Are VIPS To VIP Hostess." So reads a September 1965 headline in the *Spokane Chronicle,* on a photocopied clipping that arrived in an envelope postmarked Spokane. The typeface of the address looked similar to that of the letter sent by the elusive, effusive Mrs. Grimsby. Again, the news is laudatory: "Kitty Kelley as VIP hostess at the General Electric Progressland at the New York World's Fair greets many a celebrity. . . . It is a role in which Kitty must be well versed in the background of the individual she is entertaining."

The article goes on about Miss Kelley's touching kindness to a crippled child visiting the fair. In a perky cap and uniform, the 23-year-old Miss Kelley led visitors like Julie Andrews and Margaret Truman on private tours of the GE Pavilion and a show narrated by its spokesman, Ronald Reagan. It was her first opportunity to feel, up close and personal, the kind of celebrity heat that would fuel her career. Later, Kelley would remember that she thought one of her VIPs, Jacqueline Kennedy, seemed so human. She got out of the car with a run in her stocking!

When the fair closed, Kelley moved to Washington, where she got a temporary job in the office of Senator Eugene McCarthy; she ended up staying almost four years. It has been alleged by one of her publishers and in print that Kelley overstated that job on subsequent résumés, calling herself McCarthy's press secretary. The book jacket for *Jackie Oh!* was corrected once the error was discovered. But talk to the senator himself, and it appears to have just been part of the social confusion that was the '60s. What did Kelley do for him?

"She was affable and friendly," says McCarthy "A good receptionist."

He thinks she may have distributed press releases, photocopied them, that sort of thing. But he has no problem with whatever she called herself. He remembers an aide asking what titles he should give office staffers. "I said let them call themselves anything they want to. I think I had only one woman who called herself a secretary."

But press secretary?

"I don't think that was in order." He hesitates. "If Kitty called herself press *person*, it would have been quite all right."

Her years on the Hill were lean ones, and Kelley was still financially strapped when, after the '68 election, she found a job as a researcher on *The Washington Post* editorial page in early 1969. Donna Mackie was a secretary in the newsroom when they became friendly.

"Everybody knew her on the paper in those days," says Mackie. "She's easily one of the most outgoing, sparkly, friendly, energetic persons in the world. It's almost theatrical. I'm reminded of Shirley Temple's mama, who would always caution Shirley to sparkle before she went on camera. And Kitty has always sparkled."

She was "not cut out for support work," says Mackie, and wanted to become more than a researcher. Asked about his daughter's writing career, William Kelley offers what he believes to be the truth: "She was really an investigative reporter for *The Washington Post*." He says he wishes she'd stuck with it.

In fact, in 1971, after two years as a research assistant on the editorial page of the *Post*, Kelley was called to task for taking excessive notes unrelated to her duties during editorial meetings. She was asked to tender her resignation by Phil Geyelin, then editorial page editor. In recent interviews she has said that she left to pursue a career in freelance writing.

Kitty Litter

The most puzzling communique yet arrived unsigned, typed on crumpled paper, with a D.C. postmark. It offered negative information about Kelley. Why a nasty missive following two laudatory ones? I had been warned by other recipients that the mysterious Kelley correspondents occasionally offered false and sinister information. And as I suspected, the information in the note proved untrue. But checking the matter took valuable time.

Curiouser still: The typing on this note looked remarkably similar to that on envelopes mailed from the correspondents in Spokane. And the notes had begun to fall into a pattern, paralleling my research and my travels rather closely. Clearly someone was watching, anticipating. Could the same person be operating on both coasts?

The notes were sent for analysis to Dr. David A. Crown, a forensics expert who was chief of the CIA Questioned Documents laboratory for 15 years. A renowned expert witness, Crown was called in to identify the handwriting of Nazi war criminal Josef Mengele and examine documents relating to the World War II activities of Kurt Waldheim. Often, he is consulted for his particular expertise in handwriting and handwriting analysis.

His first report (there would be more) confirmed that the same arthritic Underwood used by Mrs. Grimsby—who had mailed her note from Spokane—also typed the crumpled note mailed in D.C. And it had typed the envelope with the World's Fair news clipping sent from Spokane.

On which coast toils the energetic memoist? Does he/she have an accomplice? Who would go to the trouble of typing a note on one coast—and mailing it from another?

Crown advised perseverance. In his experience, he said, even anonymous letter writers fall into the unconscious habits we all have—styles of writing, a way of addressing an envelope. Small things undo them, in the service of greater schemes.

The Junior Leaguer

"Kitty has several things in common with Brenda Starr, including a knack for getting herself mixed up in intriguing plots and controversial situations."

—Junior League Newsletter, 1973

Donna Mackie remembers one goal her friend Kitty spoke of over and over: She wanted a house in Georgetown. Ten years before she realized that ambition, Kelley spent a good deal of time there as an active member of the Junior League.

For a bright ambitious woman aspiring to a Georgetown address, it was a nice way to network. Miss Kelley was a transfer from Spokane in 1967;

within a year she was on the newsletter committee writing copy that appeared between ads for fur storage and Kasper tennis dresses. She wrote about community service, Liz Carpenter, Jill Ruckelshaus and J. Carter Brown, "the sartorially slim [*sic*] director" of the National Gallery. In those early efforts Kelley's celebrity reporting was gentle indeed. Of Mrs. William McCormick (Deeda) Blair she gushed, "What a challenge! To emulate Deeda Blair one would have to be born gorgeous, have rich chestnut brown hair always exquisitely coiffed, be a perfect model's size 8 . . ."

Kitty Litter

"Kelly [*sic*] quit the Junior League of Washington because they didn't have any black or Jewish members." This typed explanation was offered—anonymously—stuffed in an envelope from *Fortune* magazine and postmarked Washington, D.C. It arrived several days after my visit to the Georgetown headquarters of the Junior League. The informant gave no date for when Kelley quit. She resigned in 1981, 14 years after joining the Georgetown chapter.

This letter was clearly typed on a different machine from the one that typed the Mrs. Grimsby-of-Spokane series. It was time for another consultation with forensics expert Crown. Time, too, to play a hunch. The anonymous correspondence called Kitty Litter was provided for examination along with four original samples of Kitty Kelley's business correspondence written to various people from 1979 to 1983. Some of them were typed on stationery bearing "Kitty Kelley" in embossed lettering. All bore her signature and return address.

Crown's conclusion: Three of the anonymous samples—including the letter referring to the Junior League—were typed on the same machine, one with Smith-Corona-style-typeface. The same machine, characterized by telltale broken serifs and other identifying details, typed the four samples of the correspondence of Kitty Kelley, investigative journalist. When asked whether Kelley owns such a typewriter, her attorney said that he checked with her office and was told that no such machine is owned.

Kitty's First Scoop

"When I was working at 'Entertainment Tonight,' somebody said to me, 'Do you want to do a piece on Kitty Kelley?' And I said, 'Not unless it's her obituary.'"

—Barbara Howar

Times were lean after Kelley left the *Post*. As she wrote of herself, "I'm a writer who barely pays the rent by grinding out articles like 'How To Lose Weight and Seduce a Senator.'"

Then the affair of the Howar Papers got people talking about "reporter Kitty Kelley." It percolated in this town's gossip columns in January of 1973. Folks tittered over their morning danish. But 15 years later, Howar still takes the incident very seriously. She says it cost her $16,000 in legal fees—"more money than I had"—when Kitty Kelley tried to bootleg Howar's life story. Here is what happened, according to Howar:

The living room of Howar's 31st Street Georgetown house was crowded for a well-publicized garage sale. Howar was moving, selling furniture, odds and ends. She noticed a young blonde on a couch and asked who that woman was.

"That's Kitty Kelley," someone told her. Within days, the name came up again when Howar got a call informing her that *Washingtonian* magazine had obtained the rough manuscript of her soon-to-be-published memoir, *Laughing All the Way*. That woman—Kitty Kelley—said she had bought it at the sale. Kelley's version, according to editor Jack Limpert, was that she'd found the papers in the drawer of a small Sheraton table being bought by an elderly woman, and purchased them from her for $2. The magazine intended to publish excerpts.

"*The Washingtonian* was a very small magazine back then, with very little going for it," says Limpert. "We were just trying to have some fun and get some attention. We were surprised that Barbara took it as seriously as she did."

Howar says she was bewildered. And horrified. "I was writing about my children, my husband, my life, the president—and it was in its rawest form."

She says that it was the only copy she had at home and that she had been working on the manuscript exclusively on the third floor, which was off limits during the sale. Howar says she never took the manuscript out of her study upstairs. "That I would bring it down to the basement and put it in the drawer of a table I was selling is highly unlikely." She said as much publicly. "And [Kelley] had lawyers threaten to sue me for libel."

It would be the beginning of a long string of legal skirmishes for Kitty Kelley. Though Howar says now that she probably overreacted, not realizing the strength of her position as author and owner, she spent more on legal fees than she was being paid for an excerpt of the book in *Ladies Home Journal*. All to prevent another magazine from publishing a bootleg version first.

After consulting with its lawyers, *Washingtonian* did not publish the material, but Limpert still damned it in print, saying, "It reads like a reject from *True Confessions.*" The manuscript was also provided to *Washington Post* columnist Maxine Cheshire, whom Kelley had been friendly with when she worked at the paper. It was quoted in Cheshire's column, and in effect reviewed—unkindly—months before publication.

Thus Kitty Kelley's first scoop was, for Howar, a humiliating and expensive one. Kelley stuck to her story about the elderly woman who sold her the goods, and she laughed at the fuss. "For all the furor over the matter," she said, "you'd think I purchased a copy of Dr. Teller's atomic bomb secrets."

"The real crux of explaining Kitty Kelley," says Howar, "is that she believed she owned my manuscript. That she felt she was *entitled* to it, to print excerpts to skim my book buyers, or embarrass me. If she had paid $10 million, *it wasn't hers.*"

Just whose life was it, anyway? And what was fair game?

"She has no honor whatsoever," says Howar, who then wonders aloud if Kelley might send lawyers after her again. "Darlin', I have gotten down with that dog and come up with fleas once before."

As a freelancer, Kitty Kelley was on her way. She followed the Howar flap with a feature for *The Washington Star-News* on fighting flab alongside rich matrons at the Golden Door spa. She wrote it in first-person: ". . . a moose size masseuse takes me in hand. Appraising my short, squatty body, she says, 'Well, this is bad, but I've seen worse.'"

In 1974, Kelley repeatedly, persistently sought an interview with the young, recently widowed senator from Delaware, Joe Biden. He hadn't talked to the press in the year and a half since the highway deaths of his wife and infant daughter before Christmas of '72. His staffers felt it was time, and he granted the interview.

Her story ran in *Washingtonian*, and afterward, Joe Biden would not sit for another profile for nearly 10 years. It ran with the headline "Death and the All-American Boy," and a boldface quote above his photo: "I have no illusions about why I am such a hot commodity. I am the youngest man in the Senate and I am also the victim of a tragic fate."

It caught the 31-year-old senator with his media savvy down, talking about his dating situation and his sex life with his wife. People do *talk* to Kitty Kelley, recalling her as engaging, friendly and very down to earth. What they often forget is that the other Kitty—*that woman*—will print anything they say, sometimes with her own shading. To wit: "Biden tells him [Senator Thomas Eagleton] a joke with an anti-Semitic punch line and asks that it be off the record."

There were immediate objections from Eagleton and Biden's administrative aide, Wes Barthelmes, and in a subsequent issue of *Washingtonian*, Kelley apologized for misinterpreting Biden's remark. Biden told the anecdote to illustrate—with dismay—anti-Semitism he'd encountered in a certain Delaware county.

Kelley also apologized for reporting that a photograph of a monument on Biden's wall was of his wife's tombstone. It was not.

It was the only time, says Janet Donovan, a Kelley friend since they worked together at the World's Fair, that she felt compelled to comment on her friend's work. "I called Kitty and told her it was just an awful thing to do," says Donovan. "I couldn't imagine anybody turning something so awesomely painful to their own advantage. It must have caused him enormous pain."

Scoop No. 2 did cause great distress to Biden's family, friends and staff. It earned Kitty Kelley about $500. And, says *Washingtonian* editor Limpert, "it really got people talking."

Fat City

"My agent says the only things that sell are sex, fat and violence."

—Kitty Kelley

Thus did she explain the genesis of her first book project. Agent David Obst talked her into expanding her fat farm article into *The Glamour Spas,* billed on its cover as "the spicy inside story of the fabulous fat farms where Liza Minnelli, Barbra Streisand, Joan Kennedy . . . reduce and relax."

It is a far cry from Kelley's meticulously documented Sinatra opus: Unattributed quotes outnumber identified sources by an average of 4 to 1—20 to 1 in some chapters. She explained her methodology to her home-town paper, which reported: "In order to obtain her story, Miss Kelley said she promised anonymity to spa employees and others who did the 'tattling.' However, she added, 'People in the public eye have no anonymity, of course.'"

Fair game.

Kelley described spa treatments and regimes, but much of the text concentrated on unattributed hearsay about the spas' celebrity clientele.

On Luci and Lynda Bird Johnson at the Greenhouse spa: "They arrived wearing size 13 dresses that bulged at the seams. Their hair hung in clumps, and their plastic glasses made them look like chubby cheeked owls. 'They were so bad,' says one of the employees, 'they should have been arrested.'"

On the men's spa at La Costa: "Gossip . . . runs to tattletale anecdotes about Burt Lancaster's face-lifting scars, the girdle Henry Fonda occasionally wears to camouflage his pot belly. . . ."

The book does contain excerpts from an interview with Michel Corrado, chef at the Golden Door. Handsome Michel is not shy about the physical gratuities bestowed on him by grateful clients. Michel uses many four-letter words to describe his "tips."

During her research, Kitty Kelley returned home to Spokane and played a tape of the Corrado interview for a group of women that included her mother and the mother of Marcia Gallucci. "It was really rude, real graphic sex stuff," says Gallucci. "My mother's eyes were rolling back in her head."

The girl who had been banished to a spartan cubicle at Holy Names laughed and laughed.

Lyle's Way

Larry King: "Since you are now a public figure would you like a book done on your private life?"

Kitty Kelley: "Yes, I would, if a Kitty Kelley did it."

Kitty Kelley got her start as a celebrity biographer under the tutelage of a wily independent publisher named Lyle Stuart, who quarters his company in the odiferous swamps of Secaucus, N.J. A former business manager for *Mad* magazine, Stuart had scored big with *The Sensuous Woman,* by "J." He published celebrity bios, movie books, diet books. The industry press is given to calling Stuart a renegade publisher. "I do *anything,*" he says.

It was more than 10 years ago that Stuart coaxed Kelley into beginning *Jackie Oh!,* and this spring, he hopes to publish another Jackie book, along with *Bimbo: The Kitty Kelley Story.* He thinks the symmetry is sweet.

He sits behind his desk in a Great Wall of China T-shirt stretched over a stomach not even the bookshelf stack of Pritikin diet foods can keep in check. A geriatric poodle snuffles underfoot. Lyle Stuart is a gambling man, a Vegas high roller. And he says he just had a hunch Kitty Kelley was the right one to go after the president's widow. Forty-three Jackie books had already been done when he proposed the idea to her.

"She said, 'Oh, no, I don't even know her.'"

Stuart laughs at the nascent biographer's naiveté. His voice slides into the ersatz southern accent that often colors Kelley's speech: "Why, Laaaahle, nobody's going to talk to me."

He said he'd teach her how to get them to say things. "I said, 'Look, you go to these people and say there's been so much garbage being written about Mrs. Onassis. We'd like to get the real, true story.'" He pauses, adopts a casket salesman's most sincere tone. "'She *deserves* better than what she's had.'"

Kelley was still reluctant.

"Cinderella sells," he told her. "Cinderella *sells*."

Stuart gave Kelley a $3,000 advance and cut a deal with Onassis' famous tormentor, *paparazzo* Ron Galella, for the photos.

Kelley worked very hard. Her friends remember her as determined, but quite nervous. Would anyone close to Jackie talk? Would she stop her friends from talking? Would she sue? It is a pattern of anxieties that has persisted through subsequent books, says Donna Mackie: "There's always great angst and concern. But I think that's just the way she works. Kitty is not a calm person. Maybe a little hyper."

Kelley has said she was despairing, until Liz Smith offered her files containing five years of research. "I'd been going to write a book [on Onassis] and then I'd given up," Smith says.

Kelley has acknowledged a debt to Smith: "When I saw the bulging cardboard boxes sitting in her apartment, I knew I could do it."

The Kelley Methodology—a relentless accumulation of original, old and borrowed information—took shape. She canvassed friends, servants, friends of friends. Hunting up fresh material she followed the slimmest lead. "She seemed particularly obsessed," remembers a Washington friend, "with finding out about these medical things. That's all she talked about. She especially wanted to find the guy we called the zaperooney."

Getting the tip was a fluke. An old friend of Kelley's, a physician who was in D.C. for a convention, had let it slip that his cousin was married to an anesthesiologist who worked with "zaperooneys"—doctors who administered shock treatments. His cousin had said her husband anesthetized Jackie Kennedy for electroshock therapy when she was being treated for depression in a Massachusetts clinic. Kelley hired a private detective to go with her to Massachusetts and brace the man in his home. Don Uffinger, a strapping former D.C. cop, confirms that he did accompany Kelley on the mission. He has worked for her on other matters he declines to discuss.

In an article describing their odyssey, Kelley wrote about how Uffinger coached his nervous client. He bought a packet of rubber bands and insisted she bind up her curly bleached hair in a bun, call herself Katherine, quit chain-smoking and let him do the talking if it got dicey. Finding only the doctor's wife at home, they informed her that they knew she had leaked the information to her cousin. They told her they would go to her husband to ascertain the facts. "The interview turned into an interrogation," Kelley wrote.

Terrified of her husband's reaction, the woman confirmed that the treatments had been administered at a private clinic called Valleyhead—then ordered them out of her home. Kelley had her zaperooney.

Lyle Stuart was impressed. And he felt Kelley had truly mastered his lessons when she ensnared former senator George Smathers of Florida, a longtime Kennedy friend.

"Oh, she got me good," Smathers says from his Florida law office. He says she came in to his Washington office saying exactly what Lyle Stuart had taught her, that it was to be a laudatory book.

Smathers was quoted on Jack Kennedy's healthy libido, as well as their adventures when the two maintained a Potomac love nest before JFK was married. He described the president's perfunctory sexual technique with an allusion to barnyard animals. Kelley has recalled that she "giggled at every outrageous anecdote." But Smathers is still not amused.

"She was charming, I guess," he says. "Squatty little thing but okay in the face. In those days they didn't tape. She was writing very vigorously." But what she did get him to admit, he says, was skillfully extracted. He was ensnared by solid, true information that Kelley had collected researching *The Glamour Spas*. It was unusable dross at the time, but for *Jackie Oh!* it was pure gold.

"It seems she'd been my ex-wife's roommate at a fat farm," says Smathers. "Oh, I can see those two yakking until the wee hours. She walked in here and said, 'I know all about when you and Jack went to Vendôme in 1956.'"

When the book came out, Kennedy stalwarts castigated Smathers. Some shunned him. "Kitty Kelley has made my life miserable for the last 10 years," he says.

All of this put Lyle Stuart in six-figure raptures. His hardcover did gangbusters, and in paperback, *Jackie Oh!* became Ballantine's biggest book of the year. Stuart remembers checking his author into the Plaza Hotel in Manhattan for a "Today" show appearance.

"She walked up the steps [of the Plaza], she suddenly turned to me, and she was crying. She said, 'Would you believe this is the first night I've ever stayed in a first-class hotel in my life?'"

For three glorious months, the Lilac Princess was queen of the best-seller nonfiction list. And she had done it against all the odds, burying the nearly four dozen books that had already been done. During the arduous research, right through her post-publication interviews, Kelley had endured serious medical problems. She announced in *Women's Wear Daily* that she was having a hysterectomy the following week, a fact that deeply saddened Kelley and her husband. (She married Michael Edgley, a media director, in August 1976).

There would be no children, no large family like her own. But she had a bona fide best seller and a shower of royalty checks that more than made up for Stuart's stingy advance. Around town, Kelley and Edgley were seen wearing matching sweat shirts with hot pink *Jackie Oh!* logos. They began to look at choice real estate. In Georgetown.

Within months of her triumph, Kelley was at war with Stuart. There was a lawsuit by a *Jackie Oh!* source. Worse, there was a nettlesome option clause on her next project that Stuart would not release her from. She wanted to do her next book about Elizabeth Taylor; Stuart didn't want that book, but he wanted Kitty Kelley.

"I said, 'The next book you do is going to bring a fortune. You could put *garbage* between two covers and get a lot of money from a paperback house.'"

Kelley was equally hardheaded. It had to be Liz. Three times she tried her Taylor proposal on Stuart, and each time he refused. Finally, Kelley submitted what is known as an "option buster" manuscript, a novel called *Reunion*. It was, says Stuart, "dreadful." Stuart believed it was written by Kelley's husband, an unpublished novelist. When he rejected the novel, Kelley sold it to Simon and Schuster, the company that also intended to pay a $150,000 advance for her Liz Taylor book. The sale of the novel proved it publishable, thereby "busting" Stuart's option. However, when Simon and Schuster actually began editing the novel for publication, Kelley abruptly bought it back, returning her $25,000 advance. At the time, she stated that she did not wish it published under her name.

In a court deposition, Kelley was asked repeatedly if her husband wrote

Short-Form Biography

any part of *Reunion*. The first time, she answered, "No," then, "It's hard to answer that, because most everything I write my husband goes over and edits." A third time, she responded, "Possibly."

Arbitration settled the option matter between Stuart and Kelley, and after much legal and personal unpleasantness, he released her from her contract.

And now, *Bimbo*. Is this the protégé throttled by her jealous Svengali? Hoist by her own pushy pants petard? "We're not doing this for malice," insists Stuart. "We're just doing this for fun." *Bimbo*'s author is a staff writer for the supermarket tabloid, *The Star*. George Carpozi Jr. has written, at last count, 71 books. Since Stuart announced the book plans, Carpozi says, he has been getting mysterious letters and harassing phone calls. He finds the interest "encouraging." He says he wanted to call his book *Down and Dirty with Kitty Kelley*, but Stuart insisted on *Bimbo*.

Isn't he worried about a lawsuit?

"I haven't heard from her lawyers yet," says Stuart. "I'd love to. I thrive on that."

Lawsuits sold books when he published the memoirs of porn star Linda Lovelace. Thus he is not afraid of lawsuits. He thinks Kelley's reputation as a "scalp-hunting biographer" can only work against her.

"Here's a woman who has attacked *everyone*. I can't see any jury coming in and giving her a penny. I'm not concerned at all." He grins, and rubs his ample stomach.

"She's made herself a public figure."

Fair game?

"You bet."

The profile by Calvin Trillin, titled "Covering the Cops," appeared in the February 17, 1986, issue of *The New Yorker* magazine. It is copyright © 1986 by Calvin Trillin and reprinted here with permission.

In the newsroom of the *Miami Herald*, there is some disagreement about which of Edna Buchanan's first paragraphs stands as the classic Edna lead. I line up with the fried-chicken faction. The fried-chicken story was about a rowdy ex-con named Gary Robinson, who late one

Sunday night lurched drunkenly into a Church's outlet, shoved his way to the front of the line, and ordered a three-piece box of fried chicken. Persuaded to wait his turn, he reached the counter again five or ten minutes later, only to be told that Church's had run out of fried chicken. The young woman at the counter suggested that he might like chicken nuggets instead. Robinson responded to the suggestion by slugging her in the head. That set off a chain of events that ended with Robinson's being shot dead by a security guard. Edna Buchanan covered the murder for the *Herald*—there are policemen in Miami who say that it wouldn't be a murder without her—and her story began with what the fried-chicken faction still regards as the classic Edna lead: "Gary Robinson died hungry."

All connoisseurs would agree, I think, that the classic Edna lead would have to include one staple of crime reporting—the simple, matter-of-fact statement that registers with a jolt. The question is where the jolt should be. There's a lot to be said for starting right out with it. I'm rather partial to the Edna lead on a story last year about a woman about to go on trial for a murder conspiracy: "Bad things happen to the husbands of Widow Elkin." On the other hand, I can understand the preference that others have for the device of beginning a crime story with a more or less conventional sentence or two, then snapping the reader back in his chair with an abbreviated sentence that is used like a blunt instrument. One student of the form at the *Herald* refers to that device as the Miller Chop. The reference is to Gene Miller, now a *Herald* editor, who, in a remarkable reporting career that concentrated on the felonious, won the Pulitzer Prize twice for stories that resulted in the release of people in prison for murder. Miller likes short sentences in general—it is sometimes said at the *Herald* that he writes as if he were paid by the period—and he particularly likes to use a short sentence after a couple of rather long ones. Some years ago, Gene Miller and Edna Buchanan did a story together on the murder of a high-living Miami lawyer who was shot to death on a day he had planned to wile away on the golf course of La Gorce Country Club, and the lead said, ". . . he had his golf clubs in the trunk of his Cadillac. Wednesday looked like an easy day. He figured he might pick up a game later with Eddie Arcaro, the jockey. He didn't."

These days, Miller sometimes edits the longer pieces that Edna Buchanan does for the *Herald,* and she often uses the Miller Chop—as in a piece about a lovers' spat: "The man she loved slapped her face. Furious, she says she told him never, ever do that again. 'What are you going to do, kill me?' he asked, and handed her a gun. 'Here, kill me,' he challenged. She did."

Now that I think of it, that may be the classic Edna lead.

There is no dispute about the classic Edna telephone call to a homicide detective or a desk sergeant she knows: "Hi. This is Edna. What's going on over there?" There are those at the *Herald* who like to think that Edna Buchanan knows every policeman and policewoman in the area—even though Dade County has twenty-seven separate police forces, with a total strength of more than forty-five hundred officers. "I asked her if by any chance she happened to know this sergeant," a *Herald* reporter once told me. "And she looked at her watch and said, 'Yeah, but he got off his shift twenty minutes ago.'" She does not in fact know all the police officers in the area, but they know her. If the desk sergeant who picks up the phone is someone Edna has never heard of, she gives her full name and the name of her paper. But even if she said, "This is Edna," there aren't many cops who would say, "Edna who?" In Miami, a few figures are regularly discussed by first name among people they have never actually met. One of them is Fidel. Another is Edna.

It's an old-fashioned name. Whoever picks up the phone at homicide when Edna Buchanan calls probably doesn't know any Ednas he might confuse her with. Edna is, as it happens, a rather old-fashioned person. "She should have been working in the twenties or thirties," a detective who has known her for years told me. "She'd have been happy if she had a little press card in her hat." She sometimes says the same sort of thing about herself. She laments the replacement of typewriters at the *Herald* with word processors. She would like to think of her clips stored in a place called a morgue rather than a place called an editorial reference library. She's nostalgic about old-fashioned criminals. As a girl growing up around Paterson, New Jersey, she used to read the New York tabloids out loud to her grandmother—a Polish grandmother, who didn't read English—and she still likes to roll out the names of the memorable felons in those stories: names like George Metesky, the Mad Bomber, and Willie Sutton, the man who robbed banks because that's where the money was. She even has a period look about her—something that recalls the period around 1961. She is a very thin woman in her forties who tends to dress in slacks and silk shirts and high heels. She wears her hair in a heavy blond shoulder-length fall. Her eyes are wide, and her brow is often furrowed in concern. She seems almost permanently anxious about one thing or another. Did she neglect to try the one final approach that would have persuaded the suspect's mother to open the door and have a chat? Will a stray cat that she spotted in the neighborhood meet an unpleasant end? Did she forget to put a quarter in the meter? Despite many years spent among people who often find themselves resorting to rough language—hookers, cocaine cowboys, policemen, newspaper reporters—her own conversation tends to sound like that of a rather demure secretary circa 1952. Her own cats—she has five of them—have names like Misty Blue Eyes and Baby Dear. When she is particularly impressed by a bit of news, she is likely to describe it as "real neat." When she discovers, say, a gruesome turn in a tale that might be pretty gruesome already, she may say, "That's interesting as heck!"

Among newspaper people, Edna's line of work is considered a bit old-fashioned. Daily police reporting—what is sometimes known in the trade as covering the cops—is still associated with that old-timer who had a desk in the station house and didn't have to be told by the sergeant in charge which part of the evening's activities to leave out of the story and thought of himself as more or less a member of the department. Covering the cops is often something a reporter does early in his career—an assignment that can provide him with enough war stories in six months to last him through years on the business page or the city desk. Even Gene Miller, a man with a fondness for illegalities of all kinds, turned rather quickly from covering the cops to doing longer pieces. The *Herald*, which regularly shows up on lists of the country's most distinguished dailies, does take a certain amount of pride in providing the sort of crime coverage that is not typical of newspapers on such lists, but it does not have the sort of single-minded interest in juicy felonies that characterized the New York tabloids Edna used to read to her grandmother. When Edna Buchanan began covering the cops for the *Herald*, in 1973, there hadn't been anyone assigned full time to the beat in several years.

In the dozen years since, Edna has herself broken the routine now and then to do a long crime piece or a series. But she invariably returns to the daily beat. She still dresses every morning to the sound of a police scanner. Unless she already has a story to do, she still drops by the Miami Beach department and the Miami municipal department and the Metro-Dade department on the way to work. She still flips through the previous night's crime reports and the log. She still calls police officers and says, "Hi. This is Edna. What's going on over there?"

Short-Form Biography

Like a lot of old-fashioned reporters, Edna Buchanan seems to operate on the assumption that there are always going to be any number of people who, for perverse and inexplicable reasons of their own, will try to impede her in gathering a story that is rightfully hers and delivering it to where God meant it to be—on the front page of the *Miami Herald,* and preferably the front page of the *Miami Herald* on a Sunday, when the circulation is at its highest. There are shy witnesses who insist that they don't want to get involved. There are lawyers who advise their clients to hang up if Edna Buchanan calls to ask whether they really did it. (It could be libelous for a newspaper to call someone a suspect, but the paper can get the same idea across by quoting his denial of guilt.) There are close-mouthed policemen. There are television reporters who require equipment that gets in the way and who ask the sort of question that makes Edna impatient. (In her view, television reporters on a murder story are concerned almost exclusively with whether they're going to be able to get a picture of the authorities removing the body from the premises, the only other question that truly engages them being whether they're going to get the picture in time for the six o'clock news.) There are editors who want to cut a story even though it was virtually ordained to run at least sixteen inches. There are editors—often the same editors—who will try to take an interesting detail out of the story simply because the detail happens to horrify or appall them. "One of them kept saying that people read this paper at *breakfast,*" I was told by Edna, whose own idea of a successful lead is one that might cause a reader who is having breakfast with his wife to "spit out his coffee, clutch his chest, and say, 'My God, Martha! Did you read this!'" When Edna went to Fort Lauderdale not long ago to talk about police reporting with some of the young reporters in the *Herald's* Broward County bureau, she said, "For sanity and survival, there are three cardinal rules in the newsroom: Never trust an editor, never trust an editor, and never trust an editor."

Edna likes and admires a lot of policemen, but, listening to her talk about policemen, you can get the impression that they spend most of their energy trying to deny her access to information that she is meant to have. Police officers insist on roping off crime scenes. ("The police department has too much yellow rope—they want to rope off the world.") Entire departments switch over to computerized crime reports, which don't accommodate the sort of detailed narrative that Edna used to comb through in the old written reports. Investigators sometimes decline to talk about the case they're working on. (Edna distinguishes degrees of

reticence among policemen with remarks like "He wasn't *quite* as paranoid as the other guy.") Some years ago, the man who was then chief of
the Metro-Dade department blocked off the homicide squad with a buzzer-
controlled entrance whose function was so apparent that it was com-
monly referred to as "the Edna Buchanan door." Homicide investigators
who arrive at a scene and spot Edna talking intently with someone assume that she has found an eyewitness, and they often snatch him away
with cautioning words about the errors of talking to the press rather than
to the legally constituted authorities. Edna discusses the prevalence of
witnessnapping among police detectives in the tone of voice a member of
Citizens Commission on Crime might reserve for talking about an alarming increase in multiple murders.

Once the police arrive at a crime scene in force, Edna often finds it
more effective to return to the *Herald* and work by telephone. The alternative could be simply standing behind the yellow rope—an activity she
considers fit for television reporters. She may try calling the snatched
witness. With a cross-indexed directory, she can phone neighbors who
might have seen what happened and then ducked back into their own
house for a bolstering drink. She will try to phone the victim's next of
kin. "I thought you'd like to say something," she'll say to someone's be-
reaved wife or daughter. "People care what he was like." Most reporters
would sooner cover thirty weeks of water-board hearings than call a murder victim's next of kin, but Edna tries to look on the positive side. "For
some people, it's like a catharsis," she told me one day. "They want to talk
about what kind of person their husband was, or their father. Also, it's
probably the only time his name is going to be in the paper. It's their last
shot. They want to give him a good sendoff."

There are people, of course, who are willing to forgo the sendoff just to
be left alone. Some of them respond to Edna's call by shouting at her for
having the gall to trouble them at such a time, and then slamming down
the telephone. Edna has a standard procedure for dealing with that. She
waits sixty seconds and then phones back. "This is Edna Buchanan at the
Miami Herald," she says, using her full name and identification for civil-
ians. "I think we were cut off." In sixty seconds, she figures, whoever
answered the phone might reconsider. Someone else in the room might
say, "You should have talked to that reporter." Someone else in the room
might decide to spare the upset party the pain of answering the phone
the next time it rings, and might be a person who is more willing to talk. A

couple of years ago, Edna called the home of a TV-repair-shop operator in his sixties who had been killed in a robbery attempt—a crime she had already managed to separate from the run-of-the-mill armed-robbery murder. ("On New Year's Eve Charles Curzio stayed later than planned at his small TV repair shop to make sure customers would have their sets in time to watch the King Orange Jamboree Parade," Edna's lead began. "His kindness cost his life.") One of Curzio's sons answered, and, upon learning who it was, angrily hung up. "Boy, did I hate dialing the second time," Edna told me. "But if I hadn't I might have lost them for good." This time, the phone was answered by another of Curzio's sons, and he was willing to talk. He had some eloquent things to say about his father and about capital punishment. ("My father got no trial, no stay of execution, no Supreme Court hearing, nothing. Just some maniac who smashed his brains in with a rifle butt.") If the second call hadn't been productive, Edna told me, she would have given up: "The third call would be harassment."

When Edna is looking for information, slamming down the phone must sometimes seem the only way of ending the conversation. She is not an easy person to say goodbye to. Once she begins asking questions, she may pause occasionally, as if the interrogation were finally over, but then, in the sort of silence that in conventional conversations is ended with someone's saying "Well, O.K." or "Well, thanks for your help," she asks another question. The questioning may not even concern a story she's working on. I was once present when Edna began chatting with a Metro-Dade homicide detective about an old murder case that he had never managed to solve—the apparently motiveless shooting of a restaurant proprietor and his wife, both along in years, as they were about to enter their house. Edna would ask a question and the detective would shake his head, explaining that he had checked out that angle without result. Then, after a pause long enough to make me think that they were about to go on to another case, she would ask another question. Could it have been a mistake in the address? Did homicide check out the people who lived in the equivalent house on the next block? Did the restaurant have any connection with the mob? How about an ex-employee? What about a bad son-in-law? Over the years, Edna has come across any number of bad sons-in-law.

Earlier in the day, I had heard her use the same tone to question a young policewoman who was watching over the front desk at Miami

Beach headquarters. "What do you think the rest of Bo's secret is?" Edna said as she skimmed log notations about policemen being called to a loud party or to the scene of a robbery or to a vandalized garage. "Is Kimberly going to get an abortion?" At first, I thought the questions were about cases she was reminded of by the log reports. They turned out to be about "Days of Our Lives," a soap opera that both Edna and the police-woman are devoted to. Fifteen minutes later, long after I thought the subject had been dropped, Edna was saying, "So is this new character going to be a friend of Jennifer's—the one in the car wreck?"

Bob Swift, a *Herald* columnist who was once Edna's editor at a paper called the *Miami Beach Sun*, told me that he arrived at the *Sun*'s office one day fuming about the fact that somebody had stolen his garbage cans. "I was really mad," he said. "I was saying, 'Who would want to steal two garbage cans!' All of a sudden, I heard Edna say, in that breathless voice, 'Were they empty or full?' "

"Nobody loves a police reporter," Edna sometimes says in speeches. She has been vilified and shouted at and threatened. Perhaps because a female police reporter was something of a rarity when she began, some policemen took pleasure in showing her, say, the corpse of someone who had met a particularly nasty end. ("Sometimes they try to gross you out, but when you're really curious you don't get grossed out. I'm always saying, 'What's this? What's that?' ") When Edna was asked by David Finkel, who did a story about her for the *St. Petersburg Times*, why she endured the rigors of covering the cops, she replied, "It's better than working in a coat factory in Paterson, New Jersey." Working in the coat factory was one of several part-time jobs that she had as a schoolgirl to help her mother out. Aside from the pleasures Edna associates with read-ing crime stories to her Polish grandmother, she doesn't have many happy memories of Paterson. Her other grandmother—her mother's mother—was a member of the Daughters of the American Revolution; Edna still has the membership certificate to prove it. That grandmother, in the view of her D.A.R. family, married beneath her—her husband was a Paterson schoolteacher—and her own daughter, Edna's mother, did even worse. She married a Polish factory worker who apparently had some local renown as a drinker and carouser, and he walked out when Edna was seven. As soon as Edna finished high school, an institution she loathed, she joined her mother in wiring switchboards at the Western Electric plant. Eventually, she transferred to an office job at Western Electric—

still hardly the career path that normally leads to a reporting job on the *Miami Herald.*

The enormous change in Edna's life came partly because a clothes-horse friend who wanted to take a course in millinery design persuaded her to come along to evening classes at Montclair State Teachers College. Edna, who had been interested in writing as a child, decided to take a course in creative writing. She remembers the instructor as a thin, poetic-looking man who travelled to New Jersey every week from Greenwich Village. He may have had a limp—a war wound, perhaps. She is much clearer about what happened when he handed back the first short stories the students had written. First, he described one he had particularly liked, and it was Edna's—a sort of psychological thriller about a young woman who thought she was being followed. Edna can still recall what the teacher said about the story—about what a rare pleasure it was for a teacher to come across such writing, about how one section reminded him of early Tennessee Williams. It was the one radiant New Jersey moment. The teacher told her about writers she should read. He told her about paragraphing; the first story she turned in was "just one long paragraph." She decided that she could be a writer. Years later, a novelist who had been hanging around with Edna for a while to learn about crime reporting recognized the teacher from Edna's description and provided his telephone number. She phoned him to tell him how much his encouragement had meant to her. He was pleasant enough, Edna told me, but he didn't remember her or her short story.

Not long after the writing course, Edna and her mother decided to take their vacation in Miami Beach, and Edna says that as she walked off the plane she knew she was not going to spend the rest of her life in Paterson, New Jersey. "The instant I breathed the air, it was like coming home," she told me. "I loved it. I absolutely loved it. I had been wandering around in a daze up there, like a displaced person. I was always a misfit." Edna and her mother tried to get jobs at the Western Electric plant in South Florida; when they couldn't arrange that, they moved anyway. While taking a course in writing, Edna heard that the *Miami Beach Sun* was looking for reporters. The *Sun*, which is now defunct, was the sort of newspaper that hired people without any reporting experience and gave them a lot of it quickly. Edna wrote society news and local political stories and crime stories and celebrity interviews and movie reviews and, on occasion, the letters to the editor.

Now, years later, Edna Buchanan may be the best-known newspaper reporter in Miami, but sometimes she still sounds as if she can't quite believe that she doesn't work in a factory and doesn't live in Paterson, New Jersey. "I've lived here more than twenty years," she said recently. "And every day I see the palm trees and the water and the beach, and I'm thrilled with how beautiful it is. I'm really lucky, coming from a place like Paterson, New Jersey. I live on a waterway. I have a house. I almost feel, My God, it's like I'm an impostor!"

When Edna says such things, she sounds grateful—a state that an old newspaper hand would tell you is about as common among reporters as a prolonged, religiously inspired commitment to the temperance movement. Edna can even sound grateful for the opportunity to work the police beat—although in the next sentence she may be talking about how tired she is of hearing policemen gripe or how irritated she gets at editors who live to pulverize her copy. She seems completely lacking in the black humor or irony that reporters often use to cope with even a short hitch covering the cops. When she says something is interesting as heck, she means that it is interesting as heck.

Some years ago, she almost went over to the enemy. A Miami television station offered her a hundred and thirty-seven dollars more a week than she was making at the *Herald,* and she had just about decided to take it. She had some ideas about how crime could be covered on television in a way that did not lean so heavily on pictures of the body being removed from the premises. At the last moment, though, she decided not to accept the offer. One reason, she now says, is that she faced the fact that crime could never be covered on local television with the details and the subtleties possible in a newspaper story. Also, she couldn't quite bring herself to leave the *Herald.* If I had been eighteen, maybe I would have done it, she says. But the *Herald* is the only security I ever had.

Even before the appearance of "Miami Vice," Miami was the setting of choice for tales of flashy violence. Any number of people, some of them current or former *Herald* reporters, have portrayed Miami crime in mystery novels or television shows or Hollywood movies. Some of the show-business types might have been attracted mainly by the palm trees and the beach and the exotica of the Latin drug industry: The opening shots of each "Miami Vice" episode are so glamorous that some local tourist-development people have been quoted in the *Herald* as saying that the overall impact of the series is positive. But the volume and the variety of real crime in Miami have in fact been of an order to make any

Short-Form Biography

police reporter feel the way a stockbroker might feel at a medical conven-tion: Opportunities abound. Like most police reporters, Edna specializes in murder, and, as she might express it in a Miller Chop at the end of the first paragraph, so does Miami.

When Edna began as a reporter, a murder in Miami was an occasion. A woman who worked with Edna at the *Miami Beach Sun* in the days when it was sometimes known as "Bob Swift and his all-girl newspaper" has recalled the stir in the *Sun* newsroom when a body washed up on the beach: "I had a camera, because my husband had given it to me for Christmas. The managing editor said, 'Go take a picture of the body.' I said, 'I'm not taking a picture of a washed-up body!' Then I heard a voice from the other end of the room saying, 'I'll do it, I'll do it.' It was Edna."

In the late seventies, Miami, like other American cities, had a steady increase in the sort of murders that occur when, say, an armed man panics while he is robbing a convenience store. It also had some political bombings and some shooting between outfits that were, depending on your point of view, either running drugs to raise money for fighting Fidel or using the fight against Fidel as a cover for running drugs. At the end of the decade, Dade County's murder rate took an astonishing upturn. Around that time, the Colombians who manufactured the drugs being distributed in Miami by Cubans decided to eliminate the middleman, and, given a peculiar viciousness in the way they customarily operated, that sometimes meant eliminating the middleman's wife and whoever else happened to be around. Within a couple of years after the Colom-bians began their campaign to reduce overhead, Miami was hit with the Mariel-boat-lift refugees. In 1977, there were two hundred and eleven murders in Dade County. By 1981, the high point of Dade murder, there were six hundred and twenty-one. That meant, according to one homi-cide detective I spoke to, that Miami experienced the greatest increase in murders per capita that any city had ever recorded. It also meant that Miami had the highest murder rate in the country. It also meant that a police reporter could drive to work in the morning knowing that there would almost certainly be at least one murder to write about.

"A personal question," one of the Broward-bureau reporters said after Edna had finished her talk in Fort Lauderdale. "I hope not to embarrass you, but I've always heard a rumor that you carried a gun. Is that true?"

"I don't carry a gun," Edna said. "I own a gun or two." She keeps one in the house and one in the car—which seems only sensible, she told the reporters, for someone who lives alone and is often driving through unpleasant neighborhoods late at night. It also seems only sensible to spend some time on the shooting range, which she happens to enjoy. ("They let me shoot an Uzi the other day," she once told me. "It was interesting as heck.") A lot of what Edna says about her life seems only sensible, but a lot of it turns out to have something to do with violence or crime, the stuff of an Edna story. Talking about her paternal grandfather, she'll say that he was supposed to have killed or maimed someone in a barroom brawl and that his children were so frightened of his drunken rages that the first sign of an eruption would send some of them leaping out of second-floor windows to escape. As an example of her nearsightedness, she'll mention some revelations in Paterson that seemed to indicate that she had been followed for months by a notorious sex criminal without realizing it. When Edna talks about places where she has lived in Miami, she is likely to identify neighbors with observations like "He lived right across the street from this big dope dealer" or "He was indicted for Medicare fraud but he beat it."

Edna's first marriage, to someone she met while she was working at the *Miami Beach Sun,* could provide any number of classic Edna leads. James Buchanan had some dealings with the anti-Castro community, and was close to Frank Sturgis, one of the Watergate burglars. Edna says that for some time she thought her husband was simply a reporter on the *Fort Lauderdale Sun-Sentinel* who seemed to be out of town more than absolutely necessary. The story she sometimes tells of how she discovered otherwise could be written with an Edna lead: "James Buchanan seemed to make a lot of unexplained trips. Yesterday, at the supermarket, his wife found out why. Mrs. Buchanan, accompanied by a bag boy who was carrying a large load of groceries, emerged from the supermarket and opened the trunk of her car. It was full of machine guns. 'Just put the groceries in the back seat,' she said."

Edna tried a cop the next time, but that didn't seem to have much effect on the duration or quality of the marriage. Her second husband, Emmett Miller, was on the Miami Beach force for years, and was eventually appointed chief. By that time, though, he had another wife, his fifth—a wife who, it turned out, was part owner of what the *Herald* described as "an X-rated Biscayne Boulevard motel and a Beach restaurant alleged to be a center of illegal gambling." The appointment was approved by the Miami Beach City Commission anyway, although one commissioner, who stated that the police chief ought to be "above suspicion," did say, "I don't think we're putting our city in an enviable position when we overlook this."

Since the breakup of her marriage to Miller, Edna has almost never been seen at parties or *Herald* hangouts. "I love to be alone," she says. One of the people closest to her is still her mother, who lives not far from Edna and seems to produce ceramic animals even faster than she once turned out fully wired switchboards. Edna's house is a menagerie of ceramic animals. She also has ceramic planters and a ceramic umbrella holder and a ceramic lighthouse—not to speak of a watercolor and a sketch by Jack (Murph the Surf) Murphy, the Miami beachboy who in 1964 helped steal the Star of India sapphire and the deLong Star Ruby from the American Museum of Natural History—but ceramic animals are the predominant design element. She has penguins and turtles and horses and seagulls and flamingos and swans and fish and a rabbit and a pelican. She has a ceramic dog that is nearly life-size. She has cats in practically every conceivable pose—a cat with nursing kittens, a cat carrying a kitten in its mouth, a curled-up cat. Edna is fond of some of the ceramic animals, but the fact that her mother's productivity seems to be increasing rather than waning with the passing of the years has given her pause.

All of Edna's live animals are strays. Besides the cats, she has a dog whose best trick is to fall to the floor when Edna points an imaginary gun at him and says, "Bang! You're dead!" Some colleagues at the *Herald* think that a stray animal is about the only thing that can distract Edna from her coverage of the cops. It is assumed at the *Herald* that she takes Mondays and Tuesdays off because the weekend is traditionally a high-crime period. (Edna says that the beaches are less crowded during the week, and that working weekends gives her a better chance at the Sunday paper.) Around the *Herald* newsroom, Edna is known for being fiercely proprietary about stories she considers hers—any number of *Herald* reporters, running into her at the scene of some multiple murder or major disaster, have been greeted with an icy "What are *you* doing here"—and so combative about her copy that a few of the less resilient editors have been reduced almost to the state in which they would fall to the floor if Edna pointed an imaginary gun at them and said, "Bang! You're dead!" Edna's colleagues tend to speak of her not as a pal but as a phenomenon. Their Edna stories are likely to concern her tenacity or her superstitions or the remarkable intensity she maintains after all these years of covering a beat that quickly strikes many reporters as unbearably horrifying or depressing. They often mention the astonishing contrast between her apparent imperviousness to the grisly sights on the police beat and her overwhelming concern for animals. While I was in Miami, two or three *Herald* reporters suggested that I look up some articles in which, as they remembered it, Edna hammered away so intensely at a retired French-Canadian priest who had put to death some stray cats that the poor man was run out of the country. When I later told one of the reporters that I had read the *Herald*'s coverage of the incident and that almost none of it had been done by Edna, he said, "I'm not surprised. Probably didn't trust herself. Too emotionally involved."

Policemen, Edna told the young reporters in Fort Lauderdale, have an instinctive mistrust of outsiders—"an 'us-and-them' attitude." Edna can never be certain which category she's in. Any police reporter these days is likely to have a less comfortable relationship with the police than the one enjoyed by the old-fashioned station-house reporter who could be counted on to be looking the other way if the suspect met with an accident while he was being taken into custody. Since Watergate, reporters all over the country have been under pressure to cast a more suspicious eye on any institution they cover. Partly because of the availability of staggering amounts of drug money, both the Miami and the Metro-Dade departments have had serious scandals in recent years, making them particularly sensitive to inspection by critical outsiders. The *Herald* has covered police misconduct prominently, and it has used Florida's public-records act aggressively in court to gain access to police documents—even documents involved in Internal Affairs investigations. A lot of policemen regard the *Herald* as their adversary and see Edna Buchanan as the embodiment of the *Herald*.

Edna says that she makes every effort to portray cops as human beings—writing about a police officer who has been charged with misconduct, she usually manages to find some past commendations to mention—but it has never occurred to anybody that she might look the other way. Edna broke the story of an attempted coverup involving a black insurance man named Arthur McDuffie, who died as a result of injuries suffered in an encounter with some Metro-Dade policemen—policemen whose acquittal on manslaughter charges some months later touched off three nights of rioting in Miami's black community. There are moments when Edna seems to be "us" and "them" at the same time. Keeping the picture and the press release sent when someone is named Officer of the Month may give Edna one extra positive sentence to write about a policeman the next time she mentions him; also, as it happens, it is difficult to come by a picture of a cop who gets in trouble, and over the years Edna has found that a cop who gets in trouble and a cop who was named Officer of the Month are often the same person.

"There's a love-hate relationship between the police and the press," Mike Gonzalez, one of Edna's best friends on the Miami municipal force, says. A case that Edna covers prominently is likely to get a lot of attention in the department, which means that someone whose name is attached to it might become a hero or might, as one detective I spoke to put it, "end up in the complaint room of the property bureau." Edna says that the way a reporter is received at police headquarters can depend on "what you wrote the day before—or their perception of what you wrote the day before."

Some police officers in Dade County won't talk to Edna Buchanan about the case they're working on. Some of those who do give her tips— not just on their own cases but on cases being handled by other people, or even other departments—won't admit it. (According to Dr. Joseph Davis, the medical examiner of Dade County, "Every police agency thinks she has a direct pipeline into someone else's agency.") Cops who become known as friends and sources of Edna's are likely to be accused by other cops of showboating or of trying to further their careers through the newspaper. When I mentioned Mike Gonzalez to a Metro-Dade lieutenant I was talking to in Miami, he said, "What Howard Cosell did for Cassius Clay, Edna Buchanan did for Mike Gonzalez."

Gonzalez is aware of such talk, and doesn't show much sign of caring about it. He thinks most policemen are nervous about the press because they aren't confident that they can reveal precisely what they find it useful to reveal and no more. Edna's admirers among police investigators—people like Gonzalez and Lloyd Hough, a Metro-Dade homicide detective—tend to admire her for her skill and independence as an investigator. "I'd take her any time as a partner," Hough told me. "Let's put it like this: If I had done something, I wouldn't want Edna investigating me. Internal Affairs I don't care about, but Edna . . ." They also admire her persistence, maddening as it may sometimes be. Hough nearly had her arrested once when she persisted in coming under the yellow rope into a crime scene. "She knows when she's pushed you to the limit, and she'll do that often," Hough told me. "And I say that with the greatest admiration."

Telling the Untold Story

A police detective and a police reporter may sound alike as they stand around talking about past cases—recalling the airline pilot who killed the other airline pilot over the stewardess, or exchanging anecdotes about the aggrieved bag boy who cleared a Publix supermarket in a hurry by holding a revolver to the head of the manager—but their interests in a murder case are not necessarily the same. If an armed robber kills a convenience-store clerk, the police are interested in catching him; Edna is interested in distinguishing what happened from other killings of other convenience-store clerks. To write about any murder, Edna is likely to need details that wouldn't help an investigator close the case. "I want to know what movie they saw before they got gunned down," she has said. "What were they wearing? What did they have in their pockets? What was cooking on the stove? What song was playing on the jukebox?" Mike Gonzalez just sighs when he talks about Edna's appetite for irrelevant detail. "It infuriates Mike," Edna says. "I always ask what the dog's name is, what the cat's name is." Edna told me that Gonzalez now advises rookie detectives that they might as well gather such details, because otherwise "you're just going to feel stupid when Edna asks you."

There are times when Edna finds herself longing for simpler times on the police beat. When she began, the murders she covered tended to be conventional love triangles or armed robberies. She was often dealing with "an up-front person who happened to have bludgeoned his wife to death." These days, the murders are likely to be Latin drug murders, and a lot fewer of them produce a suspect. Trying to gather information from Cubans and Central Americans, Edna has a problem that goes beyond the language barrier. "They have a Latin love of intrigue," she says. "I had a Cuban informant, and I found that he would sometimes lie to me just to make it more interesting." It is also true that even for a police reporter there can be too many murders. Edna says that she was "a little shell-shocked" four or five years ago, when Dade murders hit their peak. She found that she barely had time to make her rounds in a thorough way. "I used to like to stop at the jail," she has said. "I used to like to browse in the morgue. To make sure who's there."

Edna found that the sheer number of murders overwhelmed each individual murder as the big story. "Dade's murder rate hit new heights this week as a wave of unrelated violence left 14 people dead and five critically hurt within five days," a story bylined Edna Buchanan began in June of 1980. After a couple of paragraphs comparing the current murder figures with those of previous years, the story went on, "In the latest wave of violence, a teenager's throat was cut and her body dumped in a canal. A former airline stewardess was garroted and left with a pair of scissors stuck between her shoulder blades. Four innocent bystanders were shot in a barroom gun battle. An 80-year-old man surprised a burglar who battered him fatally with a hammer. An angry young woman who 'felt used' beat her date to death with the dumbbells he used to keep fit. And an apparent robbery victim was shot dead as he ran away from the robbers." The murder rate has levelled off since 1981, but Edna still sometimes writes what amount to murder-roundup stories. "I feel bad, and even a little guilty, that a murder no longer gets a story, just a paragraph," she says. "It dehumanizes it." A paragraph in a roundup piece is not Edna's idea of a sendoff.

On a day I was making the rounds with Edna, there was a police report saying that two Marielitos had begun arguing on the street and the argument had ended with one shooting the other dead. That sounded like a paragraph at most. But Edna had a tip that the victim and the killer had known each other in Cuba and the shooting was actually the settling of an old prison score. That sounded to me more like a murder that stood out a bit from the crowd. Edna thought so, too, but her enthusiasm was limited. "We've already had a couple of those," she told me. Edna has covered a few thousand murders by now, and she's seen a couple of most things. She has done stories about a man who was stabbed to death because he stepped on somebody's toes on his way to a seat in a movie theatre and about a two-year-old somebody tried to frame for the murder of a playmate and about an eighty-nine-year-old man who was arrested for beating his former wife to death and about a little boy killed by a crocodile. She has done stories about a woman who committed suicide because she couldn't get her leaky roof fixed and about a newspaper deliveryman who committed suicide because during a petroleum shortage he couldn't get enough gasoline. She has done stories about a man who managed to commit suicide by stabbing himself in the heart *twice* and about a man who threw a severed head at a police officer twice. She has done a story about two brothers who killed a third brother because he interrupted a checkers game. ("I thought I had the best-raised children in the world," their mother said.) She has done a story about a father being killed at the surprise birthday party given for him by his thirty children. She has done a story about a man who died because fourteen of the eighty-two double-wrapped condom packages of cocaine he tried to carry into the country inside his stomach began to leak. ("His last meal was worth $30,000 and it killed him.") She has done any number of stories about bodies being discovered in the bay by beachcombers or fishermen or University of Miami scientists doing marine research. (" 'It's kind of a nuisance when you plan your day to do research on the reef,' fumed Professor Peter Glynn, of the university's Rosenstiel School of Marine and Atmospheric Science.") Talking to Edna one day about murder cases they had worked on, a Metro-Dade homicide detective said, "In Dade County, there are no surprises left."

Edna would agree that surprises are harder to find in Dade County these days. Still, she finds them. Flipping through page after page of routine police logs, talking to her sources on the telephone, chatting with a homicide detective, she'll come across, say, a shopping-mall murder that might have been done against the background of a new kind of high-school gang, or a murderer who seemed to have been imprisoned with his victim for a time by a sophisticated burglar-gate system. Then, a look of concern still on her face, she'll say, "That's interesting as heck."

CHAPTER SIX

The Promise and Peril
of Investigative Biography

These days, sensible investigative biographers write only about persons long dead. Those of us who write about the living or the recently deceased, especially the influential, famous or wealthy, increasingly do so at our peril.

Within the cottage industry of investigative biographers delving into the lives of the living, my experience—while unique in some ways—is all too common in its broad outlines. Armand Hammer—tycoon, philanthropist, citizen-diplomat, sometimes called the most powerful person in Los Angeles—used his influence to shut doors during the five years I researched his life. He told employees and acquaintances to keep away from me. He sued the federal government to stop the release of information to me. He pressured my U.S. and British publishers to kill the book. When that failed, he sued my British publisher and me in London. Only his death in December 1990 halted his unpleasant tactics.[1]

A recent book about the craft is titled *Biography as High Adventure.* The title was apt when the book appeared in 1986, but it has taken on an unfortunate new meaning since then. Lately, the "adventure" too often is arduous—as the subjects of biographies take authors and publishers to court, as judges issue unprecedented restrictions, as custodians of records (including the federal government) withhold more information for longer periods, as subjects or their partisans withhold information, as well-meaning sources provide inaccurate accounts, as uninformed or venal reviewers dash off hasty criticisms that undermine years of careful research, as biographers receive threats of bodily harm.[2]

Besides me, biographers of J. D. Salinger, Igor Stravinsky, L. Ron

201

Hubbard, Anne Sexton, Saul Bellow, Richard Wright, Sylvia Plath, John Connally, Henry Kissinger, Arnold Schwarzenegger, Walter Lippmann, John Lennon, Aleksandr Solzhenitsyn, Howard Hughes, Malcolm X, Sam Shepard, Harry Chapin, John Belushi, J. Edgar Hoover, Frank Sinatra, Jacqueline Kennedy Onassis, John Gotti, Katharine Graham, Pete Rose, Martha Gellhorn, Robert Maxwell, H. Ross Perot, Johnny Carson, Jim Bakker, Gloria Steinem, Mikhail Gorbachev, Pablo Picasso, Barbara Walters, Roy Cohn, Lyndon LaRouche, Elton John, Madonna, Michael Jackson, Jack Kent Cooke, Diana Ross, and Lillian Hellman—to name only a small percentage—have come close to shipwrecking on the shoals of modern life-writing.[3]

One result is that book publishers who prefer to shy away from controversy are deciding against contracting with authors for biographies that cry out to be done. Some publishers have watered down, withdrawn, or pulped biographies rather than fight an unhappy subject with deep pockets. This is not a parochial matter. The true losers are readers—and history.

Any discussion about the perils of contemporary biography has to start with the case of reclusive fiction writer J. D. Salinger. His successful attempt to suppress portions of an unauthorized biography changed the rules of the genre.

It happened like this: In 1983, Ian Hamilton, a British biographer, wrote Salinger of his intent to research his life. Salinger, who had not published since 1965 and had refused interview requests since 1953, not surprisingly refused to cooperate. At that point, Hamilton ran through the catalog of doubts besetting any unauthorized biographer with a conscience: "He wanted to be left alone. He'd kept his side of the bargain—by not publishing, by refusing all interviews, photographs and so on. . . . Didn't he have the same right to privacy as you and I? Well, yes. But then again, not quite."[4]

Hamilton and Random House, his publisher, decided to proceed. Many contemporary biographies are unauthorized; in fact, many biographers and publishers believe such versions are more honest and salable than authorized versions in which the subject or the heirs exercise control. Hamilton's previous experience as a biographer had been with an authorized life of Robert Lowell. The poet's widow and still-living ex-wife were approving, as were his literary executors. But, Hamilton discovered, authorization "can be a narrow license. I had access, to be sure, to papers and to people. But papers that have not found their way into libraries (and some which have) can often be withheld, and people sometimes tell you lies. With Lowell, I found I almost had too much material—too many eyewitness accounts, too many items passed on to me in confidence, too many special interests. . . . For all that you enjoyed this magic-sounding right of access, you still had to be endlessly judging and rejudging limits of propriety. And to some extent you were always having to play one witness off against another. There were too many tightropes, too many injurable sensitivities, and later, when the book was done, too many denials and recriminations. Lowell had been loved by several people, but few of these people loved, or even liked each other. And yet all of them believed that their version of the man was the authentic one."[5]

Because of Salinger's secretiveness, Hamilton, like other unauthorized biographers, had to be especially resourceful. He located previously unpublished letters written between 1939 and 1961 by Salinger to editors, friends, neighbors, and fellow authors. The recipients of those letters had over the decades donated their personal papers to Harvard University, Princeton University, and the University of Texas. Access to the letters was easy. Like any other researcher, Hamilton signed a form restricting publication of the letters without permission from the library and Salinger. At the time, he paid little attention to the restrictions: "I signed . . . because otherwise I would not have been allowed to see the letters. At the back of my mind, though, I was skeptical about the legal weight of these enforced undertakings . . . I suspected that in spite of all this bureaucracy it would still be possible for me to use some small amount of the material I'd come to study."[6]

Until recently, most biographers felt the same way, as I did when I located correspondence between Hammer and former U.S. senators who had donated their papers to New England College, Middle Tennessee State University, the University of Missouri, and the University of Arkansas. I read the legal boilerplate provided by the archivists, and I signed. I assumed that in the end I would be able to quote directly from the letters because everybody involved wanted an accurate, compelling biography.

In Hamilton's case, quotations from the Salinger letters eventually were peppered throughout the manuscript, which he delivered to Random House in July 1985. The publisher's lawyers questioned whether the extensiveness of direct quotations from the unpublished letters would stand a legal challenge. Hamilton responded that he had quoted only a tiny amount of the total; the lawyers were satisfied. Random House set publication for autumn 1986.

In May 1986, Salinger received a copy of the bound galley pages through his agent, who had obtained it from a publishing source. Salinger was dismayed by the inclusion of quotations from the letters; he apparently had been unaware that they were available to biographers. He took two unusual steps—registering seventy-nine of the letters for copyright protection, and telling his lawyer to stop Hamilton's book until previously unpublished quotations from the letters were deleted.

Despite misgivings, Hamilton and Random House cooperated, deleting or paraphrasing most of the material from the letters. It was a shame; the incisiveness of Salinger's language was lost, especially unfortunate in a biography of a prose stylist. For example, Salinger had written a letter expressing his distress at Oona O'Neill (whom he had dated) marrying Charlie Chaplin: "I can see them at home evenings. Chaplin squatting grey and nude, atop his chiffonier, swinging his thyroid around his head by his bamboo cane, like a dead rat. Oona in an aquamarine gown, applauding madly from the bathroom. Agnes (her mother) in a Jantzen bathing suit, passing between them with cocktails. I'm facetious, but I'm sorry. Sorry for anyone with a profile as young and lovely as Oona's." Hamilton's paraphrase read: "At one point in a letter to Whit Burnett, [Salinger] provides a pen portrait of the Happy Hour Chez Chaplin—the comedian, ancient and unclothed, is brandishing his walking stick. Attached to the stick and horribly resembling a lifeless rodent, is one of Chaplin's vital organs. Oona claps her hands in appreciation and Agnes, togged out in a bathing suit, pours drinks. Salinger goes on to say he's sorry—sorry not for what he has just written, but for Oona, far too youthful and exquisite for such a dreadful fate."[7]

The revised manuscript, ready in September 1986, quoted only about two hundred words from the letters. But Salinger remained unmollified. On October 3, 1986, he sued Hamilton and Random House, charging not only copyright infringement but also unfair competition and breach of contract. The unfair competition claim complained that because Hamilton had introduced so many of the paraphrases with "Salinger states" or a similar attribution, book buyers might think they were reading Salinger's exact words. Salinger based the breach of contract claim on the forms Hamilton had signed at the libraries.

It was a brazen move, with little apparent chance of success. For two hundred years, U.S. courts had refrained from halting publication based on objections to unauthorized use of unpublished materials. The only exception anybody could locate was an 1841 case in which a judge halted a biography of George Washington because it reproduced 319 entire letters from an eleven-volume commercial compilation of the first president's correspondence. Despite the egregious copying, even that judge banned publication reluctantly, commenting, "This is one of those intricate and embarrassing questions . . . in which it is not . . . easy to arrive at any satisfactory conclusion, or to lay down any general principles applicable to all cases."[8]

More recently, during the 1960s, judges refused to permanently halt biographies of Howard Hughes and Ernest Hemingway despite claims that "fair use" of previously published or unpublished materials had been violated. Those cases seemed to settle the matter decisively in favor of biographers. In the Hughes case, for example, the court said biographies "are fundamentally personal histories and it is both reasonable and customary to refer to and utilize earlier works dealing with the subject . . . and occasionally quote directly from such works. This practice is permitted because of the public benefit in encouraging the development of historical and biographical works and their public distribution."[9]

Despite all the contrary precedent, Salinger pressed ahead. Random House was anxious. It had promised the biography to reviewers and bookstores. Further delay could harm the publisher's credibility and sales. Federal judge Pierre Leval, sitting in New York City, moved quickly. He ruled on November 5, 1986, that Hamilton's quotations were within the boundaries of "fair use," that the paraphrases were unlikely to be misunderstood as Salinger's words, and that the library agreements had been honored adequately.[10]

With Leval's opinion in hand, Random House readied the book for shipment. Salinger appealed, however, causing Leval to temporarily prohibit Random House from publishing the biography until the U.S. Court of Appeals for the Second Circuit could rule. The ruling came January 29, 1987. Three appeals judges had studied the case, but one had died three weeks earlier, leaving Jon Newman and Roger Miner. They overturned Leval's decision, thus prohibiting publication. The two judges saw the case differently from Leval, commenting, "To deny a biographer like Hamilton the opportunity to copy the expressive content of the letters is not . . . to interfere in any significant way with the process of enhancing public knowledge of history or contemporary events. The facts may be reported. Salinger's letters contain a number of facts that students of his life and writings will no doubt find of interest, and Hamilton is entirely free to fashion a biography that reports these facts. But Salinger has a right to protect the expressive content of his unpublished writings for the term of his copyright."[11]

Random House asked the U.S. Supreme Court to overturn Newman and Miner, but the Supreme Court, in October 1987, refused to hear the case. Hamilton and Random House started over, eventually issuing a book titled *In Search of J. D. Salinger,* which was as much about the biographer's frustrations as about the writer's life.

By then, the chilling effect had begun. Based on the Salinger ruling, publishers were insisting on greater caution among biographers. The author's guide from my publisher (Little, Brown and Company), composed before the Salinger decision, had been chilling enough, stating: "You should assume that the copyright to unpublished material of any kind, such as letters, journals, diaries and manuscripts, is owned by the writer or his or her heirs. Quotations from this type of material can present complicated permission problems. It is almost always necessary to get written permission to quote from unpublished material, no matter when it was created. . . . The person or institution who received a letter or who presently possesses [it] . . . controls only whether you may have access to it, not whether you may publish it." As for already published material, the manual said authors should obtain written permission and pay any fees if planning to quote more than three hundred words from a book, one hundred and fifty words from a magazine article, or fifty words from a newspaper article. Furthermore, the manual explained the onerous procedure for obtaining permission to use information from in-person or telephone interviews. After Salinger, word came from Little, Brown that even stricter standards would henceforth apply. Other biographers were receiving similar messages from their publishers.[12]

I was worried. Already, I had found numerous unpublished letters written by Hammer—to U.S. senators and presidents, among others. They were hardly prose masterpieces, but many passages were revealing. If I were forced to paraphrase, readers would lose the essence of the man. I hoped Little, Brown would let me quote from the letters, fighting any Hammer lawsuit that might result and maybe overturning the Salinger precedent. But I knew that possibility was remote. (My fears turned out to be correct; Little, Brown followed the prudent, conservative course. I had to paraphrase Hammer's words, rather than share his own language with readers.)

The reactions of other publishers did nothing to set my mind at ease, either. In July 1987, Macmillan decided against issuing a group biography already under contract, *The Binghams of Louisville* by Pulitzer Prize–winner David Leon Chandler. In a cryptic news release, the publisher cited "serious disagreements" over Chandler's interpretation of his research, adding that the cancellation was "not based upon legal considerations and is, in fact, contrary to Macmillan's own commercial interests."

According to Chandler and his wife, Mary Voelz Chandler, who assisted with the book, Macmillan's decision "was a surprise to us. Until that day, we had never been told by Macmillan that we had disagreements, interpretative or research, substantive or otherwise." The Chandlers never received further explanation, but said intimidation by Barry Bingham, Sr., longtime publisher of the *Louisville Courier-Journal*, was a reasonable hypothesis, although Bingham had cooperated initially: "Macmillan made its decision after Barry Bingham became alarmed by our conclusions that Barry's father, Judge Robert Worth Bingham, had caused the death of his second wife, Mary Lily Kenan Flagler, in 1917 by having her drugged with morphine. . . . Our book was based in small part on documents written by the Judge and donated by his son Barry to the Filson Club, a private museum in

Louisville which is partly supported by Bingham philanthropy and which had given us permission to use the documents. After seeing *The Binghams of Louisville* in manuscript, however, Barry, Sr., began his assault by copyrighting those documents approximately one year after we had used them and just prior to book publication." Crown Publishers, in this instance gutsier than Macmillan, issued the book in December 1987 with the controversial material intact.[13]

Amid the controversies over the Salinger and Bingham books, Judge Leval issued a ruling that effectively suppressed a biography of composer Igor Stravinsky by John Kobler. Robert Craft filed the complaint against Kobler and his publisher, Macmillan, after manuscript copies had already reached reviewers; a few magazines aimed at the book trade already had published reviews based on the manuscript.

But Craft refused to accept the book as a fait accompli. For the last two decades of Stravinsky's life, Craft had been his confidant and amanuensis. Fifteen books resulted, some by Craft alone, some by Craft and Stravinsky together—books that Kobler quoted. The books were out of print, and Craft expressed no desire to write further about Stravinsky. Under the circumstances, many authors would have been flattered to have their work cited with approval in a biography. Not Craft. Because Stravinsky had willed his copyright to Craft, the coauthor had standing to sue Kobler, and did so.

Leval's burden was to compare Kobler's biography to various Craft-Stravinsky writings, examining the 230 passages at issue line by line. Kobler had directly quoted about two thousand words scattered from throughout fifteen books, with no more than five hundred words taken from any single book. Any responsible biographer would have considered that fair use. Leval concluded otherwise, saying Kobler had crossed the invisible boundary between fair use and copyright infringement. Distribution of the book would have to stop. "This ruling does not kill Kobler's biography but may require revisions reducing the use of Stravinsky's prose," the judge said. In fact, the ruling did kill the biography; Macmillan never published the book.[14]

Copyright infringement, two years earlier near the bottom of the list when biographers discussed perils, was at the top by 1988. Even when authors and publishers prevailed, the victories seemed Pyrrhic. That was the case with *Bare-Faced Messiah: The True Story of L. Ron*

Hubbard, written by Russell Miller and published by Henry Holt and Company. An arm of Hubbard's Scientology Church alleged copyright infringement, asking that the biography of its deceased high priest be withdrawn. The case was a hostile one, as evidenced by testimony from the executor of Hubbard's estate, Norman Starkey: "That scum bag book is full of bullshit, man, and you know it. It is full of bullshit . . . goddamn, fucking bullshit."

Judge Leval was at center stage again. He had ruled for Salinger's biographer, then was overturned. He had ruled against Stravinsky's biographer; that book had died. What would Leval do this time? By the time the church filed its lawsuit on May 5, 1988, about twelve thousand copies of Miller's book had been distributed, with a second printing scheduled to begin the next day. Leval refused to stop the second printing. But when the church agreed to pay Holt for its losses should the publisher prevail in court, Leval ordered on May 20 that distribution of the second printing cease. The order stayed in effect until Leval's ruling on August 9, 1988.

In his decision, Leval summarized the publisher's position: "Holt contends there is powerful justification for Miller's quotations from Hubbard's letters and journals. It argues that these are not appropriations of Hubbard's efforts and talents in literary expression, but demonstrations through Hubbard's words of his flaws of character. The thesis of *Bare-Faced Messiah* is that Hubbard was dishonest, pretentious, boastful, paranoid, cowardly, cruel, disloyal, aggressive, bizarre and finally even insane in his pseudo-scientific fantasies and obsessions. Defendant argues that a portrait of these qualities is almost impossible to convey without reliance on the subject's own words."

Essentially agreeing with Holt, Leval worked through numerous direct quotations, including Hubbard's sentence, "The trouble with China is, there are too many Chinks here." Leval commented, "It would be preposterous to restrict Miller to writing something like 'Hubbard used a derogatory epithet exhibiting snobbish bigoted disdain for the Chinese.' That would be at once unfair to the biographer, the subject and the readership, which can reasonably demand to know 'What did he say? Let us be the judge of whether it was vulgar, snobbish or bigoted.'"

Leval said Miller had used Hubbard's writings skillfully to help prove a thesis; almost surely, *Bare-Faced Messiah* would have passed all legal tests before the appeals court ruling against the Salinger biography. But, Leval said, "given [the Salinger case's] strong presumption against a finding of fair use for unpublished materials, I cannot conclude that the Court of Appeals would accord fair use protection to all of Miller's quotations, or that the biography as a whole would be considered non-infringing." Despite that finding, Leval refused to halt further distribution: "As a practical matter, an injunction would kill this informative book. As the book is already in print, the expense and waste involved in republishing after deleting infringing material would be prohibitive. The injury to freedom of speech would be significant."

The Scientologists went to the Court of Appeals for the Second Circuit, the same forum that had issued the troublesome Salinger ruling. Two of the judges disagreed with Leval, making it clear they would have halted the book if the church had filed a more timely lawsuit. The stern language meant a hollow victory for biographers and publishers. As the Association of American Publishers noted in petitioning the U.S. Supreme Court: "In the wake of the decision below, no prudent publisher can afford to risk even very limited quotation from unpublished materials—no matter the degree of their prior dissemination or how compelling the purpose—since to do so invites injunction of the entire work."

The appeals court language led another federal judge to stop a second Hubbard biographer from publishing his book because of an alleged copyright infringement. That biographer, Jon Atack, a very disillusioned Scientologist, and the Carol Publishing Group appealed. The appeal went to the judges of the Second Circuit, as usual, but Atack and Carol were fortunate to draw a different panel this time. Those three judges decided Atack had stayed within the boundaries of fair use in *A Piece of Blue Sky: Scientology, Dianetics and L. Ron Hubbard Exposed.* Hubbard's partisans appealed to the U.S. Supreme Court, but it refused to accept the case.

All in all, the victories of Miller and Holt and Atack and Carol were mixed, at best. They spent several years and hundreds of thousands of dollars to place the books into stores. But they left behind judicial language discouraging to responsible biographers.[15]

Unhappy subjects of critical biographies moved into the breach. Novelist Saul Bellow's displeasure convinced St. Martin's Press to delay *Saul Bellow: A Biography of the Imagination* by Ruth Miller; the publisher cited the Salinger/Hubbard precedents among its reasons. Miller's book, already sent to reviewers in the form of uncorrected galley proofs, was scheduled to be in stores in May 1990. St. Martin's took the unusual step of recalling reviewers' copies, and then delayed the book. It eventually appeared in March 1991.

Before the recall, Bellow had talked to *Chicago Tribune* writer John Blades. Blades reported that Bellow had urged Miller to write the book, giving her access to his papers at the University of Chicago. Blades characterized the galley-proof version as "neither voyeuristic nor scandalous." He said the book was "both a highly personal and rigorously academic pastiche of biographical vignettes, reminiscences and excerpts from Bellow's speeches and letters. . . . Although Miller is decidedly sympathetic toward Bellow, making frequent references to his formidable intellect, incandescent style and irrepressible humor, she does not flatter the mercurial author or spare criticism of either his literary or his private life."

Blades speculated Bellow bridled at publication because of Miller's suggestion "that the increasingly misogynistic tone of his work . . . was the direct result of the breakup of his second marriage. Afterward, Miller says that Bellow 'thrashed about wildly from bed to bed.' Using correspondence from the Bellow file at the Regenstein Library as collaborative evidence, Miller goes on to give the first names of a dozen Bellow paramours. Later, she also provides a 'cast list' that identifies real people who have appeared as characters in Bellow's fiction."

Before the book's appearance, St. Martin's published a rare paragraph in its catalog: "Despite Miller's long acquaintance with Bellow, this is not an authorized biography; Bellow has not approved the book and apparently disagrees with much of its contents, even going so far as to object through legal counsel. Though this has resulted in a delay in the book's publication, the author has maintained the integrity of her opinions and interpretation."[16]

In another case, Ellen Wright, widow of author Richard Wright, tied up biographer Margaret Walker and her publisher, Warner Books, for years over copyright-infringement claims involving Walker's *Rich-*

ard Wright: Daemonic Genius. A federal court entertained the case even though the widow's claim involved letters written by Richard Wright to Margaret Walker herself. On September 19, 1990, the judge ruled in favor of the biographer and publisher. In 1991, a federal appeals court upheld the ruling, giving biographers a bit of breathing room, at least temporarily.[17]

Ellen Wright's lawsuit illustrates Judge Leval's concern that a "ban on fair use of unpublished documents establishes a new despotic potentate in the politics of intellectual life—the widow censor. A historian who wishes to quote personal papers of deceased public figures now must satisfy heirs and executors for 50 years after the subject's death. When writers ask permission, the answer will be 'Show me what you write. Then we'll talk about permission.' If the manuscript does not exude pure admiration, permission will be denied."[18]

Widower censors exist alongside the widows, as the Sylvia Plath tempest shows. Ted Hughes, the widower of the dead poet, owns her copyrights; Hughes's sister, Olwyn, is the literary executor. The Hugheses allegedly used their control over Plath's papers to influence biographies by Linda Wagner-Martin and Anne Stevenson.

After the *New York Times Book Review* paid attention to Wagner-Martin's biography, Olwyn Hughes complained in a letter to the editor: "The preface of Linda Wagner-Martin's [book] yelps about the Plath estate's suppressive tactics. These, Ms. Wagner-Martin claims, resulted in her having to limit quotations in her book. Though she does not say so, she did quote a not inconsiderable 5000 or so words by Plath (including 2000 words of hitherto unpublished prose, and all the book's chapter headings) for which she obtained no permission and made no payment."

Accusing Wagner-Martin of shoddy scholarship, Hughes commented, "Quite what representatives of literary estates like myself can do about such unauthorized biographers, without spending half our lives attempting to correct them and the other half in court, I don't know. They seem to recognize no proper standards. . . . The reputations of living people are damaged, the public is deceived and publishers break the copyright law vital to their own and their authors' long-term interests. It's the last straw when, to publicize their shoddy wares, these authors clamor their outrage at 'suppressive' literary estates."[19]

The subject of a book by James Reston, Jr., on the other hand, was very much alive as the biographer was trying to finish his unauthorized life of John Connally, published by Harper and Row as *The Lone Star*. Connally tried to play censor by asking friends to stay away from Reston, requesting payment for his own cooperation, and placing restrictions on access to his papers at the Lyndon Baines Johnson Library in Austin, according to the author. Reston observed restrictions on quotations, writing afterward of his frustration: "Since the letters [I wished to quote] came from opened files in a presidential library, it felt as if to discover rich, unpublished material in a kind of research coup was dangerous; to use it was a crime. Good research was a form of entrapment. Better and safer, the law . . . seemed to be saying, that you rehash the stale stuff that has already appeared in print. . . . I was informed . . . that a hostile subject of a biography could not stop publication for supposed libel, but he could enjoin publication for copyright infringement. No author, in my view, could bear that risk."[20]

Author Ken Englade, piecing together biographical profiles of two suspected murderers for his book *Beyond Reason*, planned to quote directly from letters between the young woman and her boyfriend. The police had found the letters, which were made public during the woman's sentencing hearing. Englade was pleased, but not for long. "My problem arose," he wrote, "when I incorporated quotes from these documents in my manuscript. The in-house counsel for my publisher, St. Martin's Press, absolutely forbade me to use direct quotes," citing the Salinger and Hubbard cases. "At first, I couldn't believe this applied in my case. The documents I wanted were, after all, part of the court record, some of them even entered by the defense. Many of them had been read aloud on the witness stand. Excerpts had been published in newspapers and magazines and broadcast on both TV and radio. But the St. Martin's lawyer said it did not make any difference."[21]

Bruce Perry, author of *Malcolm*, a biography of Malcolm X, wrote in distress to several U.S. senators while the work was still in progress that he had "been forced to delete a great deal of material from a biography I have been working on for more than a decade. The deleted parts . . . are based on letters that Malcolm X . . . wrote while he was in prison. Some were written in an effort to win new recruits to the so-called Nation of Islam. Some were love letters to Gloria Strother, whom Malcolm wanted to marry. Others were letters he wrote during the Korean War in a two-pronged attempt to persuade the penal authorities to parole him and the military authorities not to draft him." Perry said he had considered trying to "separate the factual aspects of the unpublished letters from their expressive aspects. But, as Judge Leval has observed, it can't be done when the letter writer's state of mind is the fact in question. His choice of words is what indicates his state of mind."[22]

Clearly, there was cause for alarm. In an attempt to resurrect verisimilitude in biography and history, three members of Congress introduced corrective legislation. Bills from U.S. Senators Paul Simon and Patrick Leahy and U.S. Representative Robert Kastenmeier would have added four words to the U.S. Code. Those four words would have removed unpublished material from the protected status carved out in court decisions. The appropriate House and Senate committees held a hearing, but the legislation failed to pass during 1990 and 1991, partly because of unexpected opposition from the computer software industry.[23]

At the 1990 hearing, members of Congress listened to Pulitzer Prize–winning authors Taylor Branch and J. Anthony Lukas, among others. Branch was working on the second volume of his Martin Luther King, Jr., epic; the first volume, *Parting the Waters: America in the King Years, 1954–1963*, appeared in 1988, just as the Salinger decision was beginning to have an impact. "I had previously worked on the understanding that many factors controlled the extent to which I could quote or paraphrase historical sources," Branch said. "But now, my editors tell me, there is no amount of unpublished material that I can safely quote or even paraphrase without obtaining permission from those who participated in the events I write about, or their heirs. This rule will inevitably and unnecessarily impede readers' understanding and appreciation of the past."

Branch wondered how much of *Parting the Waters* would have survived in the current legal atmosphere: "In addition to the costs of bargained-for content control are the more prosaic burdens of having to locate and gain permission from the holders of rights of works that have long reposed in libraries and archives. Not all the holders are famous or easy to find. Indeed, most of mine have been obscure people. Many are dead, with scattered heirs. And please allow me to stress the logistical nightmares these rulings pose for the research phase of work such as mine. As thick as my book is . . . the text and all 77 pages of footnotes represent only a small fraction of the research material collected. At what point should a historical writer seek permission for quotation from an unpublished source? Before taking the first notes? Before making the first photocopies from material that may not be used? If so, work such as mine could not be done in a lifetime and would be abandoned in advance. Or should a writer wait until a quotation appears in the final draft of a book manuscript, when time pressures and potential difficulties in permissions might threaten the substance or publishing schedule of a book?"

Lukas, author of *Common Ground: A Turbulent Decade in the Lives of Three American Families,* explained how he would have been forced to omit compelling information from the book if the Salinger precedent had been in effect. He said the need for a new law is not merely the pleading of selfish biographers and publishers. "The biggest losers are your constituents . . . who, if this ruling is permitted to stand . . . will increasingly find fewer works of compelling history and biography available on their bookshelves and eventually in their libraries."

The court rulings, Lukas said, displayed "a fundamental misunderstanding of the role of unpublished materials in responsible scholarship. The very unpublished materials whose use the Second Circuit would discourage are the essential raw materials of the historian's and biographer's work . . . no serious scholar or journalist can afford to rely heavily on secondary sources. . . . If I tell the current high school student, who may know next to nothing about Adolf Hitler, that the Fuhrer was a mad beast, a raging megalomaniac, who wreaked havoc in the world for more than a decade, the student may or may not accept what I tell him. But if I ask him to read *Mein Kampf,* the findings of the Nuremberg Tribunal, the reports of correspondents who visited the concentration camps after the war . . . I am much more likely to be believed."

James L. Oakes, chief judge of the Second Circuit Court of Appeals, testified in favor of the legislation aimed at overturning the decisions of his colleagues. The court's language had "effectively put critical biographers and current historians out of the business of using direct quotations to illustrate a point, a characteristic or quality. . . . Unpublished works should not be entitled to any different treatment than published works."[24]

Biographers face numerous other problems today in addition to determining what they can quote. I will consider ten such problems that must be included in any catalog of major obstacles.

First, unexpected, time-consuming, expensive lawsuits by secondary characters. Michael Drosnin's *Citizen Hughes* was bound to be controversial, even though Howard Hughes had been dead nearly a decade. But Drosnin and his publisher, Holt Rinehart and Winston, could not have foreseen that former Hughes aide Robert A. Maheu would sue on the grounds that memorandums quoted by Drosnin actually belonged to Maheu. The documents had been stolen in 1974 from a warehouse owned by the Hughes empire—eleven years before Maheu filed his claim. Drosnin said that through assiduous detective work, he had discovered the identity of the thief and convinced him to turn over the papers during 1977. Maheu said Drosnin's use of the documents diminished their value to him, and that publication of details invaded his privacy. Drosnin and his publisher prevailed in the Maheu litigation, but victory took more than three years in two California courts, at great expense.[25]

Don Shewey, the biographer of playwright Sam Shepard, faced a libel suit by Charles Mingus III, a friend of Shepard's who had talked to Shewey about drug use. The court dismissed the complaint against Dell Publishing, finding that Shewey had been responsible overall and accurate in his rendering of drug experimentation by Shepard and Mingus. Such dismissals are better than losing, of course, but the filing of such lawsuits in the first place hurts the bottom lines of publishers and works financial hardship on biographers who cannot afford libel insurance to absorb the legal fees.[26]

Bob Woodward wrote *Wired*, the biography of actor John Belushi, with help from his widow, Judy Jacklin Belushi. After reading the book, she felt betrayed, having believed it would be more sympathetic. So she looked for grounds to sue, choosing alleged copyright infringement of one photograph. She asked publisher Simon and Schuster to halt distribution, placing a cloud over the book. The court refused to grant the request.[27]

So far, no lawsuit by anybody other than Armand Hammer has bedeviled me. But state laws have varying statutes of limitations, and federal courts have allowed cases to proceed years after the fact. As a result, many biographers never relax, hanging onto their interview notes and documents for life.

Second, information withheld or delayed by the federal government under the Freedom of Information Act. Writers often must wait years to receive an answer after requesting documents under the 1966 law. If the answer is no, appeals can take years more. The law says government agencies must respond within ten working days, but almost never do they provide a substantive answer in that span. A twice-monthly newsletter called *Access Reports* published by Harry Hammitt chronicles the horrors (and occasional triumphs) of authors trying to use the law to write complete, accurate books. One biographer who told his horror story recently in Hammitt's newsletter is Athan Theoharis, chronicler of J. Edgar Hoover's career. His original request for Hoover's previously secret FBI office file finally produced about 6,000 pages, with many (sometimes most) words blacked out. The FBI withheld another 11,700 pages in full.[28]

I am a veteran FOIA user; I have learned just about every shortcut in dealing with government agencies. Yet I had to wait years for the State Department, Federal Bureau of Investigation, and other bureaucracies to make decisions about which documents I could see. One of the key agencies was the Securities and Exchange Commission. I requested tens of thousands of pages of documentation from the agency's four major investigations of Hammer's Occidental Petroleum Corp. The agency was willing. But Hammer sued the agency to halt the release of documents to me. After inconclusive rulings by two courts, the matter returned to the agency. About eighteen months after publication of my book, my request was still being processed.[29]

Third, physical threats. Wendy Leigh, the author of *Arnold: An Unauthorized Biography,* about actor/bodybuilder Arnold Schwarzenegger, said she received nasty telephone calls after publication, on the heels of attempts by the subject to control the content of the book and then to suppress it. According to Leigh, a security consultant suggested to her "that I avoid standing in front of a lighted window, always check underneath the car for bombs and never fail to test the brakes." Leigh decided to write the book hidden away in Colorado, to shred documents daily, and to place interview tapes in bank vaults.[30]

Albert Goldman, the biographer of Elvis Presley and John Lennon, said he called the Federal Bureau of Investigation after receiving "a particularly alarming and savagely anti-Semitic screed." Months later a bullet passed through the window of Goldman's New York City office, almost hitting him while he talked on the telephone. The police said it might have been a random shooting. Goldman wondered.[31]

Hammer's minions said some nasty things about me, once in a while to my face, usually behind my back. Their words were vicious; none constituted a physical threat, however.

Fourth, sources who lie (intentionally or otherwise), sources who refuse to talk without some kind of consideration, and sources who question a biographer's motives. Philip Ziegler, the authorized biographer of Lord Mountbatten, told of how, when working on the book, he "was confronted by elderly grandees of total rectitude who recounted stories that not merely sounded wrong but that the logic of geography or chronology proved to be false. An admiral, for instance, described in detail a highly important conversation he had held with Mountbatten in Singapore. . . . His recapitulation of Mountbatten's views was surprising but not impossible and would have been well worth quoting had it not been for the fact that Mountbatten never visited Singapore while the admiral was in residence there and did not even become chief of the defense staff until after the admiral had retired."[32] I heard so many inaccurate statements about Hammer being passed off as true by well-intentioned sources that I could have filled a second book with them.

James Reston, Jr., was shocked when his subject, John Connally, asked about being paid for his cooperation. Potential sources asked for payment when I contacted them for my Hammer biography. Rather than register shock, I said I would consider the requests. Each time, upon reflection, I said no. It would set a bad precedent for future biographers, something I had no right to do. Paying for information can taint it—a source will say the "right" thing to earn the money, thinking that the "wrong" words will mean no payment. Like me, Reston encountered sources who questioned his motives, despite his writing in advance that he was interested in positive anecdotes. Reston commented that calls to Connally's friends often began "with a question I grew to despise. 'Is this an authorized or an unauthorized biography?' they would ask."[33]

Thomas Powers, biographer of Central Intelligence Agency director Richard Helms, said, "Just about everyone I talked to while working on this book wanted to know where I stood. Did I intend to attack or defend? Was I going to write an indictment or an apology? A short answer was desired. The question made me uneasy; it implied that my mind was firmly made up before I began."[34]

I empathize with Reston and Powers. Sometimes it seemed the only neutral person on the subject of Armand Hammer was me. Almost everybody I talked to thought Hammer either walked on water or was the devil incarnate. Almost nobody believed that I could believe otherwise.

Fifth, another biographer writing on the same subject at the same time, or the subject releasing an autobiography at the same time. Simultaneous books complicate relationships with sources; they also result in sharing precious book-review space with the other author. That has happened recently to, among others, John Dinges and Frederick Kempe, simultaneous biographers of Manuel Noriega; Roger Morris and Stephen Ambrose, writing about Richard Nixon's life; as well as Alanna Nash and Gwenda Blair, chroniclers of Jessica Savitch's career.[35]

Before signing a contract for a Hammer biography, I investigated the possibility that there might be other biographers. I turned up two names; both, I heard, might have begun their research. I called each, explaining how much work I had completed. One was cool; he said he would think about what I had said and maybe get back to me. He never did call, but I learned a few months later that he apparently had begun work on an unrelated topic. The second potential competitor listened politely to me, promising to call back. He did soon thereafter, suggesting collaboration. I politely said that I work better alone. At that point, he put his Hammer research on the back burner, turning to a different project.

I already knew that Hammer himself was working on an autobiography (the fourth authorized version of his life). Putnam's published it more than two years before my biography was ready. Hammer's book got mostly lukewarm or negative reviews; mine received almost entirely positive reviews. But his made the best-seller list; mine sold poorly.[36]

Sixth, the subject's circumstances change in midstream. When Roger Kahn and Pete Rose agreed in 1986 to work together on the ultimate baseball life, Rose was an idol. By the time *Pete Rose: My Story* was published, Rose was on the path to prison, Kahn had gone through a divorce plus lost a son to suicide, and the original publisher (Warner Books) had terminated the contract while seeking to recover its advance. When Macmillan picked up the contract and published the book, the reviews were so-so.[37]

Seventh, the biographer becomes the story. After researching attention-getting unauthorized biographies of Jackie Onassis, Elizabeth Taylor, and Frank Sinatra, Kitty Kelley was a household word pulling down multimillion-dollar advances. The *Washington Post* decided to take an in-depth look at Kelley herself. The nearly book-length unauthorized series began on a Sunday in the newspaper's magazine, continuing on Monday and Tuesday in the Style section. It was clever, well researched, compelling, and almost unrelievedly negative, much like the books Kelley writes. (The first part is reprinted in Chapter Five of this book.) After the publication of her biography of Nancy Reagan in 1991, Kelley was the subject of numerous stories, many of them unflattering. Several months later, she became the subject of a full-length muckraking biography.[38]

Biographer C. David Heymann has received intense scrutiny two different times—after his life of heiress Barbara Hutton was withdrawn from bookstores by Random House in 1983 because of inaccuracies, and after his biography of Jackie Onassis appeared in 1989 amid more charges of inaccuracy. Lyle Stuart, a maverick publisher, picked up the Hutton biography, had Heymann clean it up, and published it. As for *A Woman Named Jackie*, it became a best-seller.[39]

Eighth, a publisher withdraws a book, or forces changes. Heymann's Hutton biography is not an isolated example. Harcourt Brace Jovanovich stopped distributing and selling Deborah Davis's life of *Wash-*

ington Post publisher Katharine Graham after complaints from Graham and *Washington Post* editor Benjamin Bradlee. Davis sued Harcourt Brace, eventually receiving an out-of-court settlement. Eight years after the book was shredded, National Press, a small publisher in Washington, D.C., issued a slightly revised version of *Katharine the Great: Katharine Graham and the Washington Post*, with a new introduction by Davis.[40]

Richardson & Snyder recalled from bookstores Antoni Gronowicz's biography of Pope John Paul II after evidence surfaced that portions of it might have been fraudulent. Gronowicz later faced a mail-fraud investigation by the federal government in connection with the marketing of *God's Broker*. He refused to produce documents in response to a 1985 grand jury request, thus placing himself in contempt of court. Gronowicz died before the proceedings had run their course.[41]

John Cooney's biography of Francis Cardinal Spellman, titled *The American Pope*, went out in bound galleys to reviewers with the assertion that the late Roman Catholic archbishop of New York was a homosexual whose sex life "was a source of profound embarrassment and shame to many priests." After the galleys had reached reviewers, Times Books asked Cooney for better proof of his assertions. The finished book contained only a toned-down speculative paragraph about the cardinal's sexual proclivities.[42]

Ninth, reviewers who fail to understand the craft of biography, trash the book due to apparent conflicts of interests, or destroy years of work with unwarranted glibness. Too many reviewers simply recount the facts of the life as lived, failing to comment on whether the biographer used the best possible sources, was judicious in psychoanalyzing the subject, refrained from unfounded guesswork when gaps in the evidence existed, and so on. As a result, potential book buyers rarely know if the life has been accurately and skillfully told.

Conflicts of interests can be hard to detect. One surfaced recently when Shirley Hazzard criticized Robert Herzstein's biography of Kurt Waldheim. It turned out that Hazzard had expressed animus toward the book while doing an in-house critique for the publisher, Arbor House/William Morrow. She appeared to be upset that Herzstein had not praised her previously published magazine research on Waldheim. The editor of the *New York Times Book Review* was unaware of all the baggage Hazzard brought to the book when assigning it to her. Eventually, the book review published a letter from Herzstein setting out his complaint about her alleged bias.[43]

Joan Peyser, Leonard Bernstein's biographer, was puzzled when a reviewer commented that she seemed unable to decide whether the composer was an angel or a monster. "That's my whole point," Peyser said. "It's not a question of either one or the other. He could be both—and within minutes."[44]

When a biographer's effort is trashed by a reviewer, many keep silent, at least in public. Some join the fray. Linda Wagner-Martin, one of Sylvia Plath's biographers, wrote the *New York Times* about a mostly negative review by, of all people, Ian Hamilton, Salinger's biographer. Wagner-Martin wondered about Hamilton's emphasis on Plath's husband, Ted Hughes, seeing it as evidence of a skewed perspective: "If Mr. Hamilton finds little that is new in my biography, it is probably because he is looking for the wrong kind of events—perhaps cataclysmic happenings. Plath did not go to war. She did not take lovers and flaunt them in her partner's face. She lived her housewifely life, working also as a writer, more or less quietly. . . . I have tried to make this biography very gender specific; it chronicles a woman's life, and the details are appropriate. . . . While one might not expect Mr. Hamilton to understand the intricacies of Plath's life, one might have thought he would have understood the approach to describing it."[45]

Tenth, wrenching relationships between biographer and subject. If the author has access to the subject, the relationship is almost always bound to be wrenching. If the author has never met the subject, obsession thrives, too, only in a different way. For example, Seymour Hersh, who left the *New York Times* to write a masterful but admittedly hostile biography of former Secretary of State Henry Kissinger, ended up being denounced publicly by the diplomat as "slime."[46]

J. Randy Taraborrelli grew up near Philadelphia fascinated with Motown music and especially Diana Ross. At age ten, he met her fleetingly but got the brush-off. Undeterred, at fourteen he started an international fan club for her. Nineteen years later, less enamored, he published what was generally considered to be a nasty, unauthorized biography titled *Call Her Miss Ross*.[47]

William Wright never did understand where he stood with his subject, author Lillian Hellman. After Wright contacted her, she complained bitterly to his editor at Simon and Schuster, then announced a competing authorized biography by a writer of her choosing. Wright received a letter from her saying, in full, "I do not wish a biography of me and therefore I cannot see you." Hellman signed it "Most sincerely," including a telephone number and an address. Wright got to wondering about the telephone number. "I was fascinated. If you dismiss someone as curtly as Hellman had dismissed me, why offer a phone number? Even if her secretary added the number to her letters as a matter of course, Hellman surely would have been consulted in this case about whether or not she wished to add her private number. If it was deliberate, what had Hellman wanted? For me to call and plead? To offer myself for a tongue-lashing? To match wits? To convince her of my mettle? My persistence? Perhaps the phone number's inclusion was a clerical error, but I preferred to think it was a signal." If so, it went unanswered; Wright had failed to notice the phone number until after Hellman's death.[48]

Not being particularly introspective, I wondered little about my "relationship" with Hammer. I told questioners that I never chose him as a topic, that the idea came to me from a fellow writer. Yet from time to time, I reflect. I could have said no. Why did I say yes instead, subjecting myself to efforts at suppression and eventually a lawsuit that drained my bank account, kept me away from my wife and children, and otherwise dominated my life? Nonetheless, if it weren't for biographers willing to conduct the long search to learn about another's life, the world would be a poorer place.

NOTES

___

Fuller citations for the books mentioned can be found in the Bibliography. Most of the notes could cite far more books, articles, interviews, and/or court decisions than they do. But rather than clutter the notes, I have included only the most informative, compelling, and/or timely references.

Introduction

1. Stephen B. Oates, *Biography as History*. This pamphlet contains lectures presented by Oates at Baylor University on March 19 and 20, 1990. The first quotation is from the March 19 speech; the second is from the March 20 speech.

2. *Chronicle of Higher Education*, February 27, 1991; also see James Atlas, "Speaking Ill of the Dead," *New York Times Magazine*, November 6, 1988, and Paul Gray, "Pssst! Have You Heard the One About Augustus," *Time*, April 22, 1991.

3. *New York Times Book Review*, June 21, 1991; also see Walter Shapiro, "Nostalgia Isn't What It Used to Be: Is Anything Better Than in the Past?, *Gentleman's Quarterly*, December 1991.

4. *Washington Post*, April 15, 1991.

Chapter One: *From Plutarch to Pathography*

Portions of this chapter first appeared in the Missouri Review 12:2 (1989) *under the title "Telling Lives."*

1. Caro's publisher, Knopf, supplied me with copies of Caro's award citations.

2. Dumas Malone, *Jefferson and His Time: The Sage of Monticello*.

3. *Washington Post Book World*, October 6, 1974.

4. *Publishers Weekly*, January 15, 1988.

5. George Garrett, "Literary Biography in Our Time," *Sewanee Review* 92 (Summer 1984): 495–505. Jean Strouse's quotation comes from *Biography as High Adventure: Life-Writers Speak on Their Art*, ed. Stephen B. Oates. Also see her speech "The Real Reasons" in *Extraordinary Lives: The Art and Craft of American Biography*, ed. William Zinsser. Her thoughts on biography appear as well in *The Biographer's Gift*, ed. James F. Veninga.

225

6. Other novels with biographers as protagonists appear in the Bibliography, as do full citations for the novels mentioned in this chapter.

7. Margaret Oliphant's quote appears in *One Mighty Torrent: The Drama of Biography*, by Edgar Johnson.

8. Dumas Malone, "Biography and History," in *The Interpretation of History*, ed. Joseph R. Strayer.

9. The list of contemporary biographers writing about contemporary, controversial subjects is not complete, but I believe it is representative. Stephen B. Oates's thoughts appear in "Biography as High Adventure," in his book of the same name. His thoughts on biography also appear, inter alia, in *The Biographer's Gift*, ed. Veninga.

10. Michael Scammell, *Solzhenitsyn: A Biography*.

11. James Walter, "The Biography of a Contemporary Figure and Its Pitfalls," in *Biographers at Work*, ed. Walter and Raija Nugent-Nathan.

12. *New York Times Book Review*, July 21, 1985. Steel's further thoughts on biography appear, inter alia, in *The Biographer's Gift*, ed. Veninga, and in "Living with Walter Lippmann," in *Extraordinary Lives*, ed. Zinsser. Also see Peggy Lamson, "Writing Biography: Pitfalls and Dilemmas," *The Writer*, December 1991.

13. Deirdre Bair, "The How-To of Biography," in *Biographers at Work*, ed. Walter and Nugent-Nathan. For more on Bair's experiences, see her interview with Wendy Smith in *Publishers Weekly*, April 13, 1990.

14. Malone, "Biography and History," in *The Interpretation of History*, ed. Strayer.

15. Chapter Two of this book contains more on Caro's thoughts about chronology.

16. Leon Edel, *Writing Lives: Principia Biographica*; Geoffrey T. Hellman, "Chairman of the Board" (a profile of Edel), *New Yorker*, March 13, 1971; Gerald Clarke, "The Many Lives of Leon Edel," *Connoisseur*, January 1992.

17. Stephen E. Ambrose, *Eisenhower: The President*.

18. Milton Lomask, *The Biographer's Craft*; William Abrahams is quoted from *San Francisco Examiner* book pages, January 25, 1987.

19. Anthony Edmonds, "Men and Myth," in *Focus on Biography*, ed. Dwight W. Hoover and John T. A. Koumoulides; Elizabeth Longford is quoted from *New York Times Book Review*, August 3, 1986.

20. Adam Ulam, *Stalin: The Man and His Era*.

21. The Dreiser biographer's anecdote is mentioned in *Ultimately Fiction: Design in Modern American Literary Biography*, by Dennis W. Petrie.

22. Bernard Crick, *George Orwell: A Life*.

23. William Shirer, *The Rise and Fall of the Third Reich*.

24. Robert C. Tucker, "A Stalin Biographer's Memoir," in *Introspection in Biography: The Biographer's Quest for Self-Awareness*, ed. Samuel H. Baron and Carl Pletsch.

25. Mark Schwehn, "Henry Adams: An Intellectual Historian's Perspective Reconsidered," in *Introspection in Biography*, ed. Baron and Pletsch.

26. Ronald Steel, "Living with Walter Lippmann," in *Extraordinary Lives*, ed. Zinsser; also see Steel's *Walter Lippmann and the American Century* and John P. Sisk, "Biography without End," *Antioch Review* 48 (Fall 1990): 448–59.

27. Allan Nevins, "The Essence of Biography," in *Allan Nevins on History*, ed. Ray Allen Billington.

28. Sigmund Freud and William C. Bullitt, *Thomas Woodrow Wilson: A Psychological Profile*.

29. Gamaliel Bradford, "Psychography," in his *A Naturalist of Souls*; William McKinley Runyan, "Progress in Psychobiography," *Journal of Personality* 56:1 (March 1988): 295–326.

30. Oates, *Biography as History*.

31. Edel, *Writing Lives*.

32. Mark Schorer, "The Burdens of Biography," *Michigan Quarterly Review* 1 (Autumn 1962): 249–58, as reprinted in *Biography as High Adventure*, ed. Oates. Also see Schorer's *Sinclair Lewis: An American Life*.

33. Crick, *George Orwell*.

34. Justin Kaplan, a biographer of Samuel Clemens/Mark Twain, quotes the passage in "The Real Life," an essay from *Studies in Biography*, ed. Daniel Aaron. Also see Kaplan's *Mr. Clemens and Mark Twain*.

35. *Publishers Weekly*, June 5, 1987, interview with Joan Peyser.

36. Joseph Wall, "A Second Look at Andrew Carnegie," in *Introspection in Biography*, ed. Baron and Pletsch.

37. Paul Mariani, "Reassembling the Dust," in *Biography as High Adventure*, ed. Oates.

38. Victoria Glendinning, "Lies and Silences," in *The Troubled Face of Biography*, ed. Eric Homberger and John Charmley; Crick, *George Orwell*, plus his "Orwell and Biography" in *biography* 10:4 (1987).

39. Paul Murray Kendall, *The Art of Biography*. Part of the book is reprinted as "Walking the Boundaries," in *Biography as High Adventure*, ed. Oates.

40. Stephen B. Oates, *Texas Observer*, June 3, 1983.

41. The simultaneous Savitch and Noriega volumes were reviewed together in dozens of outlets, some of which are cited in Chapter Six.

42. Philip Ziegler, "The Lure of Gossip, the Rules of History," *New York Times Book Review*, February 23, 1986.

43. Ibid.

44. Schorer, "The Burdens of Biography," in *Biography as High Adventure*, ed. Oates.

45. Ziegler, "The Lure of Gossip, the Rules of History," *New York Times Book Review*, February 23, 1986.

46. Doris Kearns, "Angles of Vision," in *Telling Lives: The Biographer's Art*, ed. Marc Pachter. Her biography is *Lyndon Johnson and the American Dream*.

47. *Washington Post Book World*, July 20, 1986. Also see Peter Stansky, "History and Biography: Some Personal Remarks," *Pacific Historical Review* 59 (February 1990): 1–14.

48. Kendall, "Walking the Boundaries," in *Biography as High Adventure*, ed. Oates.

49. Jacques Barzun and Henry F. Graff, *The Modern Researcher*, 4th ed. Also see Barzun's essay "History, Popular and Unpopular," in *The Interpretation of History*, ed. Strayer. A more recent essay is by Lynn Z. Bloom, "Popular and Super-Pop Biographies: Definitions and Distinctions," in *biography* 3:3 (1980): 225–39.

50. See Barbara Grizzuti Harrison, "Terrified and Fascinated by His Own Life," *New York Times Book Review*, November 2, 1986.

Chapter Two: *Up from the Newsroom*

1. Caro's books are *The Power Broker: Robert Moses and the Fall of New York*; *The Path to Power*, vol. 1 of *The Years of Lyndon Johnson*; and *Means of Ascent*, vol. 2 of *The Years of Lyndon Johnson*. Nicholas von Hoffman, in his profile titled "Robert Caro's Holy Fire," *Vanity Fair*, April 1990, discusses the reason for Caro's switch from newspapering to book writing. Numerous other profiles of Caro and reviews of Caro's books contain similar passages about Caro's thinking. In addition, I drew him out on this point and many others during numerous telephone interviews, the longest of those occurring on July 20 and 28, 1990, and March 24, 1992. The direct quotation used here comes from the second telephone interview.

2. To gauge the breadth, depth, and quality of the debate, I searched for profiles of Caro, book reviews, op-ed pieces, editorials, and the like. I received clippings from the libraries of newspapers in every major Texas city, compiled book reviews listed in various indexes, located magazine articles through periodical indexes, checked a reference work that shows in which academic writings Caro's books are cited, and conducted an electronic database search using the vendor Dialog. The result of all that was approximately two hundred separate writings about Caro and his books.

3. Biographical information comes in part from the *New York Times* sketches of the 1975 Pulitzer Prize winners, May 6, 1975; Fred Bernstein's Caro profile in *People* magazine, January 17, 1983; Caro's listing in the reference book *Contemporary Authors*, volume 101 (Detroit: Gale Research Company); publicity from his publisher; and numerous other secondary sources. In addition, I verified the information with Caro.

4. My interviews with Caro.

5. Michael T. Kaufman, "Moses Rips into 'Venomous' Biography," *New York Times*, August 27, 1974. Excerpts appeared in the *New Yorker* on four consecutive weeks, beginning July 22, 1974.

6. Gore Vidal's quote appears in the *New York Review of Books*, October 17, 1974.

7. Book review in the daily *New York Times*, September 9, 1974. The *Times* Sunday book section published a separate review, September 15, 1974, by Richard C. Wade.

8. *New Republic*, September 7, 1974.

9. Edel, *Writing Lives*.

10. Caro's quotation appears in *Extraordinary Lives*, ed. Zinsser. I combined what he said then with information from our interviews.

11. *Atlantic Monthly*, October and November 1981; *Publishers Weekly*, November 25, 1983; *People*, January 17, 1983; Edel, *Writing Lives*.

12. Ronnie Dugger, *The Drive for Power: From the Frontier to Master of the Senate*, vol. 1 of *The Politician: The Life and Times of Lyndon Johnson*. Dugger

said in a telephone interview on June 16, 1990, that he still plans to write another volume, but is unsure when.

I consulted every serious, major Johnson biography that I knew about covering, inter alia, his life at least through 1948. That list includes the Paul Conkin, Robert Dallek, Ronnie Dugger, Doris Kearns, Merle Miller, and Sam Houston Johnson biographies cited elsewhere, as well as the biographies by Martin Caidin and Edward Hymoff, *The Mission* (Philadelphia: Lippincott, 1964); Rowland Evans and Robert Novak, *Lyndon B. Johnson: The Exercise of Power* (New York: New American Library, 1966); Joe B. Frantz, *Thirty-Seven Years of Public Service: The Honorable Lyndon B. Johnson* (Austin: Shoal Creek Publishers, 1974); Rebekah Johnson, *A Family Album* (New York: McGraw-Hill, 1965); Booth Mooney, *The Lyndon Johnson Story* (New York: Farrar, Straus, 1964); Clarke Newlon, *LBJ: The Man from Johnson City* (New York: Dodd, Mead, 1966); William C. Pool et al., *Lyndon Baines Johnson: The Formative Years* (San Marcos: Southwest Texas State College Press, 1965); Harry Provence, *Lyndon B. Johnson* (New York: Fleet, 1964); Philip Reed Rulon, *The Compassionate Samaritan* (Chicago: Nelson-Hall, 1981); Alfred Steinberg, *Sam Johnson's Boy* (New York: Macmillan, 1968).

13. *New Yorker,* November 6 and December 18, 1989.

14. *Vanity Fair,* April 1990.

15. Stephen Harrigan, "The Man Who Never Stops," *Texas Monthly,* April 1990.

16. Henry C. Fleisher, "The Two Sides of Lyndon Johnson," *Dissent,* Summer 1983.

17. *New York Times Book Review,* November 21, 1982.

18. Merle Miller, *Lyndon: An Oral Biography.*

19. Tom Dunkel, "The Lies behind 'Landslide' Lyndon," *Insight,* April 30, 1990.

20. *New Republic,* June 4, 1990.

21. Curt Suplee, "The Telling of a President," *Washington Post,* December 9, 1982; Charles Trueheart, "LBJ and the Historian's Scalpel," *Washington Post,* March 21, 1990.

22. *L.A. Weekly,* March 23, 1990; *Texas Observer,* April 6, 1990.

23. Caro's eulogy is excerpted in the *New York Times Book Review,* June 12, 1988; *Houston Post,* March 21, 1990.

24. Caro in *Extraordinary Lives,* ed. Zinsser.

25. Ibid.

26. Ibid.

27. John Dinges, *Our Man in Panama: How General Noriega Used the U.S.— and Made Millions in Drugs and Arms;* Frederick Kempe, *Divorcing the Dictator: America's Bungled Affair with Noriega.*

28. Caro in *Extraordinary Lives,* ed. Zinsser.

29. Edel, *Writing Lives.*

30. Caro in *Extraordinary Lives,* ed. Zinsser. Quotations from Caro in the next two paragraphs are from the same source.

31. David Donald in *New York Times Book Review,* November 21, 1982; Paul K. Conkin, *Big Daddy from the Pedernales.*

32. Dugger, *Drive for Power.*

33. *Washington Post Book World,* March 4, 1990.

34. *New York Times Book Review,* March 31, 1991.

Chapter Three: *Inquiring Minds*

Some of this chapter appeared, in different versions, in Washington Journalism Review *(October 1990) and in* Business Journalist *(December 1990).*

1. Many of the details and the conclusions in this chapter are drawn from repeated discussions and correspondence I had with Barlett and/or Steele during 1990.

2. The seven-part series appeared during December 1975 in the *Philadelphia Inquirer*. The entry form was submitted to the Business Journalism Awards at the University of Missouri School of Journalism.

3. Interviews with Barlett and Steele, February 1990.

4. Interview with Barlett and Steele, February 21, 1990.

5. Barlett's letter to me, February 24, 1990, which is the source for the quotations in the balance of this section as well.

6. The Swedish translation was supplied by Torbjorn von Krogh, a Stockholm journalist; also interview of Barlett and Steele by Jerry Rosen, *Business Journalist*, June 1989.

7. Steele's testimony to the House of Representatives Committee on Government Operations, "U.S. Government Information Policies and Practices—Administration and Operation of the Freedom of Information Act," Part 4, March 1972.

8. Steele discussed the project at the June 1976 conference of Investigative Reporters & Editors in Indianapolis. I attended that conference and have relied on my notes as well as a transcript provided by IRE.

9. Barlett and Steele interviews, February 1990; Barlett and Steele, "So Much for the Glamorous Life of an Investigative Reporter," *Quill* 65:3 (March 1977): 18–22.

10. Ibid.

11. "The Inquirer's Inquirers," *Newsweek*, December 30, 1974.

12. Bill Rainbolt, "Harnessing the Energy Anarchy," *IRE Journal* 4:1 (Winter 1981): 5–8.

13. Barlett and Steele interviews, February 1990.

14. Jonathan Alter, "Two Reporters You Don't Want on Your Tail," *Newsweek*, March 24, 1989; *Knight Ridder News*, Summer 1989. The tax series appeared in the *Philadelphia Inquirer*, April 10–16, 1988.

15. Barlett and Steele, "America: What Went Wrong?," *Philadelphia Inquirer*, October 20–28, 1991, and the book of the same title.

Chapter Four: *Telling the Untold Story of Armand Hammer*

An earlier version of this chapter appeared in the IRE Journal, *published by Investigative Reporters & Editors Inc., Spring 1990.*

1. I sent registered letters to Hammer and called him repeatedly. He never responded directly.

2. Some of the most helpful indexes to periodicals include *Business Periodicals*

Index, Legal Resource Index, Applied Science and Technology Index, Education Index, and *Public Affairs Information Service.* I also rely on indexes to specific newspapers, especially the *New York Times, Washington Post, Wall Street Journal, Los Angeles Times* and *St. Louis Post-Dispatch.*

3. To keep up with computer databases, I rely on mailings from specific vendors such as Dialog and Nexis. I also read *Online Access* magazine. To find industry-specific publications, I rely on the *Standard Periodical Directory* and the *Oxbridge Directory of Newsletters,* both available from Oxbridge Communications, as well as various directories published by Gale Research.

4. The extensive endnotes to my book, *Armand Hammer: The Untold Story,* list many more specialized publications. The best book I have seen on finding information is *The Reporter's Handbook: An Investigator's Guide to Documents and Techniques,* 2d ed., ed. John Ullmann and Jan Colbert.

5. *Dissertation Abstracts* from University Microfilms International covers most universities back to 1861. An on-line computer version goes back to 1980.

Chapter Five: *Short-Form Biography*

1. First-rate, albeit typical, histories are *The Magazine in America, 1741–1990* by John Tebbel and Mary Ellen Zuckerman and *A History of News: From the Drum to the Satellite* by Mitchell Stephens.

2. Norman Sims, "Joseph Mitchell and *The New Yorker* Nonfiction Writers," in *Literary Journalism in the Twentieth Century,* ed. Sims.

3. Loudon Wainwright, *The Great American Magazine: An Inside History of Life.*

4. Tom Wolfe, *The New Journalism.*

5. Walt Harrington's profiles have been collected in *American Profiles: Somebodies and Nobodies Who Matter.* Madeleine Blais has an anthology, too: *The Heart Is an Instrument: Portraits in Journalism.*

Chapter Six: *The Promise and Peril of Investigative Biography*

1. See Chapter Four of this book. The lawsuit was in the High Court of Justice, Queen's Bench Division, Case 1989–3292. It ended when Hammer died December 10, 1990.

2. *Biography as High Adventure,* ed. Oates.

3. Concerning the long list of other biographers in peril, in each case I have read the book or manuscript, located as much coverage as possible, studied court cases when relevant, and conducted interviews with biographers and/or agents and/or editors and/or attorneys.

4. Ian Hamilton, *In Search of J. D. Salinger.*

5. Ibid.; David Margolick, "Whose Words Are They, Anyway?" *New York Times Book Review,* November 1, 1987; John Shelton Lawrence and Bernard Timberg, *Fair Use and Free Inquiry,* 2d ed.

6. Hamilton, *In Search of Salinger.*

7. Court cases involving the Salinger book, especially the U.S. District Court, Southern District of New York, are reported at 13 Media Law Reporter 1689; and the Second Circuit Court of Appeals, reported at 811 F. 2d 90. The Supreme Court's denial of review is reported at 484 US 890.

8. The George Washington fair use case that is believed to be the earliest (1841) is reported at 9 F. Cas. 342.

9. The Howard Hughes case is reported at 366 F. 2d 303; the Ernest Hemingway case is reported at 23 NY 2d 341.

10. Salinger case, 13 Media Law Reporter 1689.

11. Salinger appeals case, 811 F. 2d 90. Interview with Salinger's lawyer, Marcia Paul, November 19, 1990; interview with the publisher's lawyer, Robert Callagy, on the same date.

12. The Little, Brown and Company manual used by me for fair-use guidance is titled "From Manuscript to Printed Book." My copy is dated 1984. About tightened restrictions, I have a letter to me from Little, Brown vice-president Judith Kennedy dated September 15, 1987.

13. Interviews with David Chandler, November 19, 1990, and Edward Chase, the original editor at Macmillan, November 28, 1990; Marie Brenner, *House of Dreams*; Thomas B. Rosenstiel, "Ghastly Drama," *Los Angeles Times,* July 3, 1987.

14. Stravinsky case, U.S. District Court, Southern District of New York, reported at 667 F. Supp 120; *Publishers Weekly* advance review of the biography, August 21, 1987; Robert Craft, *Small Craft Advisories*; interviews with John Kobler and his editor, Edward Chase, November 28, 1990.

15. The Russell Miller decisions are reported at 15 Media Law Reporter 2161 and 873 F. 2d 576. Interviews with Floyd Abrams, an outside lawyer for the publisher, November 20, 1990; Holt editor Jack Macrae, November 26, 1990; Holt legal counsel Muriel Caplan, November 28. The Jon Atack decisions are reported at 17 Media Law Reporter 1029 and 904 F. 2d 152. Interview with publisher Steven Schragis, November 20, 1990.

16. *Chicago Tribune,* March 2 and April 18, 1990; St. Martin's Press Spring 1991 catalog.

17. U.S. District Court, Southern District of New York, reported at 1990 U.S. Dist. Lexis 12320; interview with publisher's lawyer Robert Callagy, November 19, 1990; interview with widow's lawyer Andres Valdespino, November 26, 1990. Also see U.S. Court of Appeals, Second Circuit, 19 Media Law Reporter 1577, November 21, 1991, and Jack Miles's commentary in the *Los Angeles Times Book Review,* December 8, 1991.

18. Pierre N. Leval, "Commentary: Toward a Fair Use Standard," *Harvard Law Review,* March 1990.

19. Linda Wagner-Martin, *Sylvia Plath: A Biography*; Anne Stevenson, *Bitter Fame: A Life of Sylvia Plath*; Olwyn Hughes letter, *New York Times Book Review,* March 27, 1988.

20. James Reston, Jr., interview, November 28, 1990; Reston account of his experience in *Washingtonian,* January 1990.

21. Ken Englade letter, American Society of Journalists and Authors newsletter, July–August 1990; Leslie Postal article, *Lynchburg (Va.) News and Daily Advance,* February 18, 1990.

22. Bruce Perry, letter to U.S. Senator Paul Simon and others, July 4, 1990; Perry interview, November 20, 1990.

23. The proposed legislation was HR 4263 in the House and S 2370 in the Senate. I have all the testimony from the July 11, 1990, hearing.

24. Taylor Branch, J. Anthony Lukas, James L. Oakes, July 11, 1990, Congressional testimony to the U.S. House of Representatives Committee on the Judiciary, subcommittee on courts, intellectual property, and the administration of justice, and the U.S. Senate Committee on the Judiciary, subcommittee on patents, copyrights, and trademarks.

25. The Maheu-Drosnin case in the California Court of Appeals is reported at 201 Cal. App. 3d 662; see also Robert Lindsey, "Ex-Aide Files Suit on Hughes Book," *New York Times*, April 24, 1985.

26. *New York Law Journal*, February 8, 1990.

27. U.S. District Court, District of Columbia, reported at 598 F. Supp 36.

28. *Access Reports*, July 26, 1989.

29. Hammer's lawsuit against the Securities and Exchange Commission was designated as civil case 86–3428 at the U.S. District Court in Washington, D.C., and case 87–5279 at the U.S. Court of Appeals.

30. Wendy Leigh, article in the *Sunday Times* of London, August 19, 1990; interview with her publisher, Harvey Plotnick, November 28, 1990.

31. Albert Goldman's account of his travails, *Penthouse*, September 1989; *Rolling Stone*, October 20, 1988; *Newsweek*, October 17, 1988.

32. *New York Times Book Review*, February 23, 1986.

33. James Reston, Jr., *Washingtonian*, January 1990.

34. Richard Powers, *The Man Who Kept the Secrets: Richard Helms and the CIA*.

35. For further examples, see my reviews in the *Kansas City Star* of December 10, 1989, and May 20, 1990.

36. Armand Hammer with Neil Lyndon, *Hammer*.

37. Roger Kahn, "Rose Book Was a Story in Itself," *Los Angeles Times*, July 29, 1990, and reply by Laurence J. Kirshbaum, *Los Angeles Times*, September 1, 1990.

38. Gerri Hirshey, "Kitty Oh!," *Washington Post*, October 30, November 1 and 2, 1988. *Poison Pen: The Unauthorized Biography of Kitty Kelley* is by George Carpozi, Jr.

39. C. David Heymann, *Poor Little Rich Girl* and *A Woman Named Jackie*; Karen Schwarz, "Just Give Us the Facts," *Publishers Weekly*, March 2, 1984; Mike Wilson, "Jackie Book Draws Heavy Fire," *Miami Herald*, May 14, 1989.

40. Megan Rosenfeld, "Publisher Returns Rights to Biography," *Washington Post*, January 11, 1980; Alex S. Jones, *New York Times*, September 20, 1987.

41. U.S. Court of Appeals, Third Circuit, reported at 764 F2d 983.

42. Edwin McDowell, "Spellman Book Deletes Homosexual Assertions," *New York Times*, September 29, 1984.

43. See my account in "The Unruly World of Book Reviewing," *Columbia Journalism Review*, March–April 1990.

44. Interview with Joan Peyser, *Publishers Weekly*, June 5, 1987.

45. Linda Wagner-Martin's letter, *New York Times Book Review*, December 13, 1987, reacting to Hamilton's review of October 25, 1987.

46. Seymour Hersh, *The Price of Power: Kissinger in the Nixon White House;* Marylouise Oates, "Hersh v. Kissinger, a Top-Drawer Uproar," *Los Angeles Times,* June 29, 1983.

47. Gail A. Campbell, "Diana Ross Fan Becomes Her Boswell," *Washington Times,* November 20, 1989.

48. William Wright, *Lillian Hellman.*

BIBLIOGRAPHY

This Bibliography does not list every investigative biography encountered, nor every book and article written about the craft. Rather, it concentrates on quality investigative biography of contemporary subjects, by authors with journalistic backgrounds, published in the last quarter of the twentieth century. Nonetheless, some of the citations that follow refer to especially enlightening works about the craft from earlier decades, earlier centuries.

Aaron, Daniel, ed. *Studies in Biography*. Cambridge: Harvard University Press, 1978.

Alpers, Antony. *Katherine Mansfield: A Biography*. New York: Knopf, 1953.

Ambrose, Stephen E. *Eisenhower: The President*. New York: Simon and Schuster, 1984.

———. *Nixon: The Education of a Politician, 1913–1962*. New York: Simon and Schuster, 1987.

———. *Nixon: The Triumph of a Politician, 1962–1972*. New York: Simon and Schuster, 1989.

———. *Nixon: Ruin and Recovery, 1973–1990*. New York: Simon and Schuster, 1991.

Anthony, Katharine. *Margaret Fuller: A Psychological Profile*. New York: Harcourt, Brace, and Howe, 1920.

Atack, Jon. *A Piece of Blue Sky: Scientology, Dianetics and L. Ron Hubbard Exposed*. Secaucus, N.J.: Lyle Stuart/Carol, 1990.

Bair, Deirdre. *Samuel Beckett*. New York: Harcourt Brace Jovanovich, 1979.

———. *Simone de Beauvoir: A Biography*. New York: Summit Books, 1990.

Barlett, Donald L., and James B. Steele. *America: What Went Wrong?* Kansas City: Andrews and McMeel, 1992.

———. *Empire: The Life, Legend and Madness of Howard Hughes*. New York: Norton, 1979.

———. *Forevermore: Nuclear Waste in America*. New York: Norton, 1985.

Barnes, Julian. *Flaubert's Parrot* (a novel about biography). New York: Knopf, 1984.

Barnett, Lincoln. *Writing on Life: Sixteen Close-ups*. New York: William Sloane Associates, 1951.

Baron, Samuel H., and Carl Pletsch. *Introspection in Biography: The Biographer's Quest for Self-Awareness*. Hillsdale, N.J.: Analytic Press, 1985.

Barzun, Jacques, and Henry F. Graff. *The Modern Researcher*. 4th ed. New York: Harcourt Brace Jovanovich, 1985.

Bell, Susan Groag, and Marilyn Yalom, eds. *Revealing Lives: Autobiography, Biography and Gender*. Albany: State University of New York Press, 1990.

Benedict, Helen. *Portraits in Print: A Collection of Profiles and the Stories behind Them*. New York: Columbia University Press, 1990.

Benson, Jackson J. *Looking for Steinbeck's Ghost*. Norman: University of Oklahoma Press, 1988.

Berry, Thomas Elliott, ed. *The Biographer's Craft*. New York: Odyssey Press, 1967.

Billington, Ray Allen, ed. *Allan Nevins on History*. New York: Scribners, 1975.

biography, a quarterly journal. University of Hawaii, 1978–current.

Black, Lionel. *The Life and Death of Peter Wade* (a novel about biography). New York: Stein and Day, 1974.

Blair, Gwenda. *Almost Golden: Jessica Savitch and the Selling of Television News*. New York: Simon and Schuster, 1988.

Blais, Madeleine. *The Heart Is an Instrument: Portraits in Journalism*. Amherst: University of Massachusetts Press, 1992.

Boswell, James. *Life of Johnson*. Oxford: Oxford University Press, 1980 (reprint edition).

Bowen, Catherine Drinker. *Adventures of a Biographer*. Boston: Atlantic-Little, Brown, 1959.

———. *Biography: The Craft and the Calling*. Boston: Atlantic-Little, Brown, 1969.

Bradford, Gamaliel. *A Naturalist of Souls*. Boston: Houghton Mifflin, 1926. (Reprint of a 1917 edition.)

Branch, Taylor. *Parting the Waters: America in the King Years, 1954–1963*. New York: Simon and Schuster, 1988.

Brenner, Marie. *House of Dreams: The Bingham Family of Louisville*. New York: Random House, 1988.

Britt, Albert. *The Great Biographers*. New York: McGraw-Hill, 1936.

Byatt, A. S. *Possession* (a novel about biography). New York: Random House, 1990.

Cannon, Lou. *President Reagan: The Role of a Lifetime.* New York: Simon and Schuster, 1991.

Caro, Robert A. *The Power Broker: Robert Moses and the Fall of New York.* New York: Knopf, 1974.

———. *The Years of Lyndon Johnson,* vol. 1, *The Path to Power.* New York: Knopf, 1982.

———. *The Years of Lyndon Johnson,* vol. 2, *Means of Ascent.* New York: Knopf, 1990.

Carpozi, George, Jr. *Poison Pen: The Unauthorized Biography of Kitty Kelley.* Secaucus, N.J.: Barricade/Lyle Stuart, 1991.

Chandler, David Leon, with Mary Voelz Chandler. *The Binghams of Louisville: The Dark History behind One of America's Great Fortunes.* New York: Crown, 1987.

Clifford, James L., ed. *Biography as an Art: Selected Criticism, 1560–1960.* New York: Oxford University Press, 1962.

———. *From Puzzles to Portraits: Problems of a Literary Biographer.* Chapel Hill: University of North Carolina Press, 1971.

Cole, John Y., ed. *Biography and Books.* Washington: Library of Congress, 1986.

Collier, Peter, and David Horowitz. *The Fords: An American Epic.* New York: Summit Books, 1987.

———. *The Kennedys: An American Drama.* New York: Summit Books, 1984.

———. *The Rockefellers: An American Dynasty.* New York: Holt, Rinehart and Winston, 1976.

Conkin, Paul K. *Big Daddy from the Pedernales.* Boston: Twayne, 1986.

Cooney, John. *The American Pope: The Life and Times of Francis Cardinal Spellman.* New York: Times Books, 1984.

———. *The Annenbergs: The Salvaging of a Tainted Dynasty.* New York: Simon and Schuster, 1982.

Craft, Robert. *Small Craft Advisories.* New York: Thames and Hudson, 1989.

Crick, Bernard. *George Orwell: A Life.* Boston: Atlantic-Little, Brown, 1980.

Cross, Amanda. *No Word from Winifred* (a novel about biography). New York: Dutton, 1986.

———. *The Players Come Again* (a novel about biography). New York: Random House, 1990.

Cummings, John, and Ernest Volkman. *Goombata: The Improbable Rise and Fall of John Gotti and His Gang.* Boston: Little, Brown, 1990.

Dallek, Robert. *Lone Star Rising: Lyndon Johnson and His Times, 1908–1960.* New York: Oxford University Press, 1991.

Davenport, William H., and Ben Siegel, eds. *Biography Past and Present.* New York: Scribners, 1965.

Davidson, James West, and Mark Hamilton Lytle. *After the Fact: The Art of Historical Detection.* 2d ed. New York: Knopf, 1986.

Davis, Deborah. *Katharine the Great: Katharine Graham and the Washington Post.* Washington, D.C.: National Press, 1987.

Dinges, John. *Our Man in Panama: How General Noriega Used the U.S.—and Made Millions in Drugs and Arms.* New York: Random House, 1990.

Drosnin, Michael. *Citizen Hughes.* New York: Holt, Rinehart and Winston, 1985.

Dugger, Ronnie. *The Politician: The Life and Times of Lyndon Johnson,* vol. 1, *The Drive for Power: From the Frontier to Master of the Senate.* New York: Norton, 1982.

Edel, Leon. *Writing Lives: Principia Biographica.* New York: Norton, 1984.

Englade, Ken. *Beyond Reason.* New York: St. Martin's, 1990.

Epstein, William H. *Contesting the Subject: Essays in the Postmodern Theory and Practice of Biography and Biographical Criticism.* West Lafayette: Purdue University Press, 1991.

———. *Recognizing Biography.* Philadelphia: University of Pennsylvania Press, 1987.

Fischer, David Hackett. *Historians' Fallacies: Toward a Logic of Historical Thought.* New York: Harper and Row, 1970.

Freud, Sigmund, and William C. Bullitt. *Thomas Woodrow Wilson: A Psychological Profile.* Boston: Houghton Mifflin, 1966.

Garraty, John A. *The Nature of Biography.* New York: Knopf, 1957.

Gay, Peter. *Freud: A Life for Our Time.* New York: Norton, 1988.

Geyer, Georgie Anne. *Guerilla Prince: The Untold Story of Fidel Castro.* Boston: Little, Brown, 1991.

Gittings, Robert. *The Nature of Biography.* Seattle: University of Washington Press, 1978.

Goettsch, Scherrie, and Steve Weinberg. *Terrace Hill: The Story of a House and the People Who Touched It.* Des Moines: Wallace-Homestead, 1978.

Goldman, Albert. *Elvis.* New York: McGraw-Hill, 1981.

———. *The Lives of John Lennon.* New York: Morrow, 1988.

Goulden, Joseph C. *Fit to Print: A. M. Rosenthal and His Times.* Secaucus, N.J.: Lyle Stuart, 1988.

Gronowicz, Antoni. *God's Broker.* New York: Richardson and Snyder, 1984.

Bibliography

Halberstam, David. *The Best and the Brightest.* New York: Random House, 1972.

Haley, J. Evetts. *A Texan Looks at Lyndon: A Study in Illegitimate Power.* Canyon, Tex.: Palo Duro Press, 1964.

Hamilton, Ian. *In Search of J. D. Salinger.* New York: Random House, 1988.

Hammer, Armand, with Neil Lyndon. *Hammer.* New York: Putnam, 1987.

Harrington, Walt. *American Profiles: Somebodies and Nobodies Who Matter.* Columbia: University of Missouri Press, 1992.

Heilbrun, Carolyn G. *Writing a Woman's Life.* New York: Norton, 1988.

Hersh, Seymour. *The Price of Power: Kissinger in the Nixon White House.* New York: Summit Books, 1983.

Herzstein, Robert Edwin. *Waldheim: The Missing Years.* New York: Arbor House/William Morrow, 1988.

Heymann, C. David. *A Woman Named Jackie.* Secaucus, N.J.: Lyle Stuart, 1989.

―――. *Poor Little Rich Girl: The Life and Legend of Barbara Hutton.* Secaucus, N.J.: Lyle Stuart, 1984.

Homberger, Eric, and John Charmley, eds. *The Troubled Face of Biography.* New York: St. Martin's, 1988.

Honan, Park. *Authors' Lives: On Literary Biography and the Arts of Language.* New York: St. Martin's, 1990.

Hoover, Dwight W., and John T. A. Koumoulides. *Focus on Biography.* New York: Cambridge University Press, 1974.

Howarth, William L., ed. *The John McPhee Reader.* New York: Farrar, Straus and Giroux, 1976. (See especially the excerpts from A *Sense of Where You Are* and A *Roomful of Hovings.*)

Hyman, Tom. *Prussian Blue* (a novel about biography). New York: Viking, 1991.

Johnson, Edgar. *One Mighty Torrent: The Drama of Biography.* New York: Macmillan, 1937.

Johnson, Sam Houston. *My Brother Lyndon.* New York: Cowles, 1970.

Judis, John B. *William F. Buckley Jr.: Patron Saint of the Conservatives,* New York: Simon and Schuster, 1988.

Kaplan, Justin. *Mr. Clemens and Mark Twain.* New York: Simon and Schuster, 1966.

Kearns, Doris. *Lyndon Johnson and the American Dream.* New York: Harper and Row, 1976.

Keeler, Robert F. *Newsday: The Candid History of the Respectable Tabloid.* New York: Arbor House/Morrow, 1990.

Kelley, Kitty. *Elizabeth Taylor: The Last Star*. New York: Simon and Schuster, 1981.

———. *His Way: The Unauthorized Biography of Frank Sinatra*. New York: Bantam, 1986.

———. *Jackie Oh!*. Secaucus, N.J.: Lyle Stuart, 1978.

Kempe, Frederick. *Divorcing the Dictator: America's Bungled Affair with Noriega*. New York: Putnam's, 1990.

Kendall, Paul Murray. *The Art of Biography*. New York: Norton, 1965.

Kessler, Ronald. *The Richest Man in the World: The Story of Adnan Khashoggi*. New York: Warner, 1986.

King, Dennis. *Lyndon LaRouche and the New American Fascism*. New York: Doubleday, 1989.

Lawrence, John Shelton, and Bernard Timberg. *Fair Use and Free Inquiry*. 2d ed. Norwood, N.J.: Ablex, 1989.

Leamer, Laurence. *King of the Night: The Life of Johnny Carson*. New York: Morrow, 1989.

Leigh, Wendy. *Arnold: An Unauthorized Biography*. Chicago: Contemporary Books, 1990.

Lenzner, Robert. *The Great Getty: The Lives and Loves of J. Paul Getty, Richest Man in the World*. New York: Crown, 1985.

Lively, Penelope. *According to Mark* (a novel about biography). London: Heinemann, 1984.

Lomask, Milton. *The Biographer's Craft*. New York: Harper and Row, 1986.

Lukas, J. Anthony. *Common Ground: A Turbulent Decade in the Lives of Three American Families*. New York: Knopf, 1985.

Lurie, Alison. *The Truth about Lorin Jones* (a novel about biography). Boston: Little, Brown, 1988.

Maas, Peter. *Manhunt: The Incredible Pursuit of a C.I.A. Agent Turned Terrorist* (Edwin P. Wilson). New York: Random House, 1986.

Malamud, Bernard. *Dubin's Lives* (a novel about biography). New York: Farrar, Straus and Giroux, 1979.

Malone, Dumas. *Jefferson and His Time: The Sage of Monticello*. Boston: Little, Brown, 1977. (This is the sixth and last volume of Malone's Jefferson biography.)

Mandell, Gail Porter. *Life into Art: Conversations with Seven Contemporary Biographers*. Fayetteville: University of Arkansas Press, 1991.

Mariani, Paul. *William Carlos Williams: A New World Naked*. New York, McGraw-Hill, 1981.

Mason, Todd. *Perot: An Unauthorized Biography*. Homewood, Ill.: Dow Jones-Irwin, 1990.

Maurois, André. *Aspects of Biography*. New York: Appleton, 1929.

Meeker, Richard H. *Newspaperman: S. I. Newhouse and the Business of News*. New York: Ticknor and Fields, 1983.

Meyer, Philip. *Precision Journalism: A Reporter's Introduction to Social Science Methods*. Bloomington: Indiana University Press, 1973.

Meyers, Jeffrey, ed. *The Biographer's Art*. New York: New Amsterdam Books, 1989.

———. *The Craft of Literary Biography*. New York: Schocken, 1985.

Miller, Merle. *Lyndon: An Oral Biography*. New York: Putnam's, 1980.

Miller, Russell. *Bare-Faced Messiah: The True Story of L. Ron Hubbard*. New York: Holt, 1987.

———. *Bunny: The Real Story of Playboy*. New York: Holt, Rinehart and Winston, 1985.

Miller, Ruth. *Saul Bellow: A Biography of the Imagination*. New York: St. Martin's, 1991.

Millhauser, Steven. *Edwin Mullhouse: The Life and Death of an American Writer, 1943–1954* (a novel about biography). New York: Knopf, 1972.

Morris, Roger. *Richard Milhous Nixon: The Rise of an American Politician*. New York: Holt, 1990.

———. *Uncertain Greatness: Henry Kissinger and American Foreign Policy*. New York: Harper and Row, 1976.

Moss, Michael. *Palace Coup: The Inside Story of Harry and Leona Helmsley*. New York: Doubleday, 1989.

Nadel, Ira Bruce. *Biography: Fiction, Fact and Form*. New York: St. Martin's, 1984.

Nash, Alanna. *Golden Girl: The Story of Jessica Savitch*. New York: Dutton, 1988.

Neff, James. *Mobbed Up: Jackie Presser's High-Wire Life in the Teamsters, the Mafia and the FBI*. New York: Atlantic Monthly Press, 1989.

Novarr, David. *The Lines of Life: Theories of Biography, 1880–1970*. West Lafayette: Purdue University Press, 1986.

Oates, Stephen B. *Let the Trumpet Sound: The Life of Martin Luther King, Jr*. New York: Harper and Row, 1982.

Oates, Stephen B, ed. *Biography as High Adventure: Life-Writers Speak on Their Art*. Amherst: University of Massachusetts Press, 1986.

———. *Biography as History*. Waco: Baylor University Press, 1990.

O'Neill, Edward Hayes. *A History of American Biography, 1800–1935*. New York: Russell and Russell, 1935.

Pachter, Marc, ed. *Telling Lives: The Biographer's Art*. Washington: New Republic Books, 1979.

Parton, James. *The Life of Horace Greeley* (1855). New York: Arno reprint, 1971.

Perry, Bruce. *Malcolm*. Barrytown, N.Y.: Station Hill, 1991.

Petrie, Dennis W. *Ultimately Fiction: Design in Modern American Literary Biography*. West Lafayette: Purdue University Press, 1981.

Peyser, Joan. *Bernstein: A Biography*. New York: Morrow, 1987.

Plunket, Robert. *My Search for Warren Harding* (a novel about biography). New York: Knopf, 1983.

Powers, Thomas. *The Man Who Kept the Secrets: Richard Helms and the CIA*. New York: Knopf, 1979.

Reich, Cary. *Financier: The Biography of André Meyer*. New York: Morrow, 1983.

Reid, B. L. *Necessary Lives: Biographical Reflections*. Columbia: University of Missouri Press, 1990.

Reston, James, Jr. *Collision at Home Plate: The Lives of Pete Rose and Bart Giamatti*. New York: HarperCollins, 1991.

———. *The Lone Star: The Life of John Connally*. Harper and Row, 1989.

———. *Our Father Who Art in Hell: The Life and Death of Jim Jones*. New York: Times Books, 1981.

Rodden, John. *The Politics of Literary Reputation: The Making and Claiming of 'St. George' Orwell*. Oxford: Oxford University Press, 1991.

Rose, Pete, and Roger Kahn. *Pete Rose: My Story*. New York: Macmillan, 1989.

Scammell, Michael. *Solzhenitsyn: A Biography*. New York: Norton, 1984.

Schoenbaum, S. *Shakespeare's Lives*. Oxford: Oxford University Press, 1991.

Schorer, Mark. *Sinclair Lewis: An American Life*. New York: McGraw-Hill, 1961.

Schwarz, Ted. *The Complete Guide to Writing Biographies*. Cincinnati: Writer's Digest Books, 1990.

Sheehan, Neil. *A Bright Shining Lie: John Paul Vann and America in Vietnam*. New York: Random House, 1988.

Sheehy, Gail. *The Man Who Changed the World: The Lives of Mikhail Gorbachev*. New York: HarperCollins, 1990.

Shepard, Charles E. *Forgiven: The Rise and Fall of Jim Bakker and the PTL Ministry*. Boston: Atlantic Monthly Press, 1989.

Shewey, Don. *Sam Shepard*. New York: Dell, 1986.

Shirer, William. *The Rise and Fall of the Third Reich*. New York: Simon and Schuster, 1960.

Sims, Norman, ed. *Literary Journalism in the Twentieth Century*. New York: Oxford University Press, 1990.

————. *The Literary Journalists*. New York: Ballantine, 1984.

Smith, Joan. *The Polka Dot Nude* (a novel about biography). New York: Jove, 1989.

Smith, Sally Bedell. *In All His Glory: The Life of William S. Paley*. New York: Simon and Schuster, 1990.

Smith, S. Stephenson. *The Craft of the Critic*. New York: Crowell, 1931.

Stannard, David E. *Shrinking History: On Freud and the Failure of Psychohistory*. Oxford: Oxford University Press, 1980.

Steel, Ronald. *Walter Lippmann and the American Century*. Boston: Little, Brown, 1980.

Stephens, Mitchell. *A History of News: From the Drum to the Satellite*. New York: Viking, 1988.

Stevenson, Anne. *Bitter Fame: A Life of Sylvia Plath*. Boston: Houghton Mifflin, 1989.

Strachey, Lytton. *Eminent Victorians*. London: Chatto and Windus, 1918. (Still available in various reprint editions.)

Strayer, Joseph R., ed. *The Interpretation of History*. Princeton: Princeton University Press, 1943.

Talbott, Strobe. *The Master of the Game: Paul Nitze and the Nuclear Peace*. New York: Knopf, 1988.

Taraborrelli, J. Randy. *Call Her Miss Ross*. New York: Birch Lane, 1989.

Tebbel, John, and Mary Ellen Zuckerman. *The Magazine in America, 1741–1990*. New York: Oxford University Press, 1991.

Theoharis, Athan G., and John Stuart Cox. *The Boss: J. Edgar Hoover and the Great American Inquisition*. Philadelphia: Temple University Press, 1988.

Tomalin, Claire. *Katherine Mansfield: A Secret Life*. New York: St. Martin's, 1987.

Tuchman, Barbara W. *Practicing History*. New York: Knopf, 1981.

Ulam, Adam. *Stalin: The Man and His Era*. New York: Viking, 1973.

Ullmann, John, and Jan Colbert. *The Reporter's Handbook: An Investigator's Guide to Documents and Techniques*. New York: St. Martin's, 1990.

Veninga, James F., ed. *The Biographer's Gift*. College Station: Texas Committee for the Humanities, 1983.

Von Hoffman, Nicholas. *Citizen Cohn*. New York: Doubleday, 1988.

Wagner-Martin, Linda. *Sylvia Plath: A Biography*. New York: Simon and Schuster, 1987.

Wainwright, Loudon. *The Great American Magazine: An Inside History of Life*. New York: Knopf, 1986.

Walker, Margaret. *Richard Wright: Daemonic Genius*. New York: Warner, 1988.

Wall, Joseph. *Andrew Carnegie*. New York: Oxford University Press, 1970.

Walshe, Robert. *Wales' Work* (a novel about biography). New York: Ticknor and Fields, 1986.

Walter, James, and Raija Nugent-Nathan. *Biographers at Work*. Queensland, Australia: Institute for Modern Biography, 1984.

Weinberg, Steve. *Armand Hammer: The Untold Story*. Boston: Little, Brown, 1989.

———. *Trade Secrets of Washington Journalists: How to Get the Facts about What's Going On in Washington*. Washington, D.C.: Acropolis Books, 1981.

Weintraub, Stanley, ed. *Biography and Truth*. New York: Bobbs-Merrill, 1967.

Whittemore, Reed. *Pure Lives: The Early Biographers*. Baltimore: Johns Hopkins University Press, 1988.

———. *Whole Lives: Shapers of Modern Biography*. Baltimore: Johns Hopkins University Press, 1989.

Wills, Garry. *Nixon Agonistes*. Boston: Houghton Mifflin, 1970.

Winans, Christopher. *Malcolm Forbes: The Man Who Had Everything*. New York: St. Martin's, 1990.

Wolfe, Tom. *The New Journalism*. New York: Harper and Row, 1973.

———. *The Right Stuff*. New York: Farrar, Straus and Giroux, 1979.

Woodward, Bob. *Wired: The Short Life and Fast Times of John Belushi*. New York: Simon and Schuster, 1984.

Woodward, Bob, and Carl Bernstein. *The Final Days*. New York: Simon and Schuster, 1976.

Woolf, Virginia. *Orlando* (a novel about biography). London: Hogarth Press, 1928.

Wright, William. *Lillian Hellman*. New York: Simon and Schuster, 1986.

Wyden, Peter. *The Unknown Iacocca: An Unauthorized Biography*. New York: Morrow, 1987.

Ziegler, Philip. *Mountbatten*. New York: Knopf, 1985.

Zinsser, William, ed. *Extraordinary Lives: The Art and Craft of American Biography*. New York: American Heritage, 1986.

ACKNOWLEDGMENTS

Beverly Jarrett, Jane Lago, and many others at the University of Missouri Press believed in this book, then helped make it happen.

Speer Morgan, editor of the *Missouri Review*, published what is now Chapter One in an earlier version. His feedback was invaluable.

Robert Caro, the subject of Chapter Two, his wife, Ina, and his editor at Knopf, Katherine Hourigan, enlightened me as I researched and wrote.

James Steele and Donald Barlett, the subjects of Chapter Three, have helped me frequently through the years; as always, they responded when I needed assistance for this chapter, which grew out of my profile in *Washington Journalism Review*. Their generous cooperation, along with that of the *Philadelphia Inquirer*, made it possible to reprint copyrighted material.

Jennifer Josephy, my editor at Little, Brown and Company for the Armand Hammer biography, has continued to provide moral support in the years after publication. I appreciate the permission granted by the *Los Angeles Times* to reprint Bob Sipchen's article about Hammer and me.

Thanks to the generosity of certain people at the *Washington Post*, I was able to reprint Gerri Hirshey's profile of Kitty Kelley. I also want to thank Calvin Trillin and his literary agent for granting permission to reprint the Edna Buchanan profile.

Walt Harrington, *Washington Post* feature writer, book author, and friend, read the manuscript carefully—a huge favor, to say the least.

The University of Missouri School of Journalism and Investigative Reporters & Editors Inc. (based at that School) provided all manner of support. I owe special thanks to Andy Cummings, at the time a graduate student in the School of Journalism, for his computer expertise.

Needless to say, I owe gratitude beyond mere words to my wife, Scherrie Goettsch, and my children, Sonia and Seth, for making my life sane (or at least saner) as I worked through yet another book.

INDEX

___